Just You and the Page

To Antony and Hazel Wood

For Will, when the time is right

Just You and the Page

Encounters with Twelve Authors

Sue Gee

SEREN

Seren is the book imprint of
Poetry Wales Press Ltd
Suite 6, 4 Derwen Road, Bridgend, Wales, CF31 1LH
www.serenbooks.com
Facebook: facebook.com/SerenBooks
Twitter: @SerenBooks

www.serenbooks.com
facebook.com/SerenBooks
Twitter: @SerenBooks

ISBN 978-1-78172-522-1
Ebook: 978-1-78172-523-8

A CIP record for this title is available from
the British Library

The publisher works with the financial assistance
of the Books Council of Wales.

Printed by Severn, Gloucester

Contents

The secret inside painting, not to be spoken of too much, to be kept at the back of the mind so that it stays as a questioning, a searching, a hope within us.

Gillian Ayres

Find your own quiet centre of life, and write from that to the world.

Her editor's advice to Willa Cather

I hope you realise that your asking me to talk about story-writing is just like asking a fish to lecture on swimming. The more stories I write, the more mysterious I find the process and the less I find myself capable of analysing it.

Flannery O'Connor

Introduction

'I understand that this is a course called "How the Writer Writes", and that each week you are exposed to a different writer who holds forth on the subject. The only parallel I can think of to this is having the zoo come to you, one animal at a time; and I suspect that what you hear one week from the gibbon is contradicted the next week by the baboon.'

Thus, in the middle of the twentieth century, the American novelist and short story writer Flannery O'Connor addressed a group of aspiring writers. The talk she gave was later published as her wise, beautiful and uncompromising essay, 'The Nature and Aim of Fiction'.

There are writers of fiction in this book: five distinctively different novelists. There is also, in what O'Connor might well have considered an improbable grouping, a poet, a nature writer, a celebrated diarist (and historian), a translator from the Russian. There is an environmental journalist; a dramatist; a writer of both poetry and prose whose stand against the politics of her country led to her exile in this one.

It is the dramatist who stands behind this book's conception, which goes back a very long way.

Early in 1972, living in north London, I moved from a tiny attic room overlooking Hampstead Heath to a rambling two-floor flat on Highbury Fields. The move was a turning point. I had been living alone, albeit sharing a micro-kitchen with an American folk singer, and a bathroom with a Burmese economist. I was now living much more communally with six others, most in our early twenties and all still feeling our way towards the kind of lives we wanted. The sixties were not long gone, and their unworldly spirit lived on: we regarded making money as a necessity, not a goal.

Among us was a man who made everyone laugh a lot, and who announced himself as a writer. Battered cardboard folders lay on the table in his room, crammed with half-finished plays and rejected novels. We could hear him tapping away on his portable typewriter, knew he was living on the dole. The first essay here is about that man, Michael Wall, who went on to write plays for stage and radio which were way ahead of his time. He died too young, but not before he had received great acclaim. He had also become an enduring friend.

Writing and friendship are intertwined in this book, in which I explore the life and work of twelve people I know or knew well. They have very different artistic identities. All have made powerful statements:

> *When I write, I want to smash through something…*
> *Writing is something without which you die.*
> *How can the self be bigger than the nation?*
> *For a novelist, the most valuable rule when observing other people is to tell yourself that nothing is as it seems.*
> *I knew I wanted to leave Ireland…it's a love/grief relationship.*
> *My diaries are very considered pieces of writing.*
> *One of the strongest motives that drives me to write is curiosity.*
> *I always felt that words were my friends.*
> *You have to recreate, not reproduce…Translation is a new beginning.*
> *New technologies have fundamentally changed what it means to be a writer.*
> *Writing is a light inside me which nothing can turn off.*

When thinking about and trying to plan this collection I turned to other, recently published books about groups of writers, to see how it might be done. In *The Violet Hour* (2016) Katie Rophe acutely considers how Freud, John Updike,

Maurice Sendak and other great thinkers, writers and artists faced, or failed to face, their death. The biographer Lyndall Gordon, in *Outsiders* (2017) links Mary Shelley and Virginia Woolf in her eloquent account of how five women writers changed the world.

In 1964 Nell Dunn interviewed many young women who, as she had done, had 'severed themselves from some of the conventional forms of living and thinking'. They included Edna O'Brien, Ann Quinn, Paddy Kitchen. *Talking to Women*, Dunn's transcriptions of these intimate interviews, was reissued in 2018 with an introduction by Ali Smith: it is full of ideas which resonate today.

I turned from Nell Dunn to *Between the Sheets* (2010) in which Lesley McDowell explores the often fraught relationships between nine twentieth-century women writers and their lovers or husbands: Katherine Mansfield and John Middleton Murry; Jean Rhys and Ford Madox Ford; Simone de Beauvoir and Jean-Paul Sartre. Why, McDowell asks, did these women stay with these men?

Finally, I read *Rebel Writers* (2019) by Celia Brayfield, who discusses a group of 'accidental feminists', Shelagh Delaney and Edna O'Brien among them, (Edna O'Brien is everywhere, and with good reason) who were writing powerful material in an era generally characterised by the emergence of Angry Young Men.

All these thoughtful books offer insights into their subjects and the art of biography. But, by their very nature, at least two of them are about writers whom the authors did not know: the material is drawn from the work they left behind. Furthermore, each has an overarching theme: the relationship with death; living the unexpected life; choosing difficult men; falling into feminism.

The book with which I found more common ground was *Dear Shadows: Portraits from Memory* (1986), in which the poet, novelist and critic John Wain summons from the shades very different people whom in life he knew well, and with whom he'd had important relationships. They include the famous – Marshall McLuhan, Richard Burton, Nevill Coghill – and the unknown: a landlady, a Welsh hill farmer, his father. All are gone, but Wain's penetrating essays capture the individuality of their lives and, glancingly, his own, over decades.

Two of the writers in my own book now lie within the shades, both people I cared for deeply. The others are very much alive, and I have known most of them for a long time, admiring both them and their work. It is our friendship, our common ground as writers, which unifies these essays. There is also a running thread of memoir: in many, I touch on what was happening in my own life at the time we met, or as our relationship developed.

In the contemporary literary landscape of this country new voices, many once obscured or ignored, are continually emerging. I make no apology for the fact that some of the voices in my book are old: indeed, one of the things I knew I wanted to do was talk to and learn from those who have gone the distance, continuing to produce fresh, engaging work well into old age.

Their work, and this book, span decades which have seen seismic changes in the working practice of writers, literary agents, publishers and booksellers. In the early seventies, when Michael Wall could barely afford to photocopy his plays for Edinburgh Fringe productions, stern gatekeepers stood between the new writer and the publishing house. Since then, many of those houses have been absorbed within huge corporations, and discerning new, independent ones have claimed their space. Meanwhile, writers now can self-publish anything they choose, and agents look online for the best of it. A Kindle can hold twenty thousand books and not a few writers are composing their novels on smart phones.

All this we know, yet in an age when the possibilities of communicating with one another have never been greater, there remains a fascination with what is often still the very private life of the individual writer. She or he has a strange existence, negotiating time spent in two deeply contrasting modes: Go away and leave me alone, and Look what I've done.

On the whole, the focus of this book is on the former. Unfashionably, perhaps, it looks at solitude, and the midnight hour; at drafting, redrafting, deleting and throwing away, starting all over again. It looks at what made these individuals the writers they are: at the people and places of their childhood; at the writers who stand in the shadow and light behind them; at struggle, inspiration and dedication to their art: this last above all. I don't think there is anyone here who has not had to overcome something hugely important in his or her life, and not one has given up. Above all – perhaps I knew it from the beginning – this is a book about resilience. In the age of Covid, when solitude has been more required than chosen, it is not only writers who have had to develop this. And it is Covid which accounts for the book appearing much later than intended.

Within its pages lie the quietude of the Somerset Levels and the violence of Northern Ireland. The essays move through wartime Warsaw and present-day Iran; through the English abroad and the Victorian underworld; environmental politics and colonial Egypt; nineteenth-century Russia and the North Yorkshire Moors. Here, too, are London galleries and museums, offering inspiration or shaping a career.

The writers who have made such material their own have all spoken to me at length: some down the years, all in long, wide-ranging interviews. I thank them for their generosity and rich, revealing talk.

I thank, too, my agent, Laura Longrigg, who has looked after me for so many years, and Mick Felton, publishing director of Seren, who had faith in the idea from the beginning, and commissioned the book.

Finally, I thank the person who has helped me throughout the writing. I am by nature a private, not to say secretive writer, unused to talking about or showing my work to anyone until it is done. This is still the case, but in later life I have been fortunate indeed to find a partner in Timothy Day. He writes about music, an art of which I know far too little, but through his unfailing interest and continual questioning he has opened my eyes to the value and enjoyment of dialogue about work in progress.

Essentially, however, I am with Kazuo Ishiguro, who so memorably said once: 'In the end, it's just you and the page.'

The Dramatist

MICHAEL WALL

Michael Wall outside The Royal Exchange Theatre,
Manchester, 1989.

'When I write, I want to smash through something – lack of feeling, indifference, cruelty. I'm shocked by callousness or indifference.'

I

Someone is talking to himself in the bath. It seems that a soldier has returned from the front to find his wife in the arms of another man.

'But what ees zis?'

Falsetto: 'I vas going to write you a letter, darling.'

There follows much laughter, and splashing about, then the taps are turned on and the geyser roars. Eavesdropping on the long dark landing outside the bathroom door, I can't hear what became of this doomed wartime couple, though I'm dying to know.

It is the spring of 1972. We are still in the age of the geyser, and the dreaded pilot light. We are deep in the age of *Time Out*, with its yards of small ads, and five of the seven of us now sharing a vast two-floor flat on Highbury Fields, north London, have each answered one. We've been through a long selection process, as Clare and Anna, old university friends, made their choices.

We each have an airy bedroom. I paint mine purple. With a lowly job in publishing, I've come from a tiny attic in a rambling, run-down place overlooking Hampstead Heath, even larger than the one in which I now find myself, sharing with six people I'm getting to know.

Clare – dark curly hair, appealing blue gaze – has a much more impressive job in publishing. It's the age of Tom Maschler at Jonathan Cape, and she's copy-editing *The Rachel Papers*, a first novel by someone called Martin Amis. 'He's Kingsley's son.' She's also proof-read Kingsley himself. 'He won't let you change a *comma*.'

Anna has a Pre-Raphaelite cloud of red hair and lovely skin; she's teaching at Goldsmith's College, right across the city. Cultural studies, though it wasn't called that then.

Who else have she and Clare selected to live here?

Jackie is a potter, tiny, pale, with wistful-looking dark brown eyes. Improbably, she has married Jay, a tall, lanky American photographer, who yodels at the kitchen sink and at thirty is older by far than any of us.

Patrick is a post-graduate art student, treating his bedroom as a studio. Tall and loose-limbed, with long curly hair and a gorgeous smile, he spends hours listening to music with Mike: Bob Dylan, the Beatles, the Bonzo Dog Doo Dah Band, Pink Floyd.

It is Mike who talks to himself in the bath. He talks to himself all the time: we can hear him trying out scenes in his room. Brought up on a council estate in Hereford, he left school at sixteen and is the only one of us without a job, living on toast and the dole, and announcing himself as a writer.

There are books on his shelves by writers I barely know, or have never heard of: Jean Genet, Richard Brautigan. On the table there's a heap of manuscripts in ancient folders. There's also a chess set, spirited away from his last job: a packer in a gift-shop factory. On Sunday afternoons, he teaches me to play. He's good, and chess means a lot to him.

Mike is of middle height, tow-haired, with little round specs and a moustache. There's something of E.M. Forster about his appearance. His clothes are ordinary – jeans and old shirts and jumpers – but he has a wine-coloured velvet jacket for special occasions. Wearing this, with newly-washed hair, he's adorable.

The first time we kiss, the morning after a party, I remark upon the moustache – and is that a bit of a denture? He tells me that he lost a number of teeth while hitch-hiking in Europe without a toothbrush. It's not until much later that he reveals that he was born with a cleft palate and a hare-lip: the shaggy moustache conceals the scar; the denture hides the wounded, toothless palate.

I have forgotten the cat. The cat is lithe and black and adopts us from who knows where. It's Mike who gives him his name: Spassky, after the Russian chess champion. It is Mike who puts him down on the electoral roll as a merchant seaman.

But he's a serious person. 'I can't see the point of life without writing,' he said once.

It's Mike who will be the first of us to die.

This essay about those distant Highbury days is about him.

It's about you, Mike, after all this time.

Michael Robert Wall was born in November 1946, in the Herefordshire village of Hoarwithy. A wintry name, but a pretty place, lovely to grow up in. Footpaths lead across peaceful meadows, in summer massed with buttercups, down to the river Wye. Mike was born in Myrtle Cottage, to Charles James Francis Wall, of Hereford, and Joan Valerie Mary Wall, née Hopwood, from St Helen's in Lancashire.

His appearance at birth must have caused some distress, but a cleft palate and a hare-lip are treatable, and he was treated, though until he could grow a moustache in his teens the scar on his upper lip perhaps marked him out a little. And perhaps that vulnerability deepened his mother's love: quite simply, she adored him.

I never knew his father, but Mike always spoke of him with affection. The son of a Hereford master builder, at the time of his marriage in 1946 he was working as a land drainage foreman: so the Marriage Certificate announces. What work he went on to do I don't remember, but I do remember going upstairs in Highbury one evening to find Mike on the telephone, sobbing his heart out at the news of his terminal illness. He died soon afterwards, and at the family home, the night before the funeral, I met Joan for the first time.

It was not until almost the end of his own life that Mike wrote a poem which revealed the depth of his feelings for his parents, his heartache about them, and his longing to hold them in a last embrace.

For Joan Wall think Thora Hird: Lancashire in every word she spoke, with permed fair hair, beaky nose and specs, a great laugh and definite ideas. A reproach to Mike when he fooled about as a boy was, 'That's not clever or funny,' and this line, like so much of what he read, overheard, or watched on TV or at the movies, became a part of him, making us laugh years later. In different guises, his mother, the way she spoke, and his relationship with her, would appear in much of his work.

Joan, twenty-three when her only child was born, began her working life as a shorthand typist, and became, when the family moved to Hereford in 1960, a youth employment officer, with many tales to tell of the hopeless youths who ended up in her office. The irony of his mother's occupation may not have been lost on Mike: he'd been a bit of a hopeless youth himself, leaving school without an exam to his name.

Thereafter, he worked variously as grave-digger (he noted the Shakespearian nuance in later years), as van driver, civil service clerk and, on his eventual arrival in London, Harrods shop assistant. Why had he done so badly at school?

Hereford could be a rough place, and to say that Mike grew up on a council estate might suggest the rough, or at least the drab. The Whitecross estate was neither: it was pretty, grassy, quiet. Charles and Joan made good friends here, and Mike, who was fourteen at the time of the move, would have had classmates with whom to walk home at the end of the day.

Try as I may, I have not been able to find out where he was at school. Wherever he was, was he daydreaming, mucking about in class throughout his time there? Riding on the bus at the age of three, he delighted his grandfather by reading out the names of shops, and long words on posters. How was it possible – how is it still, so often – for someone so bright to fail at every academic hurdle?

He was twenty-five when he came to that Highbury flat. He'd had all these dead-end jobs, he'd hitch-hiked round Europe; now, in London, he was going to make a go of it as a writer.

How? He had no contacts and Clare, who had liked him at interview but wondered how he was going to pay the rent, didn't offer to introduce him to the exalted offices of Jonathan Cape. At home all day while the rest of us were out at work, his frequent announcement as he entered a room, 'I've not been feeling very well lately,' might have got on her nerves. Sometimes he made her laugh, sometimes he didn't. He made me laugh a lot.

'When did you first realise you weren't normal?' he asked me now and then.

Always broke, he had a made-up language which he used to get past underground ticket collectors (very fast) without a ticket. 'Something-something the transit and the paradram,' he explained airily to the collector, and was bemusedly waved through.

'No tricks, no unpleasant bending,' he'd remark now and then, for no particular reason.

And then there were the Marx Brothers. I'd hardly heard of them, but Saturdays at the National Film Theatre soon put that right. Mike had watched those old movies a hundred times, and was happy to watch them a hundred more.

We settled into cheap seats to watch *Animal Crackers, Horse Features, Duck Soup*. Groucho, Harpo and Chico made their lunatic way through all of them, but it was Groucho who was the presiding spirit over Mike's life. He cultivated the features they had in common – little round specs, moustache. He held an imaginary cigar, Groucho's trademark, and pushed it back and forth through his open lips, head on one side, eyebrows waggling madly.

'Hello, I must be going,' he announced, like Groucho, on introductions at parties, and when asked what he did for a living said he was a vet. As in a Marx Brothers film, this could lead to complications: when horse ailments got too technical, he fled.

Who matched the Marx Brothers re-runs at this time? We were all glued to Monty Python each week, and their surreal and unstoppably inventive routines may have had something to do with one of Mike's first plays, begun in Highbury: the cast list of *Eric Crubb's Terrible German Experience* includes Adolf Hitler, the Lone Ranger, and the Inner London Telephone Directory. Eric himself is turning into Germany.

And then there was the music. Bob Dylan. The Beatles. Pink Floyd. Perhaps, as Patrick detected, it wasn't only their music – important to all of us – but something else which drew Mike in particular to the Beatles. Lennon, of course, like him, had a mad surreal mind. But also, like him, the band came from lower-middle-class origins, and were, as Mike was then, largely self-educated.

'Without that surge of creativity from less privileged backgrounds which characterised Sixties pop music (and playwriting, of course),' Patrick has written to me, 'I wonder if Mike would have become a writer. I always thought of him as being very much part of that sixties zeitgeist.'

Lazy Sunday afternoons… A blurry black and white photo shows Mike and me at his table, the chess board between us, Spassky the cat at the window, the smoke of a joint rising hazily into the summer air. We both look pretty happy. There was all that, in the first year of our little community: the films, the music, supper at the kitchen table, the joint passed round, the laughter. But Mike, writing every day on a portable typewriter while we were all at work; shouting to himself in the empty flat as he made another cup of tea; piling up another unpublished novel, another unperformed play, was getting nowhere. What was to be done?

What he did, finally, was to take some A-levels. In September 1972 he began to attend evening classes, and the following summer passed English and History with good grades. He had an interview in the English Department at York and was accepted as a mature student. Those were, of course, the long-lamented days of grants.

In September 1973 he left me an affectionate note of farewell, and set out for King's Cross and the train to York. I don't think anyone saw him off.

At York, after all those years of writing into the dark, Michael Wall's life as a thinker, a writer, a comedian and, above all, as a dramatist, finally began to take real shape. And at York, among dozens of girlfriends, he met the brilliant young woman from 'a sensationally different background', as he described it later, with whom he would, eventually, settle for the rest of his life.

II

17 October 1973

Dear Suze,

I've got to read Plato's Republic for a tutorial tomorrow. I arrived at a seminar the other day & found they were discussing Merchant of Venice, *which I've never read or seen: everyone else had the book open in front of them. I dunno – I don't seem to be able to catch the notices they stick up. Things like that. The lectures are actually quite interesting... Dr Drain is a gas – about 38, grey long hair, denims; he says, 'No one gives a shit about Shakespeare,' & all the kids*

*try & look as if they hear it all the time from teachers. [He's]
crazy, but in a very Samuel Beckett way; he does drama and
runs the shoestring theatre...*

*The play is held up due to Plato & lack of Croxley typing
paper, but I have at least written it...*

Dear Sue, Dear Suzie, Dear Suze...Love, Mike.

The letters were almost always undated, the postmarks
smudged. He wrote, I wrote back; I visited. I remember a cold
little house in a country lane, a room with bare floorboards, bed,
table and chair, an empty fireplace. His housemates were charming; there were two spectacular cats.

Sometimes he came down to London. Over that first year we
were affectionate, longing, querulous, struggling to disentangle
ourselves from each other. Mike in particular was struggling,
pulled in two directions: back towards London and me and,
more powerfully and importantly, towards fulfilling himself as
an independent artist. He was ambitious and determined and, as
a mature student – funny, original, and a startling dramatist –
became a compelling and charismatic university figure. 'An
aged, undergrad lord of misrule," recalls the actor Matthew
Marsh, who became a lifelong friend.

The play Mike refers to in this early letter was almost
certainly *Experiments made on Rats*, of which only a scruffy
flyer survives. A later passing reference indicates that both
Hamlet and Groucho were in the cast, entirely possible. Within
two weeks of arrival, he was presenting it to the Drama Society.
They agreed to put it on in the spring term.

*The amount of work is incredible... The business of timing and
rehearsing difficult people, sustaining the level of enthusiasm, clearing
rooms for rehearsal, arranging lights and props... I've got a few
helpers, like set-builders, painters, publicity, etc, so I'm getting
somewhere. It's just the typing – 20 copies of 30 pages – it'll be a
costly business photostatting that lot & I can't type on a stencil. I'm
sure Pinter doesn't have this hassle...*

I remember a late-night performance in a small dark campus theatre, with someone called Henry, tall and bespectacled, looking mad and shouting his head off at the audience. This was Henry Blaxland, who later became a barrister in radical chambers.

Meanwhile, Mike's essays were coming back with a B++, '*a good 2.1. I suppose if I can keep that up, I'll be okay.*'

By the beginning of 1974 our relationship was becoming difficult: he more withdrawn, I more demanding. I began seeing someone else in London; Mike didn't like this, but in the spring confessed in a long letter that he'd been having affairs with other girls. One of them was another undergraduate reading English, but in the year below. This was the much younger Lizzie Slater.

Lizzie was one of four children of a senior civil servant, educated at a progressive independent school, accustomed to privilege, but politically aware. She was also very beautiful: small, pale-skinned and clear-eyed, with a mass of unruly, deep auburn hair. There was an intense physical attraction and a deep love of language to unite these two improbable lovers.

But what they also had in common was a fearlessness, an unflinching commitment to truth. In this, and in a refusal to compromise, they were both, in different ways, true artists: Mike as the writer who in 1986 would refuse to agree to BBC cuts to a radical new play, and saw it banned; Lizzie in becoming what another friend, the director Jeremy Mortimer, once described as an unsalaried cultural entrepreneur. She became the important 'someone else' in Mike's life; she became, in time, his true love.

But throughout his years at York Mike and I went on writing to one another: as ex-lovers; as sometimes quarrelsome, tentative friends; as readers exchanging views.

I've been sitting all day in the library reading Clarissa and thinking of writing to you...

I am reading Middlemarch & think Dorothea needs something stiff up the bum. Hope you weren't on that dreadful Moorgate train.

In September 1974 Matthew Marsh and Henry Blaxland invited Mike to join them in working on the Edinburgh Revue, which Matthew was now directing. Anthony Horowitz joined them, and the four created *A Short History of Western Culture*, which included Mike in what Matthew remembers as a brilliant Dirk Bogarde in a parody of *Death in Venice*.

And Mike's writing, Matthew thought, 'had more subtlety than the writing of the rest of us – and contained comedy about real people, rather than the more derivative stuff that Anthony and I wrote... In the summer of 1975 we took our show *A Farewell to Legs* to Edinburgh and it's fair to say we were the best reviewed and most successful student review on the fringe – there were no other types of comedy shows in those days, certainly no stand-up.'

By the time Mike joined Matthew in this enterprise an old voice from Highbury days was making itself heard once more.

I want to work on this multi-media musical about a man who eats so much that he turns into Germany. I'm really excited about this. There will be all kinds of paintings on a screen, music in the mould of Schubert plus Clara Schumann, Nietzsche, Bismarck, Hitler et al all coming into the life of Eric Grubb. Far-reaching stuff...

Eric Crubb's Terrible German Experience had its first, and I think only production at York in 1975. Matthew played Martin Boorman and an American New Age conman. As well as Hitler, the Lone Ranger and the Inner London Telephone Directory, the cast of twenty-two included the Siamese twins Willy and Eric Crubb (now separated); their benighted parents; a bus conductor and one Father O'Cattle, also played by Matthew, who recalls performing an exorcism on a ventriloquist's dummy.

'It was an anarchic surrealist drama,' he writes. 'N.F. Simpson and Milliganesque – about Eric Crubb who somehow managed to be both East and West Germany. I don't remember the plot, or even if there was one, but a lot happened and there were a lot of laughs... It was the work of a huge and fertile imagination.'

In 1976, with his good 2:1 degree, Mike left York and Lizzie, who still had another year to go, and returned to London. Behind him were three years of adrenaline-fuelled success. He had been the self-proclaimed Jonathan Miller of York, looked up to and adored.

Now what? Where was he going to live? Not in Highbury. I had moved in with my Someone Else; most of the people we'd lived with in that rambling flat had moved out. But he and Patrick had remained in touch, and in the scorching summer of that year he went to join him in a Brixton squat.

Work and focus were not the centre of things for the other people living in Villa Road, and Mike did not take kindly to 'the hippy/drop-out, dope-smoking ambience of a squat', as Patrick describes it. 'But he was naturally very popular, being easily the funniest person in the room, with a fresh angle to bring to bear on most conversations.'

He also had a fiercely competitive streak. This wasn't something which I ever witnessed, probably because his rivalry was essentially with other men: Patrick remembers a chess game played in pre-York days with a visiting old school friend, in which Mike upturned the board in a fury. Now there was another chess row with a man in the squat. It blew over, but Patrick noted it; three years later, he and Mike were to fall out dramatically over a game of tennis, something which, with one or two other things, would sever their friendship for decades.

That often difficult summer was enlivened by Matthew Marsh's arrival in London. He and Mike hired the Little Theatre Club (later to become Stringfellows) in Covent Garden, and here, for two weeks, they put on their greatest hits from York. Quite a few of us from Highbury days went to see it, and watching these two belting out their calypso-style masturbation song was not something easily forgotten.

They were invited to go to a couple of script meetings for

Radio 4's *Weekending*, but as Matthew says, they weren't really writing that kind of material and the comedy scene now everywhere in London was non-existent then. Soon after, he took off for America and Mexico, while Mike, frustrated and directionless, stayed on in Brixton.

Then Lizzie came down from York.

Their first home together was in the basement of her father's elegant house in Camden Town. After the squat, this flat must have felt like heaven to Mike, but Lizzie was restless and ambitious to see the world, and they didn't stay there long. It was she who suggested they went to Japan.

Mike's travelling until now had consisted of hitch-hiking in Germany, and that a long time ago; nothing in his background could have prepared him for such a trip, and he confessed to Patrick that he was deeply anxious about it.

'At times like that,' Patrick recalls, 'one was suddenly reminded of the child within him for whom the journey from a Herefordshire backwater to carving a name for himself on the London cultural scene was a massive journey.'

Nevertheless, with no job, no production to work on, and nothing much in view, it would also be an adventure: I think it was in late 1979 that they flew out to Tokyo.

There, Lizzie became involved with new forms of Butoh dance. She would later become deeply involved with LIFT, the biannual London International Festival of Theatre, still going strong, and in 1983 brought over a group of experimental Japanese dancers, Sankai Juku, for a stunning performance at the Roundhouse in Camden Town.

Meanwhile, in those Tokyo days, Mike supported himself by teaching English. The city, the experience, the immersion in a completely different culture, were to combine as a defining point in his life as an artist.

III

DAN: Tell me, Mrs Ogura – why do you want to learn English?

AKEMI: Why? Ah – to bring myself up.

DAN: Bring yourself up?

AKEMI: Yes. My children.

DAN: Your children, yes?

AKEMI: My children learn English in school. I must speak also so I can help them.

In *Japanese Style*, Dan is staying in a cheap Tokyo hotel with his Australian girlfriend Carol, supporting them both by teaching English to private pupils. Through Carol, Oz is presented as brash, crude, uncultured: Japan – 'a lot different to India' – is a stop-over. But Dan, travel-weary of 'clamouring Asian countries' is beguiled: by the Kabuki theatres, open all day – places of 'enchantment, exaggeration, sensation, bourgeois revenge' – and by the exquisite manners of those he meets: waitresses, girls in bars, his pupils. He loves the bow with which Akemi greets him.

Married to a computer businessman, mother of two sons, she giggles when she calls herself a housewife, but that is what she is, living on a close-packed street in the suburbs.

DAN: My name is Akemi Ogura.

AKEMI: My name is Akemi Ogura...

DAN: I am happy.

AKEMI: I am happy…

[The repetitions continue: 'sad', 'tired', 'not tired'.]

DAN: TURNS PAGES) I think we can move on a bit… Let's see…

AKEMI: I am lonely.

DAN: Pardon?

AKEMI: I am…lonely.

DAN: Lonely – you mean 'alone'? (SHORT PAUSE) When you are 'lonely' you have no friends. (SHORT PAUSE) No friends, no family, no husband. Lonely. Do you see?

This moment, a few scenes into the play, is a turning point: the first indication that Akemi's settled, ordered life is not what it seems. And *Japanese Style* represents a turning point in Michael Wall's work: the hectic, hilarious, anarchic style of *Experiments Made on Rats, Eric Crubb* and the student revues of York has gone, and what takes its place is a thoughtful, fluidly constructed two-act play, whose deepening interaction between a troubled, alluring Japanese woman and a restless young Englishman is layered with sadness and unease. The writing is poised, controlled, beautiful, full of delicate obser- vations and shot through with pain. The play culminates in the revelation of a shocking act of violence. By the end, the balance of power has shifted entirely: Akemi has revealed her rage and power; Dan, who has fallen in love with her, is adrift.

Japanese Style came into being with the encouragement of Jeremy Mortimer, an old schoolfriend of Lizzie's now working in the drama department of BBC Radio 4. On their return from their travels in 1982, Mike and Lizzie had supper with him and his girlfriend Polly Fisher, later to become his wife.

Mike talked eloquently about his experience of teaching English in Tokyo; Jeremy said it would make a brilliant radio play.

'This was on the Friday,' Jeremy recalls. 'On the Monday Mike presented me with a script which was absolutely ready to go. I could hardly believe it.'

The play went out in September 1982. Jeremy Mortimer directed it, and there began a creative partnership which would last throughout Mike's career.

Japanese Style is about many things. By the time he came to hammer it out over a weekend on his old portable typewriter, Mike had travelled extensively through Asia, and the play draws on many of his newly-awakened feelings about history, modernity and the past. It carries two yearning epigraphs, the second just two lines from the eleventh-century Japanese work *The Tale of Genji*.

'Life must end, it is a transient world.

The one thing lasting is the bond between us.'

They represent the side of Mike which was most tender, most sad and nostalgic, most longing for beauty. This aspect of his personality contrasts with the rage and violence he often expressed on the page, but is no less real. And the violence in *Japanese Style* – Akemi's terrible burning of her neighbours – is shown as the result of repression, isolation, an elaborate courtesy which conceals fear and heartache. Is this Japanese 'style'?

The play is the first in his *oeuvre* to treat the recurring theme of the Englishman abroad. Travelling for the first time, Mike had the opportunity to look back at his own country; he didn't always like what he saw. In Japan, he might have wanted to shake the English dust from his feet and assimilate a completely different culture. But, as both Carol and Dan himself acknowledge, there are unknowable things in another country: a woman who bows, offers tea, and modestly considers herself to be 'rotten English student', can perform an act of horror.

The play also explores the barriers of language: misunderstandings, double meanings, an inability to express real feeling even in your own. This is the first time Mike seriously explored relationships between men and women, and perhaps it is the only one in which the possibility of real love – 'something I never had any idea could happen' – is acknowledged, even if it ends in rejection and tragedy. Later plays figure dead-end marriages, sexploitation, hatred. The marriages in *Women Laughing* (1989) are fraught and bitter, couples clinging to each other only out of fear.

I listened to *Japanese Style* while walking in the Yorkshire

Dales with my life-partner, Marek Mayer, eventually my husband. Marek and Mike got along well, as did Lizzie and I: we made a good quartet of friends. By now Mike and Lizzie were living in a little house in Corbyn Street, Finsbury Park. We were in Highbury, not so far away: we saw quite a lot of each other.

On that holiday Marek and I were expecting our first baby, and our minds were more on that than anything. But we had taken a radio with us: Mike's first play on the BBC! Sitting on the grass, we listened to those intense, contrasting voices.

> *I am lonely… My-heart-is…*
> *I'm just an alien…*
> *Have you ever tried looking at yourself with Japanese eyes?*
> *The blinds tremble, although I know it is only the wind…*

Japanese Style had three productions: on Radio 4 in 1982; on BBC2 the following year; at the Belgrade Theatre, Coventry, in 1984. It established Michael Wall as a new and important voice: over the next seven driven and prolific years, he more than fulfilled his promise. Between 1982 and 1989 he wrote some twenty plays for radio, stage and television.

He followed *Japanese Style* with a play which returned directly to Japan and an Englishman abroad, but in a specific historical context. This was *Hiroshima: The Movie* (1985), commissioned for Radio 4 by Jeremy Mortimer to mark the fortieth anniversary of the bombing of Hiroshima in 1945. Once more, he was the director. 'It represented a leap forward in Mike's writing,' he says now. 'Sophisticated, beautifully structured, with an interesting soundscape.'

Paul, an indie movie-maker, is in Japan to observe and record the reconstructed city, with its memorial Peace Park, American tourists, ex-POWs and micro-skirted, knickerless waitresses in the Hiroshima Bar. The play, startlingly accomplished in its use of sound-effects and montage, focusses on the unknowability of another culture – and, once more, on the impossibility of a full relationship between two very different characters.

Paul is divorced, cynical, living in largely unacknowledged loneliness. 'I'm a different person in every country I visit,' he reflects. Sachiko, the tourist guide whom he films all over the city, has a much stronger identity, or so it seems.

PAUL: Why is Sachiko the centre of my film? Of course, I do not suggest she is Japan; she is more than that. Close-up... Look. The breeze is stirring her hair through the open window of the bus. Her white glove is holding the microphone. Her thoughts are moving, the camera is still. There is only Sachiko in the frame. She does not represent Japan, she substitutes herself for it. She will survive.

Unlike Akemi in *Japanese Style*, Sachiko is a working woman, divorced and independent. And sharp. 'Why you make this kind of movie?' she asks Paul in their first conversation. 'What kind of movie?' he asks her. 'Kind of movie no one will see?'

But, like Akemi, she has a hinterland of mystery. Every now and then, while Paul is filming her, she disappears, and it is not until almost the last scene, both poignant and emblematic of aspects of Japan, that we discover why. She is visiting her dying father, one of the bomb's survivors, but her hospital visits are 'not for loving reason'. She goes because he has refused to tell her the identity of her mother, who died in childbirth.

SACHIKO: Maybe my mother was low woman, maybe prostitute. There is great shame for my father... But I am determined he must tell me this before he dies.

She gives Paul a parting gift: a beautiful pre-war kimono. 'Some things were not destroyed, you see.' Moved as he is, he returns to the studio to shut his feelings away, turning his attention not to the film he has been making but to footage from Mexico.

Directed by Jeremy Mortimer, *Hiroshima: The Movie* won two major awards: a Sony for Best Drama Production, and a Giles Cooper Award for one of the best radio plays of 1985. Michael Wall, established as a considerable radio dramatist, was now taken on by an ambitious young literary agent, Micheline Steinberg. She continues to represent his work to the present day.

The Englishman abroad, beguiled by a woman from another country, returns in *The Man in the Wide-Brimmed Hat* (Radio 4, 1987). Set in 1850, against the backdrop of the Austrian occupation of Italy, its centre is the love affair between a minor Pre-Raphaelite painter, Charles Catchpole (played by Edward Petherbridge) and the dazzling Princess Malvezzi (Eleanor Bron), who commissions him to paint her portrait.

It's a beautifully constructed play, set mostly in Venice, 'a place full of whispers'. The city, where Ruskin and Effie are also staying, is evocatively realised: the bells ringing out in the Piazza San Marco; the lapping canals and the songs of the gondoliers; Verdi opera; footsteps racing through the narrow streets, all provide a seductive background to an occupied city full of political intrigue. For the Princess Malvezzi, a princess only by marriage to 'that fat fool in Savoy', is an ardent nationalist, who on her early-morning walks with Catchpole carries, he realises, a pistol in her shawl.

PRINCESS: You see Venice awakening. Luxurious houses and peaceful rios, which you call canals... But you have not seen her in her darkest hour, with the bloodshed, the broken shutters, the twisted railings and the corpse of a little girl, killed as she was out playing with friends...
CATCHPOLE: No, it's true, I haven't seen these things. I suppose my life has not had many dark hours, as you call them.
Mike was stretching his wings in this play, exploring what it

means to be political, what it means to be an artist. As the drama unfolds, and the atmosphere in the city becomes more dangerous, Catchpole learns he is suspected of being a member of 'a secret brotherhood'. The Princess confides that, not for the first time, she is planning an assassination.

It is her passionate patriotism which impels her to conceal a bomb within a bouquet, and to hurl it at the visiting Marshal Radetsky as he glides down a canal. The attempt fails, she is arrested, and taken to the Spielberg prison, but when Catchpole tries to visit her, he tells her descendant years later:

CATCHPOLE: They would admit no one. I remember banging my fist on the captain's desk and saying, 'I am an Englishman, damn you!'

This cuts no ice, and fearing for his own safety he simply gives up and goes home. His kind of Englishness, in the end, manifests itself not only through reticence, good manners, dry wit, but through his failure to engage, and his abandonment of his lover.

The *Financial Times* pronounced *The Man in the Wide-Brimmed Hat* one of the two outstanding plays of the week, with Jeremy Mortimer's production 'rich in well-chosen sound... painting a fine Venetian picture'. Edward Petherbridge won a Sony Award for his portrayal of Charles Catchpole, and Mike was very happy.

But he had treated the English abroad quite differently in the hilarious *Blue Days* (1985), a stage play starring the young Kathy Burke and performed in a Hampstead pub. A group of us, including Patrick, went to see it, and I remember laughing until it hurt.

Four young English people fetch up in a villa in Spain owned by Lee, a flashy ex-pat whose 'husband', clearly a rogue, never appears. The Villa Kassman, improbably named after another old friend from York, John Kassman, is 'like one of those places you see on the television, where people lose all their savings'. The play is full of bickering, drink and innuendo, with Sammy (Kathy Burke) a 'runaway from a mental institution' and Becky, a posh young Cambridge student, the foils for the uneducated and unemployed young couple Chrissie and Duane. The play reads now like something of a dry run for *Amongst Barbarians* (1989), but without the real brutality.

A preoccupation with what it means to be English, and what kind of country England has become, characterises many of Mike's strongest plays, but what *au fond* connects some of them is an existential despair. It's there in *Japanese Style*, in *Hiroshima: The Movie* and in *Blue Days*, whose washed-up characters don't really know what to do with their lives. And it's there in *Imaginary Wars in England* (1986) a powerful stage play only performed after his death, in which England is in the grip of a totalitarian, Soviet-style revolution.

Above all, it suffuses one of his finest radio plays, *Headcrash* (1986), so violent that it was banned.

BOY: If I hadn't discovered this record, you know what I'd be saying to myself now? Why not kill myself? Really I would. Well, I might very easily. Because I used to think it before. All I could say to myself then was – why should I kill myself when there are so many who need killing first.

Dystopian barely describes this play. By *Bonnie & Clyde* out of *Badlands*, it is a surreal hymn to nihilism. Set 'in the far future', inside a car driven wildly through a desolate, post-apocalyptic landscape by the maniacal Boy, it up-ends the road-movie for ever.

The cast includes Road Signs, Creeps, Wild Men and Scavengers. The other passenger in the car is Yuka (Toyah Wilcox), covered like a mummy from head to foot with bloodstained bandages, with slits for eyes. Like Boy, who was born 'in a highway pile-up' she is murderous.

YUKA: You missed her, Boy! You missed a pedestrian.
(FX: A SCREAM IS HEARD, DISTANT)
It's all right, a truck got her.

There are echoes of *Hiroshima* in Yuka's flayed skin, and in the rumbling atomic bomb in the horror effects, which also include screams, car horns, screeching of tyres, gunshots, roller skaters (who only come out at night, and get shot), a baying elephant and cacophonous music.

Headcrash is a tremendous piece of work, the imagination unstoppable, the writing terrific. As the bleakest allegory for the human condition, it has a weird intelligiblity, an internal coherence and integrity. The journey Boy and Yuka are making is unexplained. All we know is that they sleep in one another's arms, and are on the run. Wind blows over a high bridge, over a desolate plain. Cars drift by, or are violently rammed off the road. 'Lost cities' lie behind and ahead.

Like the Road Signs (given to weeping), these cities have human feelings, and within the mayhem the overall feeling to the play is one of enormous sadness. I would argue that within Boy, depicted as a murderous psychopath, lie shades of a dark and dangerous Peter Pan.

(FX THE WIND, CONTINUING, BUT FADE UP TELEPHONE RINGING, DISTANT)
MOTHER: Is that you, Boy?
BOY: Yes, this is Boy...
MOTHER: At last...that's a clever boy, coming to find his old mother...
BOY: What's it mean, 'mother'?

The motherless Lost Boys of *Peter Pan*, living outside the world in Neverland: it is hard not to think of them with this wondering question. Much violence is followed by a poignant farewell kiss, inside the car, on a dark and empty road. And then the poignancy is suddenly subverted: this is the mother from hell, swinging between a smothering affection and urging Boy on to kill.

MOTHER: (WHISPER) ...Go on and hate. Hate, Boly! [sic] Take it away and let all hell rip!

He does. He swats her dying laugh out of the window; he hits the road.

BOY: Try to look at me and you're dead! To kill with a flick of the eyes... All my life has led to this point!.. You keep out of my way, and make sure I don't see you, okay?
(FX: BOY'S CAR SPEEDS AWAY. SILENCE.)

The BBC's banning of this powerful, haunting play was a setback in Mike's relationship with them. (It was finally broadcast on Radio 3 in 1993, two years after his death.) It was two years before *The Wide-Brimmed Hat* was broadcast to such acclaim. But his greatest success was to come. *Amongst Barbarians* won the 1988 Mobil Award for Best Play of the Year, judged by Tom Courtenay and Albert Finney. It is based on a real event: the hanging in Malaysia in 1986 of two young men, one British, one Australian, for smuggling heroin.

BRYAN: What – foreigners hang an Englishman? Leave it out; it's a complete contradiction in terms. I mean, who gave 'em their fucking legal system in the first place?

Who are the barbarians in this drama? Those about to perform an execution, or their families, who have flown out to try to prevent it? Bryan's family have already sold the story to the papers. The play shows the English abroad at their worst: ignorant, arrogant, racist.

In a long interview in the *Independent* given to coincide with the first production of the play, Mike said he'd been shocked by public attitudes to the case.

'Everyone seemed to think they deserved it: "They knew the laws, they knew the risks, heroin's horrible, too bad." That wasn't my line at all. I felt sorry for them. That goes some way towards explaining the anger; why the play is so extreme.'

He made both young men British. Ralph, a dealer and registered addict, tunes out with headphones in the prison cell; it is Bryan, loutish and foul-mouthed, who swears at their gentle Sikh gaoler and is openly terrified of what is to come. In Act Two he pulls out a knife smuggled in by his sister.

BRYAN: Say this after me: I am a Paki Go on – 'I am a Paki.'
The GAOLER speaks calmly, as though humouring a child.
GAOLER: I am a Paki.

Meanwhile Toni, Ralph's mother, first seen in bed with the hotel barman, suggests to the female Malaysian lawyer that an introduction to the Governor would be useful: if she gets him into bed he might pardon her son.

LAWYER: I've never heard anything so outrageous in my life... What a very low opinion you must have of us! ...
TONI: Ah well...what I think is – if you are dealing with barbarians you've got to use barbarian tactics.
LAWYER: Barbarians... You know this is a terrible insult.

Toni is an ex-pat living in Spain, all bling. Like Thora Hird, like Mike's mother, she speaks posh Lancashire – 'Alan Bennett northern gentility', as one critic put it. Knowing, manipulative, canny, she's been looking out for herself for a long time. Bryan's parents are much less sophisticated: 'emotional incompetents' is how another critic described them. George is nervy, gormless, bullied by Wendy, his loud, alcoholic wife. Lilly [sic], Bryan's sister, is 'overweight, sluttish, glazed'. There are shades of Mike Leigh in all of them.

Over the course of two days tension builds both within the cell and in the hotel rooms. Everyone, it's uncovered by the end, is doing some kind of drug. It's a portrait of washed-up people, but although much of the play is about brutality, pig-headed ignorance and the failure of family life – 'It's just family talk,' says George, in a pitiful attempt to normalise hatred and resentment – there are moments when something else breaks through.

In her farewell scene with Ralph, Toni begs him to name those higher up in the syndicate: she can shop them in return for his life. He refuses, mocks her with his own name, gets up to go.

GAOLER: Ralph! Kiss your mother.
RALPH (*returning*) He's a big family man, you know. These Sikhs are like that, they don't understand us, our – understatement and all that shit. (*He laughs*) Something rather universal, kind of eternal in this scene, don't you think? Mothers and their sons – you can't beat it.

(*He goes to give her a peck on the cheek but somehow the embrace very quickly becomes impassioned: she covers him with kisses and they hold each other tightly.*)

Think *Headcrash*. Think mother and son in a last embrace, a boy speeding away into silence, leaving devastation behind him. Think of Mike himself, the only son of an adoring mother. Here the real agony of these people is on show, and it is the play's achievement that although the characters are largely held up as monstrous we also care for them.

Of the ending of this dark, despairing drama, Mike said in that long interview that he wanted it to be 'complete mayhem, absolutely shattering, everything broken up'. He compared it to *King Lear*, where 'Shakespeare smashes everything at the end... I wanted to do that – smash everything up.'

And while Ralph and Bryan are taken away to be hanged, their families drink and dance. Blood drips from a needle in Wendy's arm, Lilly lunges for the Barman, George grapples Wendy to the floor and Toni is frozen into immobility. The Lawyer enters, stops, aghast, and we hear the bodies drop. Lights out.

With the brilliant Kathy Burke playing Lilly, and Avril Elgar as Wendy, *Amongst Barbarians* had its first production in February 1989 at the Manchester Royal Exchange: the theatre which, searching for strong new writing, had sought sponsorship from Mobil for a competition. In 1988 the play had won Mike £10,000, an unimaginable sum for someone who the year before had earned perhaps £2000 from radio plays.

He and Lizzie had a celebration lunch in their garden in Corbyn Street. Jeremy and Polly (who since 1983 had been living just across the road), Marek and I all sat on rugs on the uncut grass, drinking champagne in the sun.

'Ten thousand pounds,' Mike kept saying. 'Ten thousand pounds!' There was something else to celebrate: Lizzie was pregnant.

There's something in *Amongst Barbarians* which links with Mike's own life. Toni is partly drawn from his mother, but it's not that. When Wendy is unpacking in their hotel room, George asks her to get his pills out of the case – "Got the bleeding shakes already, I have.' He struggles to read the label. 'Carbamazepine! That's the ones.'

Carbamazepine is a drug used to treat epilepsy. It might have done little for George's nerves, but it was a drug whose name Mike could use with confidence because he himself was taking it.

I'm not sure when he first began to experience symptoms of his illness, but as it developed he began to suffer seizures. It was some time before I witnessed one, but I heard about them: they were described as panic attacks, and because of them Mike had gone into two years of psychotherapy. The experience fed into his last major play, *Women Laughing*, broadcast on Radio 4 in the same week that *Amongst Barbarians* opened at Manchester. This was in February 1989.

On 5 April of that year, Marek and I accompanied Mike and Lizzie to hospital, as they had taken us when our son was on the way. Now, Nicola was born, a very beautiful, dark-eyed baby. Her arrival took Mike into a new sphere: of happiness, pure and simple.

There was little of that in his last bleak play.

MADDY: No, we weren't laughing unkindly, were we, Steph?
COLIN: Oh no, it's never unkind! Perish the thought. It's just funny, that's all. And that's the main thing, isn't it? That our wives have a good giggle. I get a panic attack – ha ha ha. I wake up in the night – ha ha ha; I get on the train to go home, it's the wrong train – ha ha ha... It's women who drive us mad and then they laugh at us when we seek help.

Why are the women laughing in the house while their husbands struggle to make conversation out in the garden? ('So how's the car running?') Because they've discovered that both men are seeing psychiatrists. Or receiving 'some form of therapy'. Ha ha ha. It's a play filled with bitterness and fear, with bemusement and hatred. And it's essentially tragic: people going under without the first idea of why. Lizzie, who throughout Mike's career was a fiercely intelligent editor of his work, described it in her introduction to the Oberon Books edition (1992) as an Anatomy of Melancholy.

Two married couples, Colin and Stephanie, Tony and Maddy, have known each other a long time but don't meet often. The two acts are both set in gardens: Act One in Ealing, home of Colin and Stephanie, Act Two in the garden, or grounds, of 'a

North London asylum'. Ealing probably stands simply for suburbia; north London is, of course, very close to home.

And I read this play as pretty close to home. Mike and his life weave in and out of it, particularly through Colin, the more extrovert of the two men. 'I was a natural mimic,' he says of his schooldays. And: 'I speak to myself sometimes.' Somewhat improbably, on a summer day out in the garden, he smokes a cigar. 'He looks a bit like Groucho Marx with that, doesn't he?' says Maddy. Groucho was, it seems clear, essentially a signature in Mike's work. When Maddy wonders at Colin's elaborate way of talking – 'You look like a deity with all her offerings' – Stephanie says, 'It's only showing off.'

COLIN: It's always 'showing off', isn't it? That's exactly what my mother used to say.

All this is pure Mike: impersonating at random, talking to himself, waggling that Groucho cigar, recalling his mother's talk, and ticking off. 'That's not clever or funny': it wouldn't be surprising to find that line of hers in here. Crucially present, of course, is his illness – insomnia, panic attacks, confusion. Catching the wrong train was just the kind of thing he began to do as illness took hold, and at the end of his life he wrote a heartbreaking poem about getting lost in a French seaside town. However far his life was removed from suburban talk of cars and garden trellis, he's there in this play, and it sprang from his suffering.

As for the fear and loathing of women: perhaps there always was a conflict within him; perhaps it lay in his relationship with his mother, so close that he had to break away, no matter how much he loved her. Or perhaps, as he fell ill, no matter how much he was supported, he felt isolated, afraid, misunderstood.

Women Laughing began life as a radio play; Mike added a second act for the stage version which followed, first performed in 1992 at the Royal Exchange Manchester, a year after his death. It won the Writers' Guild Best Regional New Play and the Manchester Evening News Best New Play; it remains the most produced of all his stage plays, most recently revived in a production at the Old Red Lion Theatre in Islington, in 2012. For all that, Jeremy Mortimer feels that the addition of a second act made it looser. 'And it's a little bit voyeuristic, it kind of makes fun of the characters.'

It does. It holds limited lives up to the light, exposing them as both pitiful and shameful. Tony has gone into group therapy 'just to take the pressure off, really...'

TONY: But the thing that – precipitated it was the sensation that – I thought – I wanted to kill my wife... I wanted to take her neck in my bare hands and squeeze and squeeze until I [could] feel the life ebbing away.
MADDY: That's just the way he is.

It's all on a cusp of pain and laughter, real feeling undercut in a flash. Like George, in *Amongst Barbarians*, these people struggle to normalise distress and dysfunction.

As in that dark play, the drama ends with a tableau, though here, in hospital, they are disco dancing: to the theme tune from *Saturday Night Fever*, which once meant a lot to them. It's a kind of dance of death.

IV

Early in 1990 Mike and I went out for supper. It was a 'Well, here we are now,' sort of evening. We talked about the past, we talked about our children. My family had moved to Stoke Newington, buying a house at last; Mike was unofficial godfather to Jamie, now seven.

We talked about our work: I had published my first novel, which Mike didn't think much of; *Amongst Barbarians* was going to be televised on BBC2, starring David Jason as George. And there was another radio play going out on Radio 4. *Do be Doo be Doo* was about a northern working-class mother and her son, who brings her down to London for a Frank Sinatra concert.

We ate, we talked. All at once Mike went very pale, and began to sweat. In moments he was in the grip of a seizure, groaning, eyes closed, unable to speak. It lasted for perhaps a couple of minutes. Then it was over: he opened his eyes and smiled.

It so happened that I had had a brush with epilepsy in my teens. It so happened that the father of one of Jamie's friends at primary school was a neurologist, working at what is now the National Hospital for Neurology and Neurosurgery, in Queen Square. I told him about Mike: he arranged for a fast-track referral.

Lizzie and I both went to see Mike there after the biopsy they performed. He was up in a post-op room, white blinds drawn against the afternoon sun, everything shady and quiet. He lay on a narrow bed, his head bandaged; he gave us a rueful smile. The diagnosis came soon afterwards: a brain tumour, inoperable.

For a while Mike and Lizzie stayed on in Corbyn Street. But London began to be stressful: too many hospital appointments and tests, too many people. With a grant of £5000 from the Royal Literary Fund – the £10,000 from the Mobil competition had long since gone – they decided to go and live in France. They had friends in Uzes, a pretty little medieval town not far from Nimes, in the south. The seaside resort of La Grande Motte wasn't far away. They could be quiet and restful; it would be warm, and good for Nicola. Their friends found them somewhere to live.

In their absence I saw Joan Wall, with whom I had always kept in touch. Marek, Jamie and I had had a farm holiday in Herefordshire for many years; I often visited Joan, and she came over to the farm for lunch one day.

'Hello, pet.' She was laughing and beaky as ever, but she knew what was going on with Mike, and it was breaking her heart. We went for a walk in the fields, soaking after rain. 'I just don't know what I'd do if he died before me.'

In August Mike wrote me a letter, impeccably typed. This is an extract.

> 29 rue Sigalon, Uzes
> 10 August 1990

Dear Sue,

I'm only just beginning to feel like writing letters again, and it's not helped by the fact that I can't altogether see *the type. My eyes have been badly affected by the treatment; I trust they'll improve. I'm feeling better more often…the fits seem to be on the way out.*

I think about my work; one of these days I'll sit down and do some.

I'm sitting here with practically nothing on – yes, rather like Hemingway, thanks to the steroids – in the top room. Lots of rooftops and street sounds… It's nice being in town: two minutes to a selection of bars, tree-lined street, two boulangeries, and a cinema almost next door. The people are soft and quite unaggressive. And you can get *things, you know.*

Got to stop…

Love, Mike X

Some of their life in France was clearly peaceful and restorative, but as his illness took hold it began to be difficult and claustrophobic. Lizzie was looking after him and Nicola, each with quite different needs, as well as trying to do her own work, and after a while she needed a break. Mike, too: 'I just want to go home to my mother and sit in front of the telly and eat chips.'

In the spring of 1991 he came back to London, where I put him on a train to Hereford. Joan found having him there very hard: within days he was in Hereford hospital. I went to visit, found him angry and distressed. And then it was back to

London, and into Queen Square again, Joan and I accompany-
ing him. He lay on a narrow bed in some kind of room,
exhausted, turning away; he was on that seesaw of home and
hospital which overtakes everyone in such circumstances, where
nothing, wherever you are, is right. Joan never saw him again.

We were having supper one May evening when the doorbell
rang. Mike was on the doorstep, wearing a very nice dark green
jacket and looking pretty happy. He'd discharged himself from
Queen Square; he was coming to stay. Oh, Mike. Are you sure?
He was very sure. Please.

We put him in the little spare room. There followed a poignant
week or so, during which time Lizzie made arrangements to
return from France. Polly and Jeremy came to visit, so did
Patrick. They had buried the hatchet between them some time
ago, but hadn't seen each other for a while. Mike was in his
dressing-gown, frail and drowsy; we sat having coffee. What to
talk about now, after quite a gap, and in this situation? As in
Women Laughing, the two men settled on cricket.

There were good days and bad days. Mike spent a great deal of
time in bed. He wanted to be read to. He wanted Milton.

> Methought I saw my late espoused saint
> Brought to me like Alcestis from the grave...

I read it to him, he read it to me; he sank back on to the pillow.
We had scrambled eggs on toast for supper: with talk about this
and that, it became a gentle pattern. One evening, with that
rueful smile, but without comment, he gave me two handwritten
poems. They reveal the depths of his distress and confusion. And
they reveal what none of us would ever have guessed at: his
relationship with God.

'Day at La Grande Motte, April 1991' is a desperately sad
account of getting lost in the seaside town not far from where he

and Lizzie had been living. 'Prayer' is addressed to the God in whom he fervently believed as a child, and denied all his adult life. Now, in his illness, with the approach of death, it concludes:

> Dear God, I love you.
> ...
> My father dead these thirty years
> lies in an unmarked grave...
> my mother...who thinks of no one but me.
>
> Will we, may we please, all lie down together
> in the long grass?

Lizzie and Nicola returned from France. Polly and Jeremy took Mike back to Corbyn Street. Nurses came in. With Lizzie at his side, Mike died there on 11 June, 1991. He was forty-four. With some twenty plays behind him he had said to another friend, 'I've hardly started.'

A great many of us went up by train to Hereford for the funeral the following week: I think his friends, and Lizzie's family, occupied an entire carriage. From Joan's house in Shakespeare Road we drove by funeral car to St Peter's, Bullinghope, a little Victorian church set in farmland some two miles out of the city.

The service could not have been more English or traditional: The Lord is My Shepherd; the Lord's Prayer; The Day Thou Gavest, Lord, is Ended. The address was given by Michael Neal, father of Lucy, one of Lizzie's closest friends from York. Then we all went out into the churchyard. The last time I had been here was when Joan and Mike buried his father, in 1972. Now Mike was to join him, in that unmarked grave.

Clouds had gathered; as we followed the coffin in silence, a wind began to rise. In little groups, we stood round the place of burial. When the committal had ended, there were two readings. Matthew Marsh read Coleridge. David Thompson, once

Lizzie's English teacher and now with the BBC, read Donne: *A 'Hymn to God in My Sickness'*. We listened, or tried to, as the wind rose higher.

A wind had made the blinds tremble, in *Japanese Style*. Through the open window of a Tokyo bus, it had stirred the hair of a Japanese woman with a secret, in *Hiroshima, The Movie*. It blew over a high bridge, over a desolate plain, as a mother arrived in *Headcrash*, asking her son for a kiss. And no one who was there that afternoon will forget how it blew now, on and on through that country churchyard, until every tree was soughing.

Lizzie had a headstone set above the grave, unlike any of those surrounding it: just a tall, slender slab of stone. On the front are inscribed the names, the dates: Michael Robert Wall 22.11.1946-11.6.1991: Writer. Beneath: With his Father: Charles James Francis Wall, On the back, a line makes an arc up the whole length of the stone:

With one bound I am free

This essay is dedicated to the memory of Lizzie Slater, who kept the flame alive, and to Nicola Slater Wall.

The Novelist

PENELOPE LIVELY

'For a novelist, the most valuable rule when observing other people is to tell yourself that nothing is as it seems.'

It is the autumn of 2007, the beginning of the academic year. A large number of us from the School of Arts and Education at Middlesex University are gathered in a lecture hall: all come to hear the inaugural lecture from the new Visiting Professor to the MA Writing Programme.

With an excellent colleague, I preside over this programme, founded in 2000, and one of what swiftly became a great number of such creative-writing MAs up and down the country. It is I who have invited Penelope Lively to take on this role of Visiting Professor, honouring both the course and university.

There's quite a buzz. Penelope is famous: almost everyone here will have read her, and her owly specs and intelligent gaze have made her, through photographs, one of the most recognisable writers in the country. Among us is our current Writer in Residence, Alison Fell, and for a moment, as I glance across at her, I feel a frisson of anxiety. She's a feisty Scot, a fine writer, a good leftie: her work and her life could not be more different. Though Penelope's own liberal-left credentials are impeccable, she is undeniably posh. What will Alison make of her, and why am I so worried about what she might think?

I need not worry about a thing. Penelope rises from her seat, where, as always, she has been using her Backfriend, the support for her arthritic spine. Dressed informally in loose jacket and trousers, she is welcomed and introduced by the Dean. And from the moment she begins to speak, walking up and down with a few hand-written notes, she has us in the palm of her hand. She's vitally present, she's honest and modest and very funny.

We hear about the writing life, its difficulties and few financial rewards; about her early days and her voracious reading. We learn of her complete lack of knowledge, when she began, of the publishing world, about which she is now drily revealing. At the end, the applause is long and loud, and when we pile into another room for tea, Alison comes up to me.

'She's a good egg.'

In several areas of life, I can vouch for this.

We first met in 2004, when Penelope agreed to be the castaway on Desert Island Books, an annual event which the novelist Charles Palliser and I ran for many years in Stoke Newington Bookshop. She wanted a lift: accordingly, on a summer evening, I drove to her house in an elegant north London square, and rang the doorbell.

I wasn't exactly nervous, but I did wonder what it was all going to be like. As soon as she opened the door I knew it was going to be fine: as with every meeting since, as with many people, her smile and warmth, the way she always greets you by your name, combine to put you at your ease and feel welcome. I felt an instant liking for her; by the time we got in the car we were away.

And she was a great hit at the bookshop. It was an event made for someone whose whole life has been shaped by her childhood passion for reading, and whose early education in Cairo consisted of little else. She told us about her love of the Greek myths, about Arthur Ransome and *Swallows & Amazons*, and the discoveries of adulthood: Henry James, Elizabeth Bowen, Henry Green. She signed copies of her own books, and then I drove her home.

Within a very short time came an invitation to lunch, and then to a supper where she introduced me to an admired literary critic and the organisers of a high-profile literary festival. Nothing came of these introductions, but I mention them as an illustration of her kindness and generosity, which she has shown time after time: coming to book launches, endorsing a book, on one memorable occasion bringing lunch when I'd been ill. I have interviewed her in public several times, and have always been struck by the way in which she draws her interviewer into the conversation. 'Well, as you know, Sue...'

And the challenge of writing about Penelope Lively now is to try to find the right light in which to show someone whose writing about her own life is so eloquent and engaging that her countless readers already feel they know her through and through. All I can do is try to draw threads together.

Penelope Lively was born in Cairo on 17 March 1933, the only child of Roger and Vera Low. Her father, the son of a Harley Street surgeon, inherited the poor sight which runs in the family, and was so was unable to join the Army when the war came in 1939. A gifted linguist, in 1933 he had joined the National Bank of Egypt, a country with which he already had a family connection. Penelope, who says she looks like him, recalls 'an absolutely lovely man. I don't think he'd ever read a novel in his life, but I can still hear his laugh, and he left a great void when he died.' He also had a gift for marrying 'very selfish women'.

Vera Reckitt was the eldest of three children, descended from the Quaker founders of Reckitt & Colman. A family firm based in Hull, they made goods which became household names – Robin Starch, Reckitt's Blue, Sylvo, Brasso, assorted polishes. Isaac and Ann Reckitt, Penelope's great-grandparents, ran the company on benevolent and idealistic lines.

Their Quaker values found their way down in particular to Rachel Reckitt, Penelope's aunt and godmother, a distinguished artist and a distinctive person. As soon as the war broke out she went to London to work for the Citizens Advice Bureau, based at Toynbee Hall in Whitechapel, which served as a relief centre for those bombed out or otherwise in need as the result of the

Blitz. In the autumn of 1940 she informed her mother, living in the spacious family home in Somerset, that a party of evacuees was on its way.

Although she has long identified herself as an agnostic, a strain of Quaker values can also be seen, I sometimes think, in Penelope herself, both in her kindness and in the occasional stern remark. And perhaps it lies somewhere deep within her work. Doors do not often slam in a Lively novel, and if people weep it is generally discreetly. There are a good many love affairs, and her women are sexually confident, even bold, but there are few real confrontations, and when a marriage or relationship ends it does so in civilised fashion, recollected, rather than dramatised. 'They became like courteous strangers,' Sarah remembers in the short story 'Comet'.

Vera Reckitt, Penelope's mother, who became Vera Low, operated, it seems, rather differently. She had always loved travel, and she made the most of colonial life in Egypt. She and Roger were both very sociable – as is Penelope – and there were lots of visitors to their house outside Cairo, including Eighth Army officers on leave. In the unbearable heat of the summer Vera would take a house in the cooler Alexandria. Penelope and Lucy, her nanny, would go with her then, but her mother is mostly defined in Penelope's memoirs by her absence.

'She was not good with children,' Penelope recalled, in the first of the two long interviews she gave for this book. 'I remember thinking that, when she was with my own children – she was not a good granny, didn't like children very much. I've wondered why I was an only child: was it because she didn't want more, or because it just didn't happen?'

They had outings together on Lucy's afternoons off, but Penelope never felt comfortable with her. Essentially, her deep relationship was with her beloved nanny. And with herself.

★

'When I was very young,' she writes in the Preface to *Making It Up* (2005) 'I made up stories – the refuge of an isolated and frequently bored child. These were fables that I told myself – long satisfying narratives that passed the time and spiced up otherwise uneventful days.'

Both before and during the war the family was living in Bulaq Dakhur, a house which Penelope has described as substantial but which others might think of as grand. It stood in an expansive garden, wherein stood glorious trees: palm, casuarina and majestic eucalyptus. With these last, in particular, Penelope had a deep relationship.

'The central and tallest tree had a large misshapen lump a foot or so across its trunk, at about my head height,' she writes in *Oleander, Jacaranda* (1994). 'This seemed to imbue it with some mystical power.' Here, for hours, she sat putting herself at the centre of Andrew Lang's Greek myths, which she read and re-read. 'I was Helen, languishing in the arms of Paris. I was Achilles, nobly dying...'

Beyond the garden lay 'a landscape that was bright green and grey-green and tawny'. It was a place of emerald-green fields, criss-crossed by dusty paths; of canals, feathery palms, tall rustling sugar-cane; village huts, columns of camels, over-laden donkeys. 'It teemed with life...'

Further yet was 'the maelstrom of Cairo, with its trams and gharries and grid-locked lines of donkey carts, the minarets against the blue sky and the wide brown river'. She and Lucy visited it once a week.

But here, on the shady upper floor of Bulaq Dakhur, they had their own domain. During the mornings, they were occupied in a strict timetable with the educational materials sent out by The Parents National Education Union. The PNEU ran schools in England but also catered through a correspondence course for the children of expatriates, sending out books, instructions, exercise books.

And Lucy, who had left school at sixteen and who had begun her life with the Lows as nanny to an infant, transformed herself, as Penelope grew older, into a governess, with a single eager pupil. 'I see now what a luxurious educational process it was...' she writes in *Oleander, Jacaranda*, 'rich in that crucial element: one-to-one attention.'

The day was divided into twenty-minute periods. Bible reading came first, each morning. 'It did not make me a Christian but it gave me a grounding in the English language for which I am profoundly grateful.' There followed Arithmetic (manageable), Geometry ('we were floundering, and we knew it'), Algebra ('had us floored from the word go'). Natural History was much enjoyed on Wednesdays – 'Even now I find that Wednesday has a slightly raffish feel.' Geography relied on Bartholomew's Atlas. 'Latin we played about with, insincerely.'

'Reading was what we were best at, and we knew it. We were happy to read till the cows came home, and did so... We read everything the PNEU suggested: Greek and Roman mythology, Norse mythology, stories from Chaucer and *Piers Plowman*, *The Arabian Nights*, *Nicholas Nickleby*...'

Penelope's reading life was as rich and nourishing as any child's could be. And her early years contained all the ingredients to nurture a future writer: solitude, endless time to read, an intense, secret relationship with the natural world. Based entirely on narrative and language, listening and re-telling, the PNEU course gave a training in comprehension, and how to express oneself: what better foundation could she have had?

The war intensified. It barely touched Penelope. In Alexandria she slept wrapped in a rug beneath the dining-room table during a bombing raid, but the bombs fell on the distant harbour. In Cairo, her impression of the British Army, represented by her parents' officer friends, was of 'a feckless lot forever in trouble with their buttons and their socks' – Lucy frequently presented them with her home-made sewing kits.

But in 1941 Rommel's army advanced across Libya, and by 1942 had entered Egypt, halting at El Alamein. This was only seventy miles from Alexandria, and it began to seem likely that there would be an assault on Cairo. Panic set in, and many civilian expatriate families prepared to leave. Roger Low remained in post at the bank; Vera followed the example of many others and took Lucy and Penelope to Palestine.

They were safe; they returned. But others were less fortunate, and the experience forms the foundation of one of Penelope's finest short stories.

In 'Mozambique Channel' (*Making It Up*) the trio of mother, nanny and little girl travel not to Palestine but South Africa, where many such families did indeed flee. Their route was patrolled by Japanese U-boats, who in two months sank twenty Allied vessels. Told from the perspective of the nanny, who has her first romance on this journey, the account of the sudden, night-time attack, the terror, the scrambling into lifeboats swung high above the pitch-black water, the terrible listing and sinking of the stricken ship, is a tense and brilliant piece of writing.

Penelope returned to Cairo. She grew. The years went by. Much of *Oleander, Jacaranda* reflects her preoccupation with the passing of time, and her awareness of it. It considers the child and adult selves which, mysteriously, coexist within us all our lives. It describes the flow of days: lessons upstairs; life in the garden with Greek myths and guinea pigs; excursions to museum, zoo and seaside. At night she and Lucy slept in the night nursery, each beneath a mosquito net. Her parents might have been largely offstage, there might have been a war on, but life with Lucy was as solid and eternal as the Pyramids.

'She was my entire emotional world.'

And then it all came to an end.

★

'You're a wicked woman,' Penelope overheard Lucy tell her mother, who was leaving her husband for another man. In the wake of the divorce, Roger Low sent his twelve-year-old daughter away from sunlit Egypt, back to damp grey England, and, when he returned there, packed her off to boarding school.

'I have every sympathy with my father,' she says in the first of our two long interviews. 'He was now a single parent, working in the City, with a child to look after. A friend recommended this dreadful school...'

This was The Downs, in Seaford, founded as The Downs Ladies School in 1901.

'I was hopeless at games, and it was a very sporty place. The term of abuse was 'brainy', and I was brainy. The worst punishment was to be sent to the library to read for an hour.' Her misery was compounded by being the child of divorced parents: in a private interview the headmistress made it clear that this unfortunate state of affairs was best not talked about.

Lonely and uprooted, she wrote agonised letters to Lucy: steadfast, loyal, beloved Lucy. Now, she was dismissed, and perhaps Roger Low knew how difficult this would be, for he had a friend come along to that final interview.

Penelope has written at length about every period of her life, except this one. She alludes to it in several places, but does not elaborate, and as an adult she destroyed those heartbroken letters to Lucy, with whom she kept in touch until her death. Nor has she ever set a novel or story in a girls' boarding school – that staple subject of mid-twentieth-century reading for girls.

'I remember thinking: I will never have to suffer like this again,' she told me. It's an extraordinarily stoical, clear-sighted thought for someone so young, and again I'm reminded of those solid Quaker values in her background. She's a very solid person now, one of the most clear-sighted people I've ever met. Nonetheless, although she is unquestionably at the heart of the literary establishment, she said in a recent interview with the

Paris Review that, 'I observe, I listen, I'm a part of it, but I often feel slightly on the edge.'

She ascribes this partly to 'the way in which, as a writer, one trains oneself to be an observer'. But there is another aspect to being 'on the edge'. It seems that spending a part of your childhood in another country will always make you something of an outsider in the place in which you settle, and a writer can use these questions of identity to advantage. Kazuo Ishiguro and Salman Rushdie are perhaps the giants here: displacement and dislocation are the great themes of our age, and post-colonial fiction and memoir have enriched British literature immeasurably.

Penelope, whose powerful themes of here and there, then and now, memory and forgetting and shifting selves inform so much of her work, is well aware of this. In *A House Unlocked* (2001) she has written memorably of what she describes as 'the most plangent literary material of our times', and cites Eva Hoffman's unforgettable memoir, *Lost in Translation* (1989) in which she describes her exile from Poland to Canada as a fourteen-year-old, where an the longed-for country of her childhood became an 'elsewhere'.

Penelope was two years younger than Eva Hoffman when she sailed away from Egypt with Lucy in 1945. Her writing about her childhood there is among her finest work, and she acknowledges that, for her, Egypt and her young life is the 'elsewhere' she notes so sensitively in other people, and whose loss she mourned so terribly in that English boarding school.

'I believe I have some idea of how the refugee feels, or the immigrant,' she writes in *Oleander, Jacaranda*. 'Once, I was thus, or nearly so... I know what it is like to be on the outside, to be the one who cannot quite interpret what is going on... I carried around inside me an elsewhere, a place of which I could not speak because no one would know what I was talking about. I was a displaced person...'

They find their way into her fictions, these people with their ghostly pasts: people 'on the edge', outsiders, travellers in a strange land. In *Moon Tiger* (1987), Claudia befriends Laszlo, who in the wake of the Russian invasion of 1956 can never return to Hungary. In *How It All Began* (2011), Charlotte, the elderly central character, has a new student in her adult literacy class: Anton, 'whose eyes are from elsewhere, central European eyes, eyes with forests in them, and Ruritanian castles, and music by Janacek or Bartok'.

Penelope Lively's lifelong preoccupation with memory and the past stems at least in part from that abrupt uprooting from Egypt, and then from Lucy, as her childhood slammed to an end. In what she describes in *Oleander, Jacaranda* as 'the raw anguish', the 'howl of abandonment and despair' expressed in those letters to Lucy, what else did she have to cling to but remembered security and love?

Penelope has variously described herself in adolescence as a lumpen misfit, a traumatised teenager, an exile, an anguished adolescent for whom the world had fallen apart. She might well have gone under. What saved her?

Partly, undoubtedly, the firm foundation which Lucy had given her. Partly her innate or inherited stoicism, and the intelligence which meant that despite everything she left Downs School with an excellent School Certificate, ready for the crammer which got her into Oxford. But essentially she was nurtured back to inner health by two remarkable women. These were her grandmothers, both over seventy when she arrived; both strong-minded, kind and accomplished, for whom Penelope now expresses whole-hearted admiration.

Her paternal grandmother: Mabel Low, was the widow of a London surgeon. Used to a rather grand life, with literary and artistic connections, she was living now in one room of their vast Harley Street house in stringent post-war conditions: 'dust covers on furniture throughout the house, windows blown out with the Blitz'. The mother of six children, 'she was not a cosy grandmother, but a down-to-earth one, who set about what she no doubt saw as the rehabilitation of this waif washed up on her doorstep. No point in wailing and gnashing of teeth. The child must learn to adapt.' The child, by now very tall – 'like a bolted lettuce' – was bought good clothes and told to wear her gloves. All this is described in *Oleander, Jacaranda*.

Her maternal grandmother lived in the west country. Beatrice Reckitt, a fine needlewoman and gardener, was the widow of an architect, Norman Reckitt, whose parents had founded Reckitt & Colman. In 1923 they had moved from St Albans to Golsoncott, an Edwardian house in the Somerset countryside. The family was to occupy this house for the next seventy years.

In the wake of Mabel Low's death, Penelope was to spend most of her school holidays in Golsoncott. The household, liberally staffed, consisted by then of her grandmother and her artist aunt. Rachel Reckitt, 'energetic, resourceful and with a streak of adventurousness', had her studio in the house and her horses in the stables, riding to hounds with great accomplishment and, after her wartime life in Whitechapel, living the life of a countrywoman to the full.

The household was ordered and tranquil. Penelope's grandmother spent her days in gardening and embroidery; Rachel spent hers in the studio, working on her distinctive paintings and wood-engravings, out riding the lanes or hunting. The calm of it all, the gentle beauty of the English landscape, the kindness – 'my grandmother always came to say goodnight to me in bed, humming as she came along the landing'; the sweeping up of this bewildered young person into 'a routine of brisk walks, gardening chores and fireside evenings'; the generous spaces of the house itself: all these gradually combined to soothe and heal.

'When I was mooching about the Somerset lanes as an adolescent, waiting for life to begin, I saw Golsoncott as a place where nothing ever happened. I thought of it fondly, but reckoned that it was elsewhere that things went on and that in due course one would go forth... And so I did, but in due course also Golsoncott became a retreat...a kind of Jamesian great good place. You could know that it would always be the same, year by year. Absence of event was now a treasured aspect.'

These words come from *A House Unlocked*, one of Penelope Lively's finest books. Her story of the house's seventy-year occupancy has two dominating themes, 'social change and the absence of change'. She writes with great perception of herself, and of how she became a rather different self; of her idiosyncratic aunt, who liked to sleep on the balcony; her impeturbable grandmother.

But essentially she is writing as an historian, following 'the shining thread of reference' as she moves in memory through the house and its surroundings, using the great Cedar of Lebanon in the garden, the village church, a gazeteer, the gong stand and the dressing room, to discuss changing forms of travel, church-going, gardening, marriage, and above all, class.

There is one other record of life at Golsoncott: the sampler which Beatrice Reckitt stitched over the course of 1946, watched by her troubled granddaughter on those fireside evenings. It shows the elegant house; the garden with lily pond, dovecot, sundial and even moles. At the very bottom, all in a row, are those wartime evacuees. This exquisite thing now stands before the fireplace in Penelope's London study, her most treasured possession.

'That dried-up bone of a woman who taught me about the Papacy at Oxford.' It is Claudia, the central character in *Moon Tiger*, who thinks thus: she's an acerbic person whose view may be very far from Penelope's view of her own time at Oxford. She had wanted very much to go there, following her father, and applied to St Anne's College to read History.

When she arrived, she had never spoken to a young man of her own age, and the ratio of men to women was 10:1. A young woman with her background of solitude and social awkwardness might have hidden in her room or gone man-mad. But Penelope found herself at last in exactly the right milieu, made friends with girls very quickly, and 'met the boys through joining things'. She seems to have swum into it all. The fact that she didn't work very hard – 'something I now regret' – and therefore didn't get a very good degree, does indicate that she was having a pretty good time, but it is not a period in her life about which she has written or talked a great deal. What she is clear about is that those three years spent reading history determined a particular mind-set, informing the novels she would eventually write.

But writing fiction was nowhere on the horizon during those days. Chiefly, what Oxford did was to lead her to the man she would soon afterwards marry.

After a year in London doing the secretarial course which almost all young women did then, Penelope returned to Oxford in 1955 with a job as research assistant to the Professor of Race Relations at St Anthony's College. Even before Jack Lively arrived a year later, to take up a post as research fellow, she told me that people were talking about him: 'There's this chap coming over from Cambridge, who's supposed to be frightfully bright.'

Penelope realised this was true when the group of college students with whom she had coffee now included him. 'I can't remember what my first impressions were at all,' she says now, 'but I do remember thinking he did talk well.' Jack seems to have noticed her at once, and very soon asked her out: 'He was determined from the word go.' They were married within a year.

On the face of it, it was the most improbable marriage: Penelope from 'the southern Gentry' and Jack the son of a Newcastle dinner lady. It was to the social upheaval of wartime evacuation, which Penelope describes in *A House Unlocked*, that he owed his education. At the age of ten he was sent away from a council estate in the city to a Lake District farm. The farmer's wife had been a schoolteacher: she realised how bright he was, and coached him for the entrance to Newcastle Grammar School, itself evacuated to Penrith. He got in. From school to Cambridge, from Cambridge to Oxford, and his first academic post.

'We met in the clear blue air of higher education,' Penelope has written in *A House Unlocked*, and of their swift alliance says now, 'I just felt he was the right person. There was always something to talk about, I was always interested in what he had to say.'

It became what was clearly a very strong, happy marriage, one in which each of them was able to fulfil what they wanted to do, though in Penelope's case it took time to realise what this was. 'Jack was very forbearing – he did marry someone who turned into somebody else. When we married I hadn't the first idea what to do with my life.'

Their first child, Josephine, was born in Oxford; their second, Adam, in Swansea, where Jack took up his first university teaching post. For Penelope, life in Swansea was not so much the pram in the hall as the books in the pram. She wheeled it to the little local library and she wheeled it back again, babies at one end, books at the other. 'I always had something propped up on the kitchen stove.' One thing was clear to her: after the experience of her own childhood, she would look after her own children. And as Lucy had read to her in Cairo, she read now to Josephine and Adam, everything from Beatrix Potter to Laura Ingalls Wilder, via *The Borrowers*.

During these years, and in the subsequent move to Sussex, where Jack was appointed lecturer, she assumed that she would end up teaching history. But now and then, she says, while reading to the children came the thought: I could have a go at this. And once both children were settled at primary school she finally began to write.

Looking back now on her extraordinary career, she has written in *Making it Up* that, 'The whole process felt fortuitous, and only gradually did writing begin to seem inevitable... What I was doing now seemed a neat reversal of what I had always done: reading became writing.' After all those years of reading to Josephine and Adam, she began with children's books.

Her first was *Astercote* (1970). Already, her interest in the interweaving of past and present is there, in the story of a modern Cotswold village haunted by its past, when Astercote was wiped out by the Black Plague. Three other titles followed in quick succession. Then, with *The Ghost of Thomas Kempe* (1973), she won the Carnegie Medal, awarded for the outstanding children's book of the year.

The Ghost of Thomas Kempe is thoroughly satisfactory: a well-judged, well-paced story with a terrific climax and touching resolution. James Harrison, an appealing ten-year-old, is the only one to realise that the family cottage is haunted. A gripping story about a furious seventeenth-century ghost teaches in the lightest way a great deal about solitary determination, friendship and family life, old age and loneliness, and the overall complexity of people – who have 'layers, like onions' James comes to realise. Published almost fifty years ago, this beautifully constructed little book is still selling nicely.

By now, Jack was back in Oxford as a Fellow of St Peter's College, and the family had moved to the Oxfordshire village of Church Hanborough. When in 1975 he became Professor of Politics at Warwick, his last post, they moved to Duck End, a beautiful old farmhouse in the Cotswolds, with enough land for the two of them to create a much loved garden. A photograph taken in about 1985 shows Penelope leaning over a gate with the most contented smile. Another is of a woman serenely beautiful.

In those busy and productive mid-life decades, she was, it seems apparent, very happy.

Some twenty-five other books for children were to follow *Thomas Kempe*, with another award, the Whitbread, for *A Stitch in Time* (1976). But Penelope was also writing stories for adults, even in the early days, and Heinemann, her first publisher, asked to see them. They published her first collection, *Nothing Missing but the Samovar*, in 1978: it won the Southern Arts Literature Prize. For someone who had known nothing about publishing, who had picked a literary agent at random from *The Writers' & Artists'Year Book*, she was off to a flying start.

A year after winning the Whitbread, Penelope published her first adult novel, *The Road to Lichfield*, (1977) partly inspired by the regular journey she and Jack used to make there to see one of his Warwick PhD students. She was forty-four. She dedicated the novel to Jack, and with Philip Larkin in the chair it was immediately shortlisted for the Booker Prize.

'In those days,' she says now, 'they told you that you hadn't won, so you could just go and enjoy the dinner.' But it meant something, did it not, to be on this shortlist? 'Oh, yes.' And was she ambitious? The answer is swift and unequivocal: 'Yes.'

The Road to Lichfield is a gentle, extremely well-made novel. It charts the course of a summer in which Anne Linton – married, two children, history teacher – travels to see her dying father and falls deeply in love with his younger friend. The narrative moves in and out of the minds of the major players, but essentially it belongs to Anne, and what lifts the whole is the rendering of passion and tenderness between her and her lover. There is also some very beautiful observation of the natural world which has the effect of filling the novel with light.

And its furniture – cathedrals, changing landscapes, a derelict cottage with its own tragic secret – signals in this first novel the overarching theme which Penelope Lively had already explored in her books for children, and was to return to over and over again: the power and importance of the past.

Over the next eight years she published four other novels, including the gloriously satirical *Next to Nature, Art* (1982) and two short story collections, winning two more awards. In 1984 she was once again shortlisted for the Booker.

If *The Road to Lichfield* is essentially thoughtful and sad, *According to Mark* is crisp and entertaining, though not without its tender, affecting moments.

'I write within the English tradition of saying serious things in a relatively light-hearted way,' Lively has said, in a statement for the British Council, with whom she travelled and lectured for many years. Serious things certainly go on in this novel, which, like *The Road to Lichfield*, describes the pain and longing of adultery. It's something which, in her own mother's case, indirectly caused the greatest unhappiness of Lively's life: she treats it here with the lightest and most stylish touch.

Mark Lamming, a forty-something biographer, married to bright Diana and living in London, is researching the life of Gilbert Strong, a writer on the fringes of Bloomsbury. In search of a cache of letters, he travels to Strong's old house in Dorset, and falls passionately in love with his mesmerising granddaughter. What follows is one-sided affair, woven into Mark's pursuit of Gilbert Strong and the truth about his life.

This idea is central to the novel: how little we may ever know about another, dead or alive, and affords plenty of opportunity to reflect on the differences between fiction and biography. Immensely engaging and enjoyable, within it Lively is trying out ideas and techniques – conflicting pieces of evidence; the notion of writing the same scene from different viewpoints – to which, three years later, she would give full rein in the novel which at last won her the Booker.

★

'I am writing a history of the world,' Claudia Hammond tells her nurses. She is old, she is dying, she has had a brilliant career: as war correspondent and distinguished author and columnist. Now, she allows her mind to roam over her own past, and through it, following threads, to reflect on the interplay between history and the self: one of Lively's great subjects, returned to repeatedly in both novel and memoir.

Moon Tiger is an ambitious, modernist novel. It privileges consciousness over incident; it plays with chronology and perspective. And though Claudia's history of the world encompasses paleolithic burials, the Pyramids, the Russian Revolution and the Hungarian uprising of 1956, by far the most important part to her is the time she spent covering the desert war in Egypt. There she met the young officer Tom Southern, who became the love of her life, and who was killed there.

Lively is here mapping wartime Egypt on to the Egypt of her childhood. Then, for her, the war took place mostly offstage, but her memories of Cairo are the wellspring of this novel. The Cathedral where Claudia prays without belief for Tom to be spared in battle; the Gezira Sporting Club, the Zoo, the donkey carts and minarets; the kites wheeling over the Nile: all this, and much more swim up through the remembered eye of childhood.

As an adult Lively layers in research to create an immensely strong picture both of the crowded city she knew and of the Egyptian desert war in 1942 of which she knew nothing except through adult conversation: the year of the Battles of Alamein, in which the Eighth Army fought against Rommel's advance.

Away from the desert – the sandstorms, the burned-out tanks, the ants crawling through corpses, the Press tents – Tom and Claudia's love affair, encompassing brief days of leave in Cairo, is done with great tenderness: naked limbs glimmer in the darkness of a hotel room, insects chirrup beyond the shutters; they make love over and over again. She will be haunted by their love, his death, for the rest of her life.

With the winning of the Booker Prize in 1987 Penelope Lively was described by a critic in the *Independent* as one of the finest British novelists now writing.

How does she work? She writes in longhand, with any pen or pencil which comes to hand. A computer makes the work look 'too finished, too soon'.

'You get this idea,' she says, 'at first very fluid and amorphous, and gradually you see: this is what the novel will be about.' She then plans, meticulously. 'I've never thought about the readers, really,' she tells me. 'I am the reader, the critic next day.'

Generally, she is using a novel to work out an idea which interests her: with *Moon Tiger* it was conflicting pieces of evidence; *How It All Began* (2011), grew from something which happened to her, a sickening fall in the street, but was developed through her interest in chaos theory. She had first tried this out in the short story 'The Butterfly and the Tin of Paint' (*Beyond the Blue Mountains*, 1997) which opens with a decorator spilling a tin of paint and ends with the resignation of the prime minister. It's Lively at her sharpest and wittiest.

'I'll have a notebook where I jot down things which might end up in the book – I'm trying to work out what kind of people the characters are.' A character has never appeared to her fully formed. 'I'm not really sure how I do it — I think I'm hacking away at the rock face, trying to get them out. For most books I think I've filled up a whole exercise book before I begin. I usually have a skeletal frame, not necessarily the ending, and then I'm trying to put flesh on it.'

Once she sets to, this notebook stays on the desk. The one she is writing in is on her lap. (She identifies with Jane Austen, quickly putting her work away when someone comes into the room.) There is nothing else which might feed into the novel: no pictures, no cuttings, no little scraps of this and that. It's tidy, it's methodical, and extremely productive. If I had to choose a single adjective to describe her style, it would be deft. That is to say, perfectly judged.

There's a scene in *Thomas Kempe* in which James, doing his homework, is quite lost to the world around him. Is this a portrait of her own absorption in writing? Does she forget herself and her surroundings?

'I'm not sure that I do, actually. Sometimes if it's going well I become really absorbed. But I never mind if the phone rings.'

Her attitude to the whole business is authoritative. 'Novelists have complete control over their material,' she writes in the Preface to *Making It Up*. '[They control] what to put in, what to leave out, how people are to behave, what is to happen. The writer is able to impose order upon chaos, to impose a pattern.'

Not for her the idea of a character telling her what to do next: like Nabokov, she is in charge of her people. She has rarely, if ever, been surprised by the turn of events in a novel.

As for the power of the unconscious, which many writers would acknowledge as working upon them as they write: it does not figure once in the account of her own process which she gave to me in our interviews.

That being said, in the Preface to *Oleander, Jacaranda* Penelope recounts a dream of extraordinary power which came to her while she was thinking about the writing of the book, which is surely about an unacknowledged fear of returning to, and excavating, her childhood years. 'Perhaps there is an eerie affinity between the strange offerings of the subconscious and the unfettered view of the child.'

Her parents, long divorced and remarried, lived to see her success, and 'Yes, they were pleased and proud.' But Penelope is firmly modest about the Booker. 'A winner is a book which a group of people can agree on. There's no such thing as a best book.'

It did, of course, change her life – and Jack's, to some extent. In 1989 he became Professor Emeritus at Warwick, taking early retirement, and it is one of Penelope's sources of happiness that with her success she was able then to support him when needed, as he had supported her in the early days. He continued his own academic writing; he also he grew wryly and affectionately accustomed to being described as Penelope Lively's husband.

Years of intense activity now began. In the decade after *Moon Tiger* she published at least ten books for children, and five further adult novels, including *Cleopatra's Sister* (1993) and *Heat Wave* (1996) republished in Penguin Modern Classics in 2011. This was also the period of *Oleander, Jacaranda* (1994) and the short story collection *Beyond the Blue Mountains* (1997).

Since 1983 she had sat on the Board of the British Library. She was now travelling a great deal – tours for the British Council, visits for foreign translations of her books, attendance at literary festivals overseas. She found herself writing on planes, in airports. She was active in the Society of Authors. 'I'm a gregarious person,' she says simply, 'which is why I've been involved with all these book-related things.'

By now she and Jack had moved to London, and her home life with him continued: deeply companionable with one another and their children, hospitable to their literary and academic friends. In 1998, all this changed. He fell ill, and nine 'long hard months' followed, in which she nursed him. In the autumn of 1998, as she writes with quiet eloquence in *A House Unlocked*, 'one evening I walked out of a hospice, alone again.'

Jack had been her 'essential partner, supporter and foil'. So wrote their close friend Anthony Thwaite in his *Independent* obituary. He described a man of enormous moral and intellectual substance; a loving and generous man, a valued colleague; someone who nurtured his students and took pride in his children. He had always been Penelope's first reader, if only once a book was completed, and his opinion mattered greatly. She had been the only child of a difficult marriage which ended in divorce; with Jack Lively she had over forty years of close, loving family life, and no matter how great the satisfactions and success of her work, no doubt, for a while, they counted for little. It was, she has said, an 'appallingly difficult' bereavement.

It was work, however, which eventually helped her through. *Spiderweb*, a novel exploring the tribes of Somerset through the eyes of a retired anthropologist, had been published in the year of Jack's death. What followed it, in 2001, was *A House Unlocked*, in which Penelope turned from fiction to write one of her most interesting books. She dedicated it to Jack, as well as to her grandmother and aunt, and it was in many ways a tribute to him and their marriage.

In 2005, in *Making It Up*, she put a version of Jack centre stage in the story 'Imjin River'. Doing National Service in 1950, he had been devastated to learn that he would have to serve in Korea, but his acceptance at St John's, Cambridge, meant that he was no longer required to do so. In the short story, the unnamed central character does go out there and, almost certainly, meets his death.

The ending is extraordinarily well done, and it must be said that Lively is very good on death. In *Moon Tiger*, as Claudia slips away, the narrative moves simply to the six o'clock news on the radio beside her bed. In *Family Album* (2009), Charles, the quasi-academic who retreats from family life in his study, one morning 'stops writing, distracted: there is a more immediate concern.' It's a quiet masterstroke.

In the years after Jack's death Penelope published not only *A House Unlocked* and *Making It Up* but two acclaimed new novels, *The Photograph* (2003) and *Consequences* (2007). Then, all at once, she fell ill. She had long endured arthritis of the spine, but drugs had kept it under control. Now she cracked a vertebra, and the ensuing surgery left her in unrelenting pain for three and a half months, unable to work or leave the house.

Few things are more miserable than being ill on your own, and her family and close friends rallied round. I am not a close friend, but I did deeply sympathise, and we were in touch during her long time of agony. Eventually, a new painkiller worked, and she recovered.

In June 2007, not long afterwards, she came to lunch; Charles Palliser joined us for coffee. He is a great one for publishing talk and gossip, and we had a pleasant time. Penelope looked drawn, but was definitely better, wry about the current stage in her writing life – not enough in royalties, books going out of print.

'And the short story has left me,' she said, in a tone half regretful, half matter-of-fact. Over the years she had published dozens, many inspired, however obliquely, by incidents in her own life. Now: nothing.

But if Penelope had felt, in the wake of a testing illness, that her career was on the wane, she entered, after *Consequences*, what looks now like a golden age. Within less than ten years she published two novels, a quite unexpected collection of short stories, an inspiring book about growing old and, in 2017, the beautifully produced *Life in the Garden*. Published when she was eighty-four – 'the advance was so small you could hardly see it' – it has been flying off the shelves ever since. In the same year, *Moon Tiger* was shortlisted for the Golden Booker, launched in the fiftieth year of the award.

In 2009, *Family Album* received rave reviews and was short-listed for the Costa Novel Award. Told in chapters which alternate past and present, moving from one character to another, it touches on all the old themes: the self we are now, the self we once were; the power and limitations of memory; the hold of the past. There's a secret, with cleverly planted clues; as quite often, there's a sly glance at her own background: Charles has a modest private income thanks to 'a godfather who made a fortune out of household cleaning products in the early part of the twentieth century... Thank goodness for Vim and Dettol and Brasso.'

All Lively's interest in chance and contingency is brought up front in *How It All Began* (2011). Her interest in chaos theory drives the plot as, from the fall which opens it, one incident sparks another, seemingly quite unrelated. The *Guardian* called her 'a sublime storyteller, who also keeps us aware of the illusion'. She followed this book with a glorious return to non-fiction.

'This is not quite a memoir. Rather, it is the view from old age.' Thus Penelope opens *Ammonites & Leaping Fish*, published in 2013. She was eighty: 'I look the same, but am not… I remember my young self and I am not essentially changed, but I perform otherwise today.' It is a book lit with wisdom and clear thinking. 'Time itself may be inexorable, indifferent, but we can personalise our own little segment: this is where I was, this is what I did.'

In contemplating the pleasures and limitations of old age, she writes, 'There is what you can't do, there is what you no longer want to do, and there is what has become of central importance.' For her, this is reading. 'What we have read makes us what we are.'

Not quite the whole of us: we are also made, she says towards the end of the book, by objects, and their associations. As in *A House Unlocked* ('self-plagiarism') she chooses from her house full of books and pictures six things which connect her, through memory and acquired knowledge, with other people, places and times.

'Two leaping fish from twelfth-century Cairo… To have this [fragment of pottery] on my mantelpiece…expands my concept of time. There is a further dimension to memory; it is not just a private asset, but something vast, collective, resonant.'

'I saw it all. I heard it all.' This is the decided voice of the Purple Swamp Hen, a bird preserved on a fresco from Pompeii who has his own tale to tell of that doomed city.

Behold: the short story had not left Penelope after all – visiting the British Museum Pompeii exhibition in the spring of 2013, she came upon this creature, learned more about him, and found him ticking away in her mind.

The Purple Swamp Hen and other stories was published in 2016. It's a collection which, after the witty and poignant excursion into ancient Rome, returns largely to familiar middle-class territory. But within this world lies a strong theme of secrecy, buried sadness or longing: people look back to the past; find their marriage in trouble; there's a powerful story about the death of a child, as well as two ghost stories and a wry look at the life of an elderly spy and her carer. The prose is as elegant as ever.

There followed the best-selling *Life in the Garden* (2017) in which, through gardens in art and literature, and those she and Jack created in the Cotswolds and in London, she reflects on the ways we have engaged with plants and gardens throughout history. Scholarly in its range, conversational in tone, it takes in Giverny and Sissinghurst, considers Manderley and Mr McGregor, sets the grandeur of Capability Brown against the pleasures of the allotment.

'As an occupation, [gardening] seems to me unparalleled: productive, beneficial, enjoyable. What more could you want?'

Cairo is there, with her memory of Bulaq Dakhur, and the intensity of her childhood reading and story-telling beneath the eucalyptus trees. Cairo will always be there: the wellspring of her life as a reader, writer, thinker.

So here she is, Penelope Lively, in old age still reading, still writing, albeit much less and more slowly; and here am I, on a January afternoon in her study, with its books and that glorious sampler, trying to get the microphone to work.

'Don't worry, take your time. I had someone here from the *Guardian* the other day and even he had to phone the next day and say something wasn't quite right.'

We have, in the end, these two long interviews. At the end of the second I put it to her that she has had every honour the literary establishment can bestow, and every success. For a moment her face shows a flicker of a frown, a flicker of something like perplexity.

'All I can say is that it doesn't feel like that. It feels very lucky, very fortunate – something you enjoy doing, and can do reasonably well: not many people have that. In a way I feel it would have been the same if I'd been a good furniture maker.'

As so often in her memoirs, she broadens out from her own life, saying how lucky she has been simply to write in the lingua franca, remembering from British Council days the writers from other countries for whom things are so much harder. 'Slovenian writers just won't get very widely known.'

Remarkably, given her position in the world, she still dreads publication. 'I do like literary festivals, and meeting readers, but I hate waiting for the reviews. Someone will always have the knives out.'

Really? It is hard to think of a writer both so prolific and so admired.

'Oh, yes, I've had the knife in me. I can remember people who've written really bad reviews.' I wonder if this has meant she has doubted herself as a writer: so much about her betokens certainty. 'No. But if it's written by somebody I respect then I do take notice. On the whole,' she adds, 'if you get a really bad review it's because they don't like the kind of thing you write, and there's not much you can do about that. Lately, I must say, people have been very kind: the short stories, *Ammonites, Life in the Garden.*'

They are all, of course, pretty good. And I ask her by which of her books she would like to be remembered. She thinks for a moment.

'I'm fond of *Thomas Kempe* because it's lasted for an incredibly long time, and *Moon Tiger*, too – people are still reading it. They've lasted the test of time, I'd stand by those two, I think.

I'm quite fond of *Ammonites*, because I was trying to do something different – life from the point of view of an eighty-year-old.'

It's late afternoon: the winter light is fading over the street beyond the window, over the garden square. I'm looking at someone who, well into her eighties, still carries within her 'an elsewhere' which has given her a lifelong preoccupation with memory and the past. I'm looking at someone who perhaps above all else demonstrates the power of the human spirit to endure and to recover: a traumatised child who became a happy, loving, outgoing, energetic and deeply creative person. She seems *bien dans sa peau*: good in her own skin, settled within herself. Settled, too, within a much broader context.

In her statement on the British Council website she says: 'I am an agnostic, and while I would not suggest the construction of fiction as an alternative to religious belief, it does seem to me that many writers – and I am certainly one – look at it as an opportunity to perceive and explain pattern and meaning in human existence.'

She's living alone, as she has done ever since Jack's death, now more than twenty years ago. Though she is loved by many people, and her first great-grandchild is on the way, she misses him still.

'You miss the companionship, you miss having someone to complain to, and he was always interested in my work, very much so.' A dry smile. 'I always wanted him to say, "That's the best thing you've ever done." There were one or two books he didn't like very much, and he was honest about that. And with practical, mundane things – he would advise me. I miss that hugely – having someone to advise me. In fact no longer having someone who is intensely interested...'

People come in to support her: a cleaner; general helpers with tasks about the house and garden. Everything in the house is pleasing to behold, well run. But still – the time comes to everyone living alone when you wonder: should I stay on here?

Some years ago she and the novelist Jane Gardam went to look at a highly regarded old people's home in Highgate. It's a comfortable, very selective place; many of north London's elderly intelligentsia put themselves down on the waiting list.

'Well,' says Penelope now. 'It was essentially fine, of course. But you know…' she begins to laugh. 'We came outside and I said, Oh, Jane, let's just hold as long as we can.'

The Poet

HILARY DAVIES

Giuseppe Urso

'How does writing change the writer? Totally. And in every domain of life A true writer cannot live without writing. It's not a pleasant Sunday afternoon entertainment, it's not therapy, it's something without which you die.'

A summer afternoon, a country church. We are in the Herefordshire village to which the seventeenth-century poet Thomas Traherne, born in Hereford, came in 1657 as Rector to St Mary's, Credenhill. He stayed for ten years, an energetic, talkative, much-loved parish priest, and a writer of intense, sometimes exalted, spiritual writings in poetry and prose. His work is less widely known than the work of his near contemporary, Henry Vaughan, or the great metaphysical poets who preceded him: John Donne, George Herbert. But he has always attracted priests, scholars, artists, other poets and general readers, and in some cases inspired real devotion.

In 1991 one such person, Richard Birt, then Vicar of Weobley, founded the Traherne Association, and a three-day annual Festival. To this little church, overlooking a great meadow full of sheep and cowslips, an interesting assortment of people come each year to hear and give papers, read Traherne's work aloud, listen to music and buy home-made marmalade.

I am here because although at the time I knew only a very little of Traherne's work, I once had the temerity to write a novel, *The Hours of the Night*, which featured a fictional descendant, the virginal and eccentric poet Gillian Traherne. Unlike most of my novels so far, it attracted some attention, won an award, and drew letters from many readers. In 1996, a year or so after publication, I came back from holiday to find a charming letter from Richard Birt, spilling out cards and bookmarks bedecked with flowers and Traherne quotations, and inviting me to attend the Festival. I did so, and have been coming on and off ever since.

It is now 2017, and Richard Birt, having raised funds for three glorious windows to Traherne in Hereford Cathedral, has retired from the Association. His place as Chair has been taken by the kindly Richard Willmott, a retired headmaster and seventeenth-century scholar. Today, after an informal session in which all comers have been invited to read their choice of Traherne's work, we are having tea at the back of the church and talking. The west door is open, and the sun is pouring through.

I'm standing by the font when Esther de Waal, writer on matters spiritual and Benedictine, introduces me to a small, animated, bird-like person: Hilary Davies, whose work I know not at all. But it soon emerges that she is the widow of the poet Sebastian Barker, and I at once remember his obituary, published in the *Guardian* three years before. With a magnetically attractive photograph, it gave an account of a charismatic man, son of the poets Elizabeth Smart and George Barker; of his life and work, and of his last reading, given in Cambridge two days before his death, when many of his poems were read by Hilary.

We begin to talk; we're joined by my partner, Timothy Day. At lunch in the village primary school next day we share a table and a conversation begins which ignites us all. Hilary is an engaging talker: wide-ranging, clever and funny. Despite her bereavement – and she makes it clear that she is profoundly bereaved – we all laugh a great deal. It transpires that she cannot stay on for the third day, so we say goodbye, with much warmth, in the car park. As Timothy and I are walking away, there's a sudden call, and we turn to find Hilary speeding back towards us, a book in her hand. It is her fourth collection, *Exile and the Kingdom*.

ACROSS COUNTRY

How it all begins: this is what gets forgotten,
Unwilled and inarticulate, the dark start in the morning,
Being carried by gods out into the starry night.
We are silent to ourselves: no familiar landscapes,
No lintel, inglenook to shape or stable space.
Just the road and its rhythms.
The reindeer saddle and the motor car,
The sighing desert and the plateau wind
Etch the first surfaces of particularity
And settle in our souls.

As in all her collections except the first, *Exile and the Kingdom* (2018) consists of sequences, and all five here explore in some way the idea of pilgrimage. The collection as a whole, she has written in the literary magazine *Agenda* (2016), 'treats of preoccupations that have been with me all my life… Our pilgrimage through life is in a very real sense an exile but how we approach it, are changed by it and by those we meet and love, is also how we may approach the kingdom.'

In Christian liturgy, and in her thinking, the kingdom is, of course, the kingdom of God, of heaven. But although her poetry is – like the poetry of Thomas Traherne, to whom Helen Dunmore once perceptively compared her – intensely spiritual, it is also fully grounded in the material world. The power and beauty of those opening lines of the first sequence, evoking the start of a journey, darkness, birth and beginning, continue thus, in the next stanza:

I tasted the cold scent of before dawn
And awoke. The streets were hollow and strange.
My father and mother threaded upriver
Past milestones shadowy in the neon lamplight,
Catford, Dulwich, Tulse Hill and Wandsworth
To the great wall of the way west at Kew.

The city tipped and hinged,
And we crossed over the frontier into a translated land.

Within this opening of 'Across Country' lie recurring themes in Hilary Davies' work as a whole. There is the telling of a story. The mixture of real and imagined places. The apprehension and evocation of something beyond – 'the sighing desert and the plateau wind' have an eternal quality which makes one think of T.S. Eliot, to whom she has also been compared. She is interested in 'the whole relationship of the material world to the transcendent world', as she expressed it when we talked, and, since childhood, in 'things, reality, what you see, [which] somehow have something in them which is more than themselves'. Here in these opening stanzas, also and importantly, are her father and mother, who were profound and beneficent influences on their only child. Here is the beauty and distillation of her lyric line; here is Wales and Welshness.

Wales is that 'translated land': 'Land of tabernacles, land of holy wells/Land where coracles sail to holy cells.' It is where her father and his family came from; south Wales is where she spent long summers as a child, and in the Brecon Beacons had her first experience of something quite outside herself: 'voices which were more than just the wind or the water of the brooks' as she has put it; something she thought might be God. At the end of 'Across Country' she locates Wales as 'the place where first I put my footstep on the holy stair'. It is the fount of 'this whole Welsh poetry thing running down the family' as she put it in our interview.

Much, therefore, about Hilary Davies is in these eighteen lines. But not everything. She is Welsh, but as a teacher, writer, thinker and traveller she is also profoundly European. She is a convert to Catholicism: a very long way from the Church in Wales. She has a profound sense of history and the past which has inspired some of her most imaginative and exciting work.

And she is a passionate lover, who with Sebastian Barker's death lost the great love of her life – 'my soul mate'. In *Exile and the Kingdom* she has published poems of love, loss and grief which I would argue are among the finest in twentieth-century poetry.

TELL ME, MY DARLING, OF THE LIFE WE HAD

Tell me, my darling, of the life we had,
Of what was unique in cosmos and in time,
Never before nor again in this place,
Nor with this face, these hands, these eyes.

Remember your strength as you lifted me skywards
In St James's Park? Did you guess how my world's poles
Rocked away from their axis, what brightness,
Sudden as the sun's arc, caught my soul?
…
Space and time hold us prisoners, or so it seems –
Those walls stretch insolent to eternity –
How shall I ever touch you again except in dreams,
Flung from your orbit into infinity?

Yet on this one brief mote hung here crosses the whole:
Our lives are crystals on creation's web;
Only now and now and through this light burns a world
Where what we are shines meaning from the dead.

Hilary Davies was born in 1954, to parents teaching in south London: her Welsh father a primary school headmaster, her mother, who had grown up very poor in the docklands, a deputy head. She grew up in an atmosphere in which books and learning were completely taken for granted, and in which, though her parents were agnostics, 'They knew their Bible – I didn't go to church but I was familiar with all the scriptures, and studied them at school.' This was Bromley High School. As a child alert to literature from an early age, and who also loved history and geography, she read voraciously, and was taken on outings by her father which fed both her mind and her sense of place.

In particular, the story of Nelson and the ships, real and model, that she saw in Greenwich and at the National Maritime Museum, were to embed themselves in her imagination, emerging decades later in *Imperium* (2005), her third collection. In its title sequence she evokes those potent childhood influences and powerfully reimagines the battles of the Napoleonic Wars. 'You could say that *Imperium* took forty years.'

The second sequence in *Imperium* is called 'The Dismembered Spirit', and the collection is dedicated to the memory of her father.

II

The mad, skittish clouds hurrahing up the river
Are this child's heart to see the vasty city
Unrolled for the taking. She spins in a shiver
Of delight: round and round the hillside hurls her, giddy

Toward the evergreen tide. You take her hand
And walk her patiently beneath the porticos
To show the force of empire, unimagined lands
Gathered like mackerel in iridescent flows.

The pathos of it: these frozen ships upon a plastic sea
She stares at, sets within a hero's frame,
Grow big with cannon as, through the sulphurous air,

You hear the wail of gunners burning, the squeal
Where thighs and abdomen rip open, decks aflame
With blood. Inside you, horror falls like driving rain.

She describes her parents as very loving. 'The older I get, the more I see it. I was the apple of my father's eye. My mother was more practical – she needed to be – but she was also very loving. It was very much a nuclear family, but always open house to my friends.' And both were good storytellers, with strong stories to tell: her mother's father gassed in World War I, her father's grandfather a bard in the local eisteddfod. Hilary knew neither, but in their small family, 'They were quite alive to me, these voices from the past.'

There was another key figure: her father's younger brother, the uncle she adored, who 'rather glittered in my imagination', but who committed suicide when she was at university. 'There's a poem about him in every collection except the second.'

Laurence Davies was a musician, a scholar, a Cardiff don, brilliant but bi-polar. Brilliant but trapped in a loveless, childless marriage and in his relationship with his domineering mother. This was the grandmother Hilary also loved, who was thrilled when she began writing poetry in her twenties, but who, she later realised, had disastrously invested all her emotions in her youngest son. 'One day he just walked into the Bristol Channel.'

Hilary was in her third year at Oxford, reading Modern Languages, when this happened. She accompanied her father to break the news to her grandmother, a terrible occasion which appears in another poem in 'The Dismembered Spirit'. The tragedy of her uncle's death was, she has written, one of the ways in which she entered adulthood: 'with a vengeance'.

During our interview, I put it to her that in a noticeable number of her poems she inhabits a male persona. She attributes this in part to the way she was educated at Oxford: 'All male dons. All female schoolteachers. I was educated at what had till then been a male college [Wadham] and I'm conscious that that changed me.' Later, talking about her work, she acknowledges that she has a muse, and that this muse is male. One man in particular at Oxford was to change her most profoundly.

By the time she went up in 1974 she was, as she describes it to me, 'a horrid little atheist – Sartre, de Beauvoir, black polo necks, the lot'. She was determined to use some of her time to deepen her knowledge of Sartre, and 'in my third year I sat down and studied him furiously. And I realised there was nothing there – so I turned. I thought, this man is a charlatan. There is no system here, this is psychology, not philosophy.' She began to realise that 'Sartre's "system" was actually profoundly uninterested in compassion and was prepared to subordinate all to an overweening intellect. And that it did not correspond to the actualities of the lived human life and was no blueprint for living it. And that coincided, curiously, with my first meeting with a Catholic priest.'

Peter Hebblethwaite, who taught French to her for a year, was a former Jesuit who had left the Jesuits to marry. Hilary met him in the wake of her uncle's death, and of her disillusion with existentialism.

'[Peter] became my friend. He showed me what kind of mind a Jesuit might possess.' In an interview with the *Church Times* 2017 she describes it as, 'The sharpest mind I ever met.' She adds to me, 'And of course he challenged my assumptions, because that's what teachers are supposed to do.' They remained friends for the rest of his life.

II

> So I remember a study,
> And coming for the first time
> Into your presence, Peter:
> You were smoking a Woodbine.
>
> In the cupboard plenty of whisky,
> Your bearing slightly quizzical;
> You opened your mind like a razor
> To interrogate upon Pascal.

He died in 1994, and these verses come from 'Elegy to Peter Hebblethwaite', a gripping, seven-page poem in her second collection, *In a Valley of this Restless Mind* (1997) which describes

the long winter journey she made to his funeral. She is travelling
to Oxford by car, leaving Wales before dawn, daunted by the cold,
the dangerous country road.

> This hour's a strange place, full of despair and brooding,
> A world cave-black and shadowless, the very pit of souls.
> I snap the headlights on...
>   ...Ease first gear in, gently release the brake.
> The hiss of exploding ice beneath the wheel marks
>   revolution.
> This is the last journey I do for your sake.

> V

> The door bangs on the chapel wall
> Dona eis requiem
> For all the dead in the mourners' minds
> Dona eis requiem
> For father and mother and uncle and brother
> Dona eis requiem...
> For your three children and your russet-haired wife
> Dona eis requiem...
> From the day when heaven and earth shall open
> Liberate them
> From everlasting death on that great day
> Liberate them...

> Give them rest
> Give us rest
> Remember them
> Remember us
> Remember me
>   So be it.

Towards the end of 'Elegy' she acknowledges:

> In your dying, Peter,
> You teach me this last thing:

We have a whole lifetime but not a moment more
To drive our road. Make haste, therefore,
Make haste, to find the key to our own city
Before we reach the gates
For there'll be no answers given
Once God has clanged the door.
You said, 'The philosophical treatise is complete';
Peter, remember me when next we meet.

By the time she came to write this poem, Hilary Davies had converted to Catholicism, an evolution for which Peter Hebblethwaite had sown the seeds. 'No one has a conversion out of the blue,' she says. 'There's always a kind of readiness and preparation for it.' At Oxford, Hebblethwaite was opening the mind of a young woman who since childhood had been 'interested in the other-worldly', who had in the wind and water of the Brecon Beacons sensed other voices, another presence. She was preparing for conversion without knowing it; the eventual experience was dramatic.

Soon after leaving Oxford in 1980 Hilary went to teach English in Paris. Here she began work on her first collection, *The Shanghai Owner of the Bonsai Shop* (1991), in which at least some of the poems were influenced by the Chinese friends she had made. 'The poems were a way for me of controlling that kind of over-emphatic language you tend to use when you're young,' she says. 'As you learn your craft you learn that less is more, but how you learn *which* less is more – that's the craft.'

Paris therefore gave her an important poet's apprenticeship, but in her first year there it also changed her spiritual life for ever.

That September she was alone, in a state of deep distress. Her life had entered a crisis from which she could see no way out. 'And the hard city not caring,' was how she described it all, decades later, in the poem 'Lauds', from *Exile and the Kingdom*.

A hostile jangle; out of turn, the dappled quays
With their enlaced lovers; out of turn,
The times you walked these boulevards in gladness...
I ran through Châtelet and Montparnasse and Clichy
Like a starving dog looking for eyes that would see my
                                                    distress.
But I was alone and dumb in the city and no one
                                                reached out.

One afternoon, after visiting an exhibition in the Hôtel de Paris, she knew that she simply had to go into a church. As she left the exhibition, she saw a huge baroque façade: she walked up and opened the door.

> One step into the gloom.
> O Lord come to our aid. O make haste to help us.

She was expecting quiet, a few old ladies, votive candles. Instead, she found a full-blown Mass in progress. The church was home to a particular order, 'a double community of monks and nuns, very rare, whose mission was within the city: Brothers and Sisters of Jerusalem, running the Mass in a particular way, very serious and beautiful. It wasn't just a parish priest officiating, but a whole congregation of religious.'

It was when a young nun read the lesson, the great words of St Paul in I Corinthians 13, that something extraordinary began to happen. In the King James version, Chapter 13 concludes: 'And now abideth faith, hope, charity; these three, but the greatest of these is charity.'

'The nun was reading, of course, in French,' says Hilary. 'When she came to "charity", she read it as "amour". This point about "charity" and "amour" is crucial. Because "charity", even to someone like me who is very aware of the history of words, nevertheless does have connotations of its modern word, "works of charity" etc, rather than its meaning in the seventeenth century of "love". But this is powerfully reinstated by the use of the French word "amour", and of course "love" is now what is used again in English versions.'

And at this moment, 'The whole church started to pulse...there was suddenly the sense of the whole church filled, from the vaults downwards.' She raises her arms high above her head as she describes it. 'And it came out of the presence of these monks and nuns. I couldn't tell you of what, but it changed the direction of my life.'

> Outside the mighty city and its traffic dim
> And time begins dilating like butterfly's wings...
> Love never ends. The soul shivers at it...
> I lie down on the floor.
> Even if I have all gifts without love I am nothing...
> The building crackles. Recognition. Terror.
> One single, constant, unadulterated note
> The greatest of these is love.
> In the church of the martyrs St Gervais and Protais
> I have come through the impossible door of asking.

> Grace falls like rain on a late summer afternoon.

'But of course it goes on – it doesn't stop there,' she continues. 'Now the two are so intimately entwined – my life and work – and that took years. I think it came very slowly. Now I just can't imagine writing anything which is not thinking about the relationship between life and the meaning of being alive, and that, for me, means thinking about our relationship to the world of the numinous, because that is part of being human. This preoccupation has got deeper and deeper over time. It changed again when Sebastian died, of course. Death puts your faith to the ultimate test, which is that you find yourself thinking: There is nothing. It's a very, very dark night of the soul.'

★

We are talking in her house in Stamford Hill, a polyglot district of north London which she has celebrated in several poems, including the sequence 'Songs from the Lea Valley'...

> As we inched up Kingsland
> O all the tongues of the world crowded in upon us
> And I opened my ears. What savannahs,
> What monkey-hung temples, turquoise gardens
> Shimmered out of those sentences,
> What accents of dread and feud and tears?

These lines from 'As I Took My Way from Islington to Stamford Hill' record a journey out of London she often used to make with her parents when she was a child, not guessing 'how one day she will stand at the gate here/And the caravanserai of grace will be home.'

The twin-towered Roman Catholic church of St Ignatius stands on the thundering high road; Hilary sings in the choir. Many residential streets run off this road to the east; hers is as quiet and ordinary as any other. Her house, however, is not ordinary: on a sunny day, with the door open, light streams from front to back, and in the hall is a table dedicated to Sebastian Barker. His books are there, with his photograph. There is a vase of flowers.

'I think of it as a place where his presence, his mind and work, are there for others to see and think about,' Hilary says. 'With a place for our work together, too.'

They met at the Poetry Society in 1988, when he was Chair and she – by now teaching French and German at St Paul's Girls' School – was serving with him on the committee. He was to hold other public posts: above the little hall table are shelves filled with copies of the *London Magazine*, which he edited between 2002 to 2008: an editorship which has been described as brilliantly creative. But it was poetry which drew him and Hilary together. They fell in love, finally marrying ten years later in 1998: two individual writers, living alongside one another in constant dialogue until his death from lung cancer in 2014.

This is the poem in which she records her falling in love with him. It comes from her second collection, *In A Valley of This Restless Mind* (1997).

THE MOMENT

That was the moment when, closing
The wicket gate behind me, I knew
That nothing would ever be the same again.
I knew I could wait before turning,
Very slowly, to look back:
An eternity to note precisely
How the falling sun would sketch
The branches, trace the millinery
Of the leaves. And then to turn
So slowly, looking backwards
At the glory of that other life
Lived not knowing what would come,
Before the eye of the storm passing
Over our heads brings us the world's
Enormity, its frailness, driving
And driving the exquisite spike
Of ecstasy into our lives.

Barker was a visionary poet, a mystical thinker, who has been compared to Blake (and perhaps also has an affinity with Traherne). Partly through knowing Hilary, partly through the development of his own spirit, he converted to Catholicism in 1997, the year before their marriage. 'It was worth waiting for – the sacramental nature of it really mattered to both of us. And now that he's dead it matters to me even more. Sacrament matters a lot.'

She pauses, then continues slowly: 'Sacraments are about thresholds, and rites of passage – in entering into them you enter into a relationship with your creator...into something that's more than yourself – or yourselves. It is saying, This is holy, rather than just something special.'

A large colour photograph of their wedding day dominates a shelf in the book-lined sitting room in which Hilary and I talk for a long, rich afternoon. On an earlier visit she had shown me the surprise of the house: right at the very top, reached by climbing narrow dark stairs, is a huge, white, gabled room which was Sebastian's study. A loft conversion, it gave ample room for bed, bookshelves and a desk overlooking the garden. It was here that he worked and wrote and thought. He died, very suddenly, in the room below, after a six-month illness. They had been together for nearly twenty-five years.

GRIEF

No-one told me how like fear grief falls,
Nor that a serpent crawls within your bowels
At midnight, eats and eats all that's loved, familiar,
Whispers to all things: no.
Grief takes the dearest intimacies you had
And hangs them in a row marked never more –
The walk upon the evening battlements,
A wine glass lifted by the sea,
Your head bowed low beneath the elder tree –
So grief draws up memories from her bottomless store
Of pain...

Grief is reliving by a thousand cuts...
A cage of longing hung beside a road.
Grief knows. She is the death in life,
Closer than our own bone.
She is the gangplank walk above the cosmos,
Our fall down through the spheres, alone.

NOTHING PREPARES US FOR THE DESCENT
OF THIS STAIR

Nothing prepares us for the descent of this stair,
Your hand on the banister, flailing:
Roar, desperation, silence.
Sunder's brute arrival.
Your loved face turned to stone
Even as the thought rose over us like a cowl.
Out of some other cosmos
Understanding sent its javelin
And I heard rise from my own mouth
The howl of the hounds of the underworld...

'He was my soulmate,' she says now, 'in every sense of the word. We were suited to one another in every way. But most important was the endeavour in the world – the writing.'

They were soulmates, but writers can live alongside one another for years, talking about but never showing their work to one another. Publication is the discovery of what has been going on in those long quiet hours: beneath the same roof but in separate spheres. How much did they share?

'I used to read bits and pieces to him. He never read any of his work to me. He was very secretive about it. But because he was [ten years] older he was a much more established poet when we met. He certainly never edited my work. I am my own editor. Having said that, I did listen to things he said, and I did make changes sometimes. He'd never say, This line is wrong. But he might say, How are you going to develop this? Much more like that.'

She and Sebastian shared much else: they travelled a good deal together, especially in the early years. In the long summer holidays they took off for France, or for the little stone house in the Peloponnese which he had found as a ruin and, inspired by his love of the modern Greek poets, bought and rebuilt in 1983, with the help of villagers. He and Hilary made, as he described it, 'a monastery for two', in a string of quiet weeks when she, the term over, could settle to her work. From these summers abroad (and she has travelled much throughout Europe on her own account) spring long, important sequences.

'I found that discrete lyrics, unconnected to any wider context, were no longer sufficient by themselves to allow me to address the themes I wanted to address,' she wrote in an article on *Exile and the Kingdom* for *Agenda* magazine [date]. 'I began to think in terms of a broader architectonic for the poems I wanted to write: each time I have embarked on new subject matter, I have sought a scaffolding, a framework, to give my work the reach I felt my chosen topic needed.'

'When the Animals Came', the sequence published in 1997 in *A Valley of This Restless Mind*, was inspired by a summer spent in south-west France, several years earlier. In 1993, Hilary and Sebastian had been lent a friend's house close to the river Dordogne, in a district not far from the caves of Lascaux. One afternoon, driving and taking in the beauty of the Vézère river scenery, they saw a sign on the outskirts of the little town of Le Bugue, pointing towards a cave which neither of them had ever heard of. With the world-famous Stone Age paintings of Lascaux in mind, they decided to go there, expecting spectacular friezes of bison and reindeer.

'It wasn't like that. An elderly lady took us in, and the first thing we saw were lots of cave bear scratches all over the wall – they used to hibernate there – and stalactites and stalagmites. To the untrained eye it was nothing remarkable, but then with her little pointer she showed us a cave bear's head *engraved*...and suddenly there were all these other animals engraved on the walls. It was another conversion experience: I was spellbound. When we came out I was not the same person.'

What so deeply affected her, Hilary has written in a long essay, 'Shamans and Psychopomps' (2018), was the feeling that the cave wall was coming alive with the spirits of all these animals – 'bears, woolly rhinos and mammoths, stubby-maned horses, bison' – as their guide showed how 'the natural curvature and accidents of the rock had suggested an imaginative landscape to the hunter-gatherers of 20,000 years ago, and spurred them to create it. A whole world of which I had known nothing burst into evocative life before me; by the time I emerged out of this strange new territory back into the sunlight, I knew I wanted to investigate what these caves could tell us about the human condition.'

There began three intense years of research. 'I do research in the same way as an historical novelist does research,' she tells me. Now, it meant reading archaeology and thinking about the sheer physicality of finding and surviving in the deepest, most remote caves in Europe; studying patterns of climate change; learning how flints, earth-paints and fire from dried mushrooms were made. It meant reading and thinking about ancient beliefs.

'In my view, most convincingly, [such paintings] have been read as a means of communicating with the spirit world which infused every action of these artists and their communities.'

All this and more stands behind 'When the Animals Came'. The poem is structured round the seasons, opening with Autumn. The cave-dwellers, whose riverside homes lie beneath towering cliffs, have come out to wait: for the arrival of a herd, and for the kill.

I

AUTUMN

When do the animals come?

After the great heat and the midge time
On the rivers are done. In the season
When the air's no longer dense with the thrum of insects

Or tern cry, the metamorphosis comes.
...
The night rains sweep in cold air;
The forest settles.

It's then that the animals come.

Their arrival is figured in sensuous and precise detail, building up the tension:

Now the air cracks: the far boom of hooves
Unrolling forwards is like the striding of a tidal wave...
...The river starts to sizzle.
At last the leader treads with caution over the cliff scree
And down; we hear the scratch of fetlocks as the deer dig in
To slow the drop. Their heat's upon us;
We can feel their breath. The young keep close
Beneath their mothers' bellies; the bulls ride, wary,
pendulous,
Along the edges of the trail.

It is a lone female, 'the mother of the herd', who is leading them all onwards, unwittingly, towards their death.

We go for the young, much easier to kill.
How they scream! How much they want to live!
Their tongues twist purple round their muzzles,
Their mothers roar a roar you never heard.
Thus we turn them under the water with harpoon,
Assegai, hourlong; the soft river
Slips away with their soft blood.

It is visceral writing. Hilary Davies has what one writer has described as 'a ferocity of imagination', and it can feel, reading her closely, as if there is nothing she cannot do: tear you apart at human and animal suffering, or meltingly describe the tenderness of lovers.

There is a love-song set within and threaded through 'When the Animals Came': the story of Sinhikole and Ezpela, which takes a whole section to evoke the old age of the leader of a tribe and his wife, recalling the passion of their youth, desiring one another still. They have a little daughter, who in spring 'runs, head-high in grasses/After the image of a crimson butterfly'. Later, that little daughter will die, after bathing in the river. Hearing the news, given him with dignity by his grieving wife, 'Sinhikole's bird-mask trembles in his hand': a move from the visceral to the delicate.

But there are much larger brushstrokes in this sequence, describing the annual return of those who have married into another tribe, and come back for a tribal festival. As quite often in Hilary Davies, there is now a shift in perspective: the impersonal narrative becomes individual, in the command 'Look,' or in the sudden introduction of a narrator – whom, here, we assume to be Sinhikole.

> You see the subtle movements through the trees,
> The slow cortège of tribe and subtribe with their
> accoutrements
> And baggage arriving through spring mist and smoke?
> I number them all, yearly, the minute differences
> Of lilt and custom...
> Here are our sisters back from every tiny gully within
> a day's walk,
> Married into new fraternities, escorting husbands,
> Or our cousins showing the various tattoos of bird or
> fox or insect
> That mark them for ever into another chain.

Daubed with ochre by Sinhikole, given small objects to accompany their journey, they enter 'the antechamber of dread'. And here, where there is 'no sound, no breath of air, but black invading every orifice', the poet makes a startling move. She is eliding time: writing both of these Paleolithic people and of herself, and her twentieth-century discovery of their mysterious art. There is another imperative, as if she is talking to herself: 'Lift your torch and run it along the gallery wall.' What follows becomes a meditation on experience and meaning.

> This is what you have come, and now must learn, to see,
> Bereft of all the things you use to define yourself outside.
> Here you have nothing but what lies within your field
> > of vision,
> Buried in the very viscera of earth.
> No one knows when we first found a distance
> Between the felt reality of bark, or pebble, or muzzle
> And a reality within the mind – call it the inability
> Not to recall, to put out of mind the presence
> Of what we cannot see. Don't think a few visits here
> Will make of you an adept; remember always
> You will never know except by exploration and
> > re-exploration
> What it is you seek.

Eliot's sonorous voice in *The Four Quartets* is surely audible in these lines, and in some of those which follow, wherein great creatures loom, and prepare to leap from the rock towards this un-named human presence, who has so much to learn from what s/he sees.

> Come to the edge: you must hang in the void
> Before you can climb down towards the last degree
> Of the transfigured earth.

In that long essay about this sequence, Hilary Davies tells us: 'Writing this poem turned out to be not just the product of my own research and imagination. My own mind was profoundly enriched and altered in the doing of it, and I can never look at my own society, its preoccupations, achievements and failures, in the same way again.'

She has brought to life a community who once lived as close to the natural world as it is possible to do, and who, through art, made of the experience something almost everlasting, if we will let it last.

'I read French and German at Oxford; I have taught these two languages and cultures all my professional life and been going to these countries regularly for nearly fifty years. They are an integral part of who I am.' These words come from an interview Hilary Davies gave to the *Church Times* in 2017. 'Europe is my home,' she adds, and it is this strong sense of belonging there which, with many other ideas, lies behind another, very different long sequence, 'Rhine Fugue', published in *Exile and the Kingdom*.

Her essay, 'How I Came to Write a Poem for Europe' (*Agenda*, 2016) deserves a wide airing in our uncertain and divided times.

'Europe. How we conjure with this name. Suddenly, shockingly to many, it has become a term of abuse, a word that is used to stoke fears of unaccountable bureaucracies in foreign languages, interference in national government and waves of unwanted immigration. This against a backdrop of ever greater disparity between the haves and the have-nots, regionally and globally, and a popular distrust of establishment institutions. And all this has been accompanied by new and disturbing lows in the level of public discourse about such matters.

'But the British Isles are indisputably and indivisibly part of Europe... Everyone in Britain has, ultimately, come from somewhere else, but our genetic bedrock, in all sorts of ways is European. This matters now and anew and urgently...'

Although its seeds were sown in Hilary's mind long before David Cameron's referendum, 'Rhine Fugue' is something of a timely and impassioned plea for unity, peace, mutual understanding and hope.

Set in seven sections, it opens with 'Night Train to Cologne', recalling her first experience of Germany. She is travelling alone for the first time, as a teenager, to meet her German exchange partner and family, who become important friends. It closes with her attending a party given decades later by other friends, on a boat going down the Rhine. The river, as she describes it, 'is one of the defining contours of Europe', acting through history as bridge and conduit, battleground and frontier.

She chooses to emphasise it as a bridge: the central sections of the poem evoke the crossing of the river in 1814 by Prussian Field Marshall Blücher, 'at dead of night on the coldest day of the year' in order to help the British: 'without him, and his German-Polish-Russian-speaking army', Britain could not have won the Battle of Waterloo the following year.

As so often in Davies' work, there are dramatic shifts of time and place. Through the historic, riverside city of Worms, the poem moves through an early pogrom, to the Reformation, to Tyndale's translation of the New Testament into English, and (offstage) his execution. 'Out of all these what interested me most was the theological and cultural melting pot of Protestant and Catholic, Christian and Jew: the tensions and creativities that have arisen from these encounters have marked all of Europe's subsequent history.'

'Worms: In the Jewish Quarter', is hauntingly rendered by a visit to the district long-since purged. Again, as often, a mysterious narrator tells the story.

> 'I dreamt I was in the city again:
> Halfway in the street, between the immaculate gables,
> And the scrubbed cobbles...
> My foot cracked in the silence but no-one answered it.
> Not one door opened, nor child's pinafore caught in
> the wind
> Flashed at a corner. The stars the moons,
> The geese and the green trees were all gone
> From the lintels, the names shorn away...
> So I leant under the lime tree and dreamed.
>
> And as I dreamed, they came.
> Crowding down to the water and chattering,

Passing the babies from sister to sister...
Little Lili Reichmann, Abigail Moses, Ruth Levine
With her fierce glances, stout Rachel Oppenheim
Always blithe...'

Now, they are all gone into the past. Not for the first time, Hilary
Davies – who no longer reads fiction – shows a novelist's ability
to conjure a place, a character, in a brushstroke that is barely
there, and yet which is indelible.

How to characterise the range and wellspring of this writer? 'A
tough poet of deep seriousness' is Timothy Day's assessment.
Her work profoundly echoes Traherne's perception of spiritual
meaning in the world around us, though she only began to read
him when another writer pointed this out. It reflects an intense
interiority, a meticulous honing and paring down, as well as a
great hinterland of reading and experience. If I were to compare
her to a painter, it might be to Winifred Nicholson, whose incan-
descent flower paintings speak of much more than flowers.
There are also affinities with Samuel Palmer and Stanley
Spencer. But if her work springs from and explores 'the whole
relationship of the material world to the transcendent world', the
ways in which this is mediated through her subjects are
immensely varied.

There is a rich sensuality and eroticism, and an immense
tenderness, in her evocation of love. Animals and birds, trees,
water and sunlight all have a meticulously observed presence in
her four collections, together with her great feeling for the
people and places of historical events: battles at sea, sudden
invasions, or simply women gathering at a well. The distant past
is conjured as only just behind us, and present everywhere. And,
of course, the liturgy, litanies and sacraments of the Church act
as an overarching frame to sequences such as 'Stations of the
Cross' (*In a Valley of This Restless Mind*), 'Exile and the

Kingdom' (title poem) and 'Seven Sacraments' (*Imperium*).

Writing mostly in free or blank verse, her occasional use of rhyme is all the more potent for its sudden, surprising arrival in just the right place. She is influenced by Eliot, whose sonorities and cadences you can hear; her work, like his, is often dense with reference and allusion. Sometimes this can feel hermetic; elsewhere there is a startling clarity and freshness.

She lists George Herbert, Henry Vaughan, Dylan Thomas, George Barker, the French poets Baudelaire and Apollinaire as other influences, but the three with whom she most strongly identifies are David Jones, Gerard Manley Hopkins and Emily Dickinson. 'If Dylan Thomas introduces you to intoxication, Dickinson shows you how to distil it.' And she points to the darkness in Dickinson's view of life and death, her haunting by the presence of death as well as her intimacy with it.

We discuss this when talking about another long sequence, 'In the Valley of this Restless Mind', the title poem of that collection, which retells the story of Abelard and Héloïse.

'Yes. There are a lot of dark things in existence, and you can't shy away from that. Very dark things. And you have to meet them... In poetry you meet them slightly at an angle, slightly askance...through what's called the Cretan glance. Sebastian and I used to call it that, I don't know where he got the expression from. But other poets have talked about the same thing. Looking at something sideways, coming at it slant. Like the Medusa's head – you can't look at it directly, or you turn to stone. And Abelard and Héloïse's story in many respects is very dark.'

But she points out that this too is a poem for our times: the influence of Héloïse's thinking, who was highly educated at a period when most women could not read or write, on that of the older and much more famous Abelard, was crucial and has been underestimated.

The darkest moment in Hilary's own life was the death of her husband. Her verses of loss speak of how the world suddenly appears an indifferent place, of the void which lies beneath human experience. She misses Sebastian in every day that passes, has written passionate poems of love and grief, and created a memorial to him in the house they shared for so long. But despite her agony at losing the 'dove of my heart', she has not lost her faith: indeed, it has evolved in ways she could not have envisaged: new friendships, new endeavours, new travels, enabling her to live without him, in what is now a monastery of one.

Each winter she goes to write in Wales. Each summer she returns to France. She is writing on her own retreats: there, and in new places she has found for herself, in Cornwall in particular.

So: she seeks out solitude, peace – it would seem, now, to be mostly peace – in which to write. But Hilary is also very much in the world. When we meet for our interview she has just returned from a festival at the University of Gdansk, where she gave two readings, and a lecture on the visionary in English poetry and painting. She travels, she gives papers, and her teaching life is not over.

She has been a Royal Literary Fund Fellow at King's College, London, and has recently fulfilled this role at the British Library, taking all comers for a day each week, reading and commenting on whatever they choose to bring her. She will continue to give seminars under the aegis of the British Library in 2020. In this RLF position she has given a number of engaging on-line talks: the uncompromising quotation which opens this essay comes from one of them.

She also reviews frequently for the *Times Literary Supplement*, *PN Review* and *The Tablet* and belongs to a number of literary associations: she is on the academic board of Temenos, is a trustee of the Winchester Poetry Festival and a member of the Vaughan Association and the Traherne Association.

At the Traherne Festival in 2018, the year after we met, she gave a fine paper on the notion of Felicity in Traherne's poetry.

On the last night she came to supper in Timothy's flat in Hereford, in a house once occupied by Elgar. When she walked into the airy drawing room which had been his study, her eyes filled with tears. 'I'm thinking of my father. He so loved Elgar. He would love to have seen this.' That weekend cemented our growing friendship.

'I have tried to make my life rich and to enrich others, trying to communicate things that I think are of vital importance in living well,' she says now. 'I've set about it, yes. That I do consciously – I don't let things happen, I try to make things happen – and then of course other things happen. People really *are* kind, and all sorts of invitations do come, because you've made it your business to go out there and be there.'

What would Sebastian say if he could see her now?

'Impossible to say. But I think he would be pleased.'

And what of her work, its place in the world? Her answer is clear-sighted.

'Your work can't change the world. But by your work you are adding to the ways in which the world may be perceived and lived.'

The Novelist

ANNA BURNS

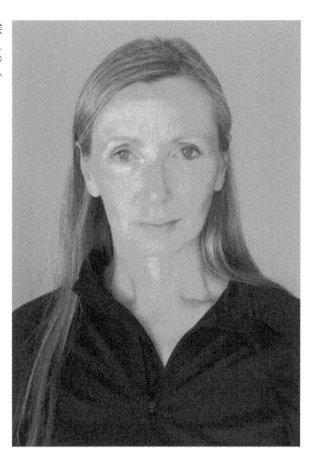

I knew I wanted to leave Ireland – I knew that from child-hood, really. I didn't know where I wanted to go. It's not that I hate Ireland: I absolutely do not. It's a kind of love/hate relationship – it's not even hate: it's a love/grief relationship.

Ardoyne, Belfast, 1976. Two teenage girls are on their way to a disco, walking down Etna Drive. The bottom of this street is the kind of place where if something awful is going to happen, it's going to happen here. They stop and go into a sweet shop. All at once, there's shooting, right by the door. When they go out they find a man writhing on the ground, blood everywhere: he's been kneecapped, and the way he's moving it looks as if he has eight legs – like a spider, writhing and whirling, grabbing at passers-by. The girls turn away, and go on to the disco.

Next day, in school, another girl says yes, he looked like a spider to me, too. They never talk about it again.

London, 1990. A young woman is starting to write. She's been here for three years, studying Russian at Queen Mary College, but mostly trying to get sober. She's been drinking for a very long time: last year she finally stopped. And now there's a space – a big, frightening space at first, which gradually fills with everything the drink has been covering up. Out it all comes on the page, dank and dark. It's not something she ever wants to look at again, or anyone ever to see. But it had to come.

London, 1995. A lot has been going on. She's had a break-down, she's living on benefits. She's started attending the Twelve Step Programme to keep herself sober; she's found a therapist. She's moved to an Islington council flat, and for the first time as an adult feels she has made a place into a home. The estate is a bit edgy, but she's used to edgy places. And now the space in her life is filled with a different kind of writing: it has a kind of light around it, it feels like creativity and playing. She starts to go to classes, to show her work to others. Pages and pages of typescript pile up on her table: unfinished pieces in no shape or sequence, but there.

London, 1997. A friend asks her to accompany her to a spiritual healing group. She has a history of insomnia, but that night, after receiving healing, she sleeps better than she's done for a long time. Something about this place seems to work for her.

London N16, Stoke Newington, 1998. She's walking back from her therapist one evening when she passes a lit-up bookshop. Charles Palliser is giving a talk on writing. She goes inside, finds a group of people: The N16 Writers Network. Charles Palliser begins to talk, and she's struck by one particular thing he says: If you can't plan your writing, go home and look at what you've got, see if there are any linking themes, or characters who keep reappearing.

She finds this really useful. Back in the flat she puts everything on the table and goes through everything, all the unfinished pieces. Many of them are about Northern Ireland, with the same group of characters reappearing under different names. She starts to put it all together, to give single names to individual characters. A lot of extraneous stuff falls away; a novel begins to take shape. At its centre is a young woman called Amelia, growing up amidst the Troubles. The voice of this novel is very strong.

London, Spring 1998 An aggressive, dysfunctional family moves on to the council estate: it's no longer a good place to live. She's still attending the Network; she and I become friends. She shows me some of her novel in progress: I know I am reading something extraordinary. And for the first time in my life I begin to understand Northern Ireland: that the place is a madhouse. Twenty years later, some scenes will still be with me.

A gang of feral children is ruling the estate, and she, a woman on her own, is a target, jeered and shouted at as she comes and goes, excrement pushed through her letter box. Life in her little flat is becoming intolerable. But she finishes the novel, and calls it *No Bones*.

London, 2001. No Bones is published by Flamingo, and receives huge critical acclaim. It is shortlisted for the Orange Prize and wins the Winifred Holtby Memorial Prize for the best regional novel. She leaves the flat, and leaves north London: we see less of each other, but visit and remain in touch.

She completes her next novel, *Little Constructions*, in our house. Nothing about this new book says Northern Ireland, but it's there, in all its meaningless violence, together with much else. It's published by Fourth Estate in 2007. One of the reviewers, Helen Brown in the *Daily Telegraph*, cannot remember when she last read prose 'so profound and so punchy, at once scattergun and forensic'. Much of it reads as if a bomb is about to go off.

In the years that follow, she is moving from place to place, house-sitting in Scotland, Cornwall and Somerset. She and I rarely meet: at one point when she's in London she tells me she's left her agent and has since written a novel called *Milkman*, which is struggling to find a publisher.

London, 2018. Milkman has been bought by Faber, through her new agent, and is shortlisted for the Booker Prize. For the first time in my life I place a bet. William Hill have never heard of this author, nor of the Booker, and *Milkman* – set, like *No Bones*, in the Troubles – is the complete outsider. I know for a certainty that it will win.

16 October. Watching the Booker Prize ceremony on BBC Arts, I leap up from my seat as a small, radiant person goes up to collect the award. She thanks everyone who has helped her, not least the woman who published her first story. 'I know you're out there.'

From tonight, the name of Anna Burns is known all over the world.

★

'The day Somebody McSomebody put a gun to my breast and called me a cat and threatened to shoot me was the same day the milkman died.'

There is a lot about names, and no names, in Anna's work. All the reviews of *Milkman*, of which this is the opening line, pointed to its nameless central character, the narrator, and her paramilitary stalker, known only as Milkman: the most innocuous of occupations naming the most dangerous and sinister of characters. Only one review, to my knowledge, pointed out the (possible) reference to the clandestine transporting of explosives in milk crates into the Catholic areas. This was in *Socialist Voice*, (2019) where Jenny Farrell noted that in north Belfast, within the Catholic enclave of Ardoyne, where Anna Burns grew up, every name reveals 'an either-or identity'. In *Little Constructions*, her second novel, names are almost fetishised: almost every character has a name beginning with J.

Throughout the novels there is also a great deal about the desire to hide, to be secret and shut away and safe. In *Milkman*, the narrator speaks of 'the privacy of the subtext of my own mind, where no one but me could witness me being me'.

And this is Amelia, in *No Bones*, hospitalised after a breakdown.

> Looking down, near the ground, she spied a tiny door. She pulled it open. Inside was black. She squeezed in and pulled it shut. And now, as long as she didn't have to think about her family, about sex or about Ireland, she could live here happily, holding her breath, for ever more.

Anna herself is in many ways intensely private and shut away. She is a warm, funny and affectionate friend, but she also needs great draughts of solitude. This is true of many writers, but with Anna perhaps more than most: the shutters come down if you seek to know too much. But we have known one another for over twenty years, and it is a mark of her generosity that in the end she agreed to a long interview: this in the midst of the huge claims on her time that winning the Booker has brought.

In the summer of 2019 we talked for a whole afternoon in my house in Highbury, Anna herself about to settle into a new home on the south coast. Many of the key moments in her life which open this essay are drawn from her own accounts, summarised or reported. What follows now is drawn from our conversation, as is the opening quotation. Amongst many other things we focussed on two of the most important: her writing life and her spiritual life. Both developed after she had finally stopped drinking: 'the hardest thing I ever did'.

We began by talking about her move to London, but she also told me a little about her early life, some of which fed into her unforgettable first novel.

Anna Burns was a daydreaming, reading child. She had – and has still – many friends, but she hated school. The middle child of seven, she grew up in an overcrowded 'tiny wee house' with few books but a reading mother, who worked as a cleaner. She would bring books back from the colleges she cleaned, and all the children would read them. After a while, to ease the overcrowding, Anna went to live with her aunt across the road – a not unusual circumstance – and was taken by her to the library. In a haphazard way, she was thus introduced to the writers she identifies as important and influential: Enid Blyton, Agatha Christie (her first childhood writing was a crime story), Gogol and Dostoyevsky.

'I didn't understand the Russians, but I was pulled along by something in their writing and their use of language, so I would read and re-read them anyway.'

In this random fashion she also discovered Shakespeare: looking down at the floor one day, she noticed a book with a picture of a woman whose hands and arms were covered in blood. She didn't know if the book was by Shakespeare or Macbeth, but she picked it up and began. A massive riot was going on outside in the street at the time.

'I remember the witches, and I remember Macbeth. And I mean he was scary, the way he turned from being someone good to someone who could kill a king.' *Titus Andronicus*, the bloodiest play in all Shakespeare, was the next, and after that she gave him a rest for a while.

Meanwhile, she was attending school. Because of the Troubles she attended several primary schools, having to go through checkpoints to attend the one built just outside Ardoyne. She was taught in all of them in an atmosphere of fear and violence. Corporal punishment was legal and used often. Anna was mitching – playing truant – quite early on. Quite early on, she began to drink.

At secondary school, the violence was more between the girls: fights out in the schoolyard and after school on the wasteground called the Bone Hills: 'fights over boys, but mainly for anything, just to have a fight'. There's a long scene about this in *No Bones*, in which the beaten-up Amelia is rescued by Vivienne Dwyer, the one girl who works hard, has her uniform tidy and her hair in plaits, and who behaves immaculately. She has also, as it happens, joined the Provisional IRA.

By now, Anna was drinking seriously, going to discos, mitching in earnest. 'I didn't like the violence but I would have liked the learning, and that's why I joined night school when I left. The happiest day of my life up to that point was leaving school at sixteen, and I remember walking over the Bone Hills filled with happiness that I'd never have to go to that awful place again.'

At night school, which features as an ambition in *No Bones* and an experience in *Milkman*, the atmosphere was calm and purposeful. These are not words which one would associate with any aspect of Anna Burns' fiction, or much of her life in that tormented city. She and her friends survived, on the whole, by turning away.

They turned away from the kneecapped man in his agony. 'It was like, This is all too much to take in, so we'll all just pretend it didn't happen.' She turned away in the chapel at the sight of a boy crying his eyes out at the funeral of one of her friends. 'I can remember thinking, *Stop that, stop that, stop that* – almost like I can't cope with people crying.'

Once, when she was out in the street with her friends, a bomb went off and she jumped so suddenly that the toffee apple she was carrying jumped right off its stick. The bomb blew the house at the end of the road to bits. They all ran into the nearest garden and hid behind a hedge – 'as if that was going to save us'. The woman in the house was furious. She, too, turned away from the blown-up house, and ordered the children out of her garden – 'And take that with you, that toffee apple!'

In scenes like this, the origins of a black-comic style – 'grimly absurdist' as one academic has described it – are not hard to see. And as for avoidance: 'We didn't want to know. We wanted to get drunk and go to clubs. And we didn't want to know, basically.' It was not until Anna was living in persecution on the council estate in London that she was able finally to feel fear for what it was, and as things were happening.

'I took [this] to be healthy in one way: that I must have got stronger, that I could let myself and my feelings be in the moment, whereas when I lived in Belfast...I just did what everybody else did, sort of blocked it off.'

This is what the narrator does in *Milkman*. When her mother's lover is attacked:

> I thought of putting on the radio to hear if he was dead but I could not ever bear radios: those voices announcing, those voices murmuring, those voices repeating on the hour, on the half-hour, in their special urgent extra bulletins, all those things I didn't want to hear. I hoped he wasn't but nearly always in these situations they were dead...

Much later, after Milkman himself has been shot: '[But] whatever he had been, and whatever he had been called, he was gone, so I did what usually I did around death which was to forget all about it.'

It was in night school, taken after days spent working as a typist, that Anna rediscovered Shakespeare, astonished to find that he had also written comedy. She found *Twelfth Night* and *The Comedy of Errors* delightful and it was those plays, and a brilliant teacher, that opened up Shakespeare and the language.

She was working for the council; as a copytaker for the newspapers; for the Civil Service. Someone suggested she should do her O-levels, and she did them. Someone else suggested A-levels, and she did French, English and Politics. Someone else said, Why don't you go to university?

In 1987 Anna left Belfast for Queen Mary College, London. She was twenty-five.

Who was she, at this point in her life? 'I don't know. I wasn't a reflective person, self-reflective, I suppose I should say. I just knew what I wanted, and I wanted out.'

It was the Russians, first encountered and enjoyed in the tiny wee house in Ardoyne, who brought her to London. 'I wanted especially to read Gogol and Dostoyevsky in Russian. I never got good enough to read Dostoyevsky but I managed some Gogol.'

Readers of Gogol's mid-nineteenth-century short stories such as 'The Nose', in which a nose falls off a face and develops a life of its own, will recognise the influence of satire, surrealism and the grotesque on Anna's novels, particularly perhaps on *Little Constructions* (2007), whose demonic or demented characters (curiously recognisable in many ways) populate the little town of Tiptoe Floorboard and are forbidden to marry if they have given birth to each other 'at some point long ago in the past'.

Anna was working in the boozy world of journalism while at QMC. Copytaking was well-paid shift work, which suited her.

She liked night shifts, so in theory could juggle it round her studies, but for much of the time she wasn't doing much studying. 'I was a terrible student,' she says with a laugh. The one strand she loved was Slavonic Linguistics, something which perhaps spoke to her acute awareness of language and wordplay, and in which she did very well. 'It was more the way my mind worked.' But she didn't discover it until the third year. 'I dropped out from the degree about fifteen minutes before the end.'

In truth, she now knows, she had left Belfast and come to London not to study, but to get sober. It took her years of on-off attempts to do so.

'We had a lot in common, Jean and I, mostly wine, but gin and vodka and Jameson's too,' says Amelia in *No Bones*, and if you want to know what the descent into drinking hell might be like, read the chapter entitled 'Battles, 1987'. Amelia and Jean meet at an AA meeting, but Anna's own recovery was something she eventually achieved in a dark, solitary struggle in a flat in Tufnell Park. It was 1989, and a great emptiness stretched before her: 'I didn't know how to be in the world any more.' A serious breakdown followed. If you need to know what a breakdown might feel like, read the chapter 'Triggers, 1991'.

Gradually, after giving up drink and before getting into recovery, she began to write: the darkest material pouring out onto the page, 'like vomiting', she tells me. As with vomiting, she felt much better afterwards: something long repressed needed to come out, and, as with vomit, she threw it away.

She was still very vulnerable, much in need of support. She didn't find it through AA, which offers help to all struggling and recovering drinkers, because she felt too fragile and distrustful to attend. But in this bleak time she discovered other Twelve Step Programmes. From 1992 she attended different groups until 1997.

The Twelve Steps involve admitting that you have become unable to control an addiction, and surrendering to God, or a higher power, as the only way to return to sanity. There was much about the programme which Anna found immensely valuable: it offered space to unburden, to talk without interruption, to tell the truth without facing judgement. It offered hope. 'And it taught me to be self-reflective.'

But her early experience of Catholicism had not been a good one. 'I found it very oppressive as a child. I hated going to Mass, just having to go and be still and not fidget. And I didn't understand, and nor was it explained to me, what was going on.' And at the Twelve Step groups, 'I could not get into the God bit, it was just not working... I was thinking: But if I think of God it's just not a very nice one, quite violent, and really, No.'

So she was attending and resisting, a difficult position to be in, for a long time.

As quite often in her life, Anna was led on to a new path by someone in need of a companion. A friend was too anxious to go by herself to a spiritual healing group: Anna went with her, and found herself at the White Eagle Lodge in High Street Kensington.

At this point in her life, despite the help she had received from Twelve Step, she was still fragile. Life on the estate had become very frightening, and neither the council nor the police did anything to stop the vandalism and persecution. 'Your estate doesn't yet have a dead body,' one policeman told her. She was struggling with fear, insomnia, nightmares.

In addition, she had suffered since childhood from a condition whose diagnostic name she discovered only in 2016: misophonia. Meaning literally 'hatred of sound', Anna says that for her it is more fear of certain sounds. The condition is characterised by an extreme and involuntary reaction to everyday noises coming from other people: coughing, chewing, breathing or eating loudly are a few examples. In sufferers they can set off real fear and panic, and the need to flee. The affliction finds its way briefly into *No Bones* and more extensively *Little Constructions*, where the young Doe children are tormented by the sounds their parents make while eating and drinking.

'I don't often talk about this,' Anna tells me, 'because people get angry, or just think I'm talking about a little irritation, and it's actually a lot more than that.' Certain very specific noises can set it off, and it means that it can be difficult to be amongst too many people. Because of this, she had sometimes been uneasy in the Twelve Step groups and was apprehensive about what might happen when she visited White Eagle Lodge. What she found was a gentle, optimistic place where she was received with great sensitivity, able to sit in the little chapel by herself until she had received healing, and then join the main group for the service.

That night she had 'the most wonderful sleep'. She has been attending White Eagle Lodge, in London and in Sussex, ever since.

'I think it was the link with spirit that was missing, that I didn't believe in. I couldn't get it from the Catholic church, and I couldn't get it from Twelve Step, although I got wonderful things from that, and I got it there. I could feel this connection, and I don't know why, really, but it worked, and I still do go when I can.'

There is barely a breath of any of this in her work.

Anna Burns has written three novels of startling originality and power. Her work is her face to the world, and although many people will want her opinion on the issues that plague our times, she is above all an artist. 'It's the world of fiction I'm looking for,' she says, 'no matter if it seems to come off real life.'

She works intuitively. 'I write down what comes', is something she says often, and her relationship with her characters is essentially one of listening.

'It's the characters [who] will tell me what's happening, and...I'm separate from it...it feels like getting hold of characters who want to tell me their story but who are also too busy with their lives to tell me their story.'

This splendid remark applies particularly to the rabble who populate *Little Constructions*, but in writing *No Bones* – begun sitting on the floor by the coffee table, using a biro – 'I felt very accompanied, I felt I wasn't alone. I felt like there were other beings in the room, but at that point I wasn't switched on enough to think, Are these characters? With my second book it was much more obvious – the characters were all over the place.'

It is not difficult to make a link between this alert, receptive mind, writing down what is given, and the kind of mind which is attuned to belief in a spirit world. At the close of *Milkman*, along with dozens of friends, Anna Burns has openly acknowledged and thanked what she simply calls Spirit. She would probably say that she found White Eagle Lodge at just the right time.

But though some might think this whimsical or New Age, there is nothing of either in her writing. An immensely strong creative mind is at work between the unheralded arrival of her characters – 'Milkman just drove up in his car,' she says, as he does in the novel – and the control of her tough, immaculate prose. Burns is a writer whose every line is quotable, and it is her bleakly satirical voice – laconically describing violence, as if telling the reader a nursery story; giving a whole new meaning to 'deadpan'; horribly funny – which, even more than her disturbing material, distinguishes her work.

'A few five-year-olds came out in the cold and rain and shouted 'Ya ya – British fuckers' and fired a few stones.'

'Eventually Mick's ma remembered that she had to go upstairs and scream her head off, and got up and left the room to do so.'

'Ten-year-old Josie said she was going to get drunk and her cousins and friends said they'd help her.'

'Mick Lovett, like most of those in the Lovett family, was not very steady in his emotions.'

'[Ma] smacked Amelia and then dropped her like a dirty duster and picked up the screaming Josephine. 'There-there-there-there-there,' she said. 'There-there-there-there- there.' She threw the baby up and down in a way that she would call soothing, which prevented her from throwing it against the wall...'

'You've turned into one cheeky wee bitch. Go to England, then, and get yourself killed.'

These lines come from *No Bones*, where life within the Lovett family is often as violent as on the streets, the dysfunctional family standing for the whole dysfunctional place that is Belfast: torn apart, traumatising those who lived there.

There are many links between this novel and *Milkman*, with *Little Constructions* erupting like a firebomb between them. As for the notion of Spirit, or some higher power which might offer hope or salvation: this might stand behind the act of writing, but if God appears at all on the page, it is only to speak in a Belfast accent.

'Things about the Troubles came out,' Anna tells me. 'I didn't have to think: I'll write about this, or I should work in this bit. If it doesn't want to come, I don't try.'

No Bones lies within the genre of the *bildungsroman*, following the growth from childhood to (some kind of) maturity of Amelia Lovett, who lives 'in the tiny old Catholic district called Ardoyne...with her ma, and her brother Mick, and her sister Lizzie and her da when he was there, though often he was not. He was in the Merchant Navy, and so this time he was in South America.' In her treasure box, along with her beloved caterpillars and paper dolls, six-year-old Amelia has thirty-seven black rubber bullets, collected from the streets 'ever since the British Army started firing them'.

Spanning the twenty-five years of the Troubles, 1969-1994,

the novel is divided into twenty-three chapters, each with a title and date. Alternating between third and first person, it puts Amelia at the centre, drily observing and recording terrible things, and opens with 'Thursday, 1969', on which day she and her little band of friends are told by the self-important Bossy that: 'There's goin' to be trouble... It's startin' tonight. It's already started in Derry. It's going to be dangerous and it means something awful. It means we won't be able to play up here any more.'

'Up here' is the top of the street. Unable to believe that anything going on in Derry – the nationalist name for Londonderry, and 'another country, another planet' – could possibly have anything to do with Belfast or with them, the children decide it must all be 'a made-up thing', and carry on with their game. Six days later, with the windows of the Lovett house boarded up, front and back doors locked and barred, Amelia is amazed to find that the Troubles are still going on. She has counted 'thirteen houses from the top of one side of her street and nine houses from the top of the other that had been burnt...so far'.

In 'An Apparently Motiveless Crime, 1969-1971', the family has a visitor. James Tone (whose name references Wolfe Tone, leader of the 1798 Rebellion against British rule) is an Anglo-Irish, Protestant-Catholic British soldier, a young man with a terrible childhood, come over from London with his regiment and bearing gifts for his distant, long-lost relations. 'Jamesey didn't understand the significance of being British in Ireland at all.' Within hours of his arrival he is murdered on the street.

'Nobody would speak about what had happened. Nothing really had happened. It was just another of those motiveless crimes that were going on all over the place.'

What follows in the novel encompasses, over the years, the fingerprinting of children, killings, counter-killings, bombs, knee-capping, suicide, anorexia, alcoholism and mental illness. Sex is an obscenity. Stray lost souls come and go.

> Mary Dolan had her baby somebody said. There'd been
> problems with it coming out maybe because of all the age
> she was. Her da was still pretending he had nothing to do
> with it and her ma was still not noticing. Nobody got in
> the doctor.
>
> She started to wheel it about in an old toy pram.

Is it, in fact, a baby? Or could it, perhaps, be a bomb?

The lost soul who first appears in that little group of Amelia's
friends, and endures to the end of the novel, is Vincent Lyttle.
Vincent's father has been murdered by Protestant thugs, an
event he repeatedly plays out in his head. His mother, who
aborts her baby in the wake of the murder, is now set on a course
of religious renewal. This involves going on holy retreats, leaving
the three-year-old Vincent to fend for himself.

> There is a scream. It happens three times with a minute
> between each. It is the boy and he is screaming because
> of the silence in the house. He does one long scream and
> then another long scream, three times, and he is
> trembling. Nobody comes... He can't move. On the third
> time he hears, for the first time, the Hum... 'Poor little
> boy,' it says. It is in the pattern of the wallpaper.

Thus begins the psychosis of this child, comforted by the
strange, benign figure of Mr Hunch, who hums, and who puts
him into psychiatric hospital for a very long time. He never fully
recovers.

Somewhere offstage in *No Bones* is a place where kitchens
gleam and people are kind. A place where people take naps, have
tea in tea shops, read storybooks, smile. All this, together with
the rarest sight of beauty in the sky above the city, lies in the
hinterland – a sliver of normal life and humanity glimpsed
through the dark, with the door slammed quickly shut. Anyone
who dares to love or hope or be happy or even to know about

such things has had that beaten out of them a long time ago. But they are referred to, now and then: Amelia's even mentioning them indicates that somewhere, if not here, they are just possible.

At the end of the novel she returns from London, where she has had her own time on a psychiatric ward, and suggests to her old friends, Vincent among them, that they should all have a day out. 'We can go sightseein', go to the beach, the hills, stroll about, not worry...'

They are shocked. 'Unbelievable. Inconceivable. And what did she mean by "not worry"?'

But they give it a go. They will visit Rathlin Island 'sad, often massacred little Rathlin' – a place freighted with the past, haunted by the ghosts of those who perished in a sixteenth-century British massacre. They row out, this bundle of fearful, damaged people, and in endless rain tramp round looking for somewhere for tea. There is nothing. They are roared at by a giant and cursed by old women. Eventually they find some orangeade and custard creams and sit down on the one place they feel safe: on the edge of a cliff. But the ending, as they row home, offers a cautious, poignant note of hope.

Anna was still suffering the after-effects of the harassment from the gangs on the Islingon council estate when she wrote her second novel, *Little Constructions*. Like *Milkman*, it opens with a gun. In this case it's a Kalashnikov, bought in a fury by Jetty Doe, off on a mission to kill her lover, the brutal gang-leader John Doe, married to her sister Janet.

'This was the annoyed Jetty Doe, the one who had knifed her mammy once, and not her less-annoyed cousin called Jotty, who hadn't.'

Also in the novel is John Doe's son, Judas. At one point 'the latest to be half-dead and tied to the torture chair', he is later killed for being an informer. There seems to be a daughter, Jane, though it transpires that Jotty Doe made her up. Julie and JanineJoshuatine [sic] are also important. A court scene late in the novel informs the reader:

> Mr J and Mr J, and Mr J – I'm sorry, but I have to do those Js for legal reasons as those particular 'Js' weren't later charged with murder – and Mr J and Mr J and Justin and Jude and Jameson and Joel and Jake and Johnny and Johnny were all looking at him.

Tom Spaders and Tom Cusack are almost the only other members of the alphabet in this anarchic, surreal work of art.

We are in the little town of Tiptoe Floorboad – a name made for secrets if ever there was one, and a place where anything can happen and does, on every page. Do these madly recurring Js reflect the Kafkaesque circumlocutions of the novel? Dreadful things pile up in past and present, and we fight to make sense of it all. As Lucy Ellmann said in her *Guardian* review (2009), 'It's a bit like watching clothes in a tumble dryer and pretending they're people: certain ones keep flopping back into view, and all of them seem to want to kill each other.'

For Anna, they 'never had any other names, ever'. Like the characters themselves, many of whom have suffered incest or trauma, they simply presented themselves to her. 'I see [them] as victims, ultimately, but I didn't give them [their] names.'

She has written an account of the writing of *Little Constructions*, as yet unpublished, but she tells me that living within the novel, despite its violence, 'felt very safe'. Once she had left London and moved to a rented cottage in Somerset, she was free to listen to what was going on in Tiptoe. 'I mean I liked these characters who would just turn up...the cottage was filled with [them] and they were all filled with light and they were all like boisterous and squabbly and – I mean I'd have to do it slant to hear them, I couldn't actually turn and look at them.'

Sometimes they would leave her. 'I'd feel first, Oh, this is going so well, don't go yet, and they'd just go. And then they'd come back when I'd be out walking, and tell me extra bits, so I always took a dictaphone and notebooks and stuff, because they'd always reappear.'

In the novel a nameless narrator mixes the urgent with the laconic, and there's a constant comic undertow. 'Tiptoe Floorboard, you see, is situated in quaintly subjective territory.'

Within this place of mayhem is a gun shop, eventually turned into a bra shop. Anna Burns has many things in her sights in this novel, and these places stand for two of them: violence and sexual abuse. Here, the sexual politics of Mars & Venus are in absurdist mode.

> 'Us men have to be bookcases,' Father would say. 'I'm a bookcase. You'll be a bookcase too, one day, son.'... What Doe meant by 'bookcase' was 'bookending'. Women were the books, and men were the bookends.

Elsewhere, she interrogates.

> Question is, if you've been abused, 'What's normal?' And if you haven't been abused, 'What's normal?' And are both 'normals' supposed to be the same thing?
>
> Are things meant to be private, or are they not meant to be private?... Take a look at incest. You can't get anything more private than incest. See? Total perplexity. And what is consensual sex if what started out as consensual sex then turns into, 'No, this doesn't feel right. It feels wrong, I've changed my mind, I don't want it any more?'

A Self-Help bookshop offers books 'on incest and child sexual abuse and on adult children of child sexual abuse and on love and lust and greed and grabbing...' and on 'Sex Which is Supposed to be Love but Which Leaves You Feeling Shame and Pain and

Lonely...' Jotty Doe, unable to have sex because 'the man she was with would turn into her da', has been lent a lot of these books, but 'hadn't got round to reading one of them, even once.'

Several of the characters know Tiptoe Under Greystone Cliff's Peninsula Mental Asylum quite well. The one place nobody wants to know is the Action Centre Hut, just around the corner from the Leprechaun Museum. It's the home of the John Doe Community Centre Group, a vicious gang. You need a five-line password to get inside, 'unless you're being taken there to be murdered'. There is no ideology here, no political affiliation: the gang kills indiscriminately.

The whole reads like a cross between *Alice in Wonderland* and Kafka, laced with Joyce and *Titus Andronicus*. Reading some of it is like being run over by a truck. Lipstick, floaty clothes and feminity break through, but always close to the threat of rape.

> She knew violence, and especially she knew the prelimi-
> naries of violence – Edgy. Safe. Edgy. Safe. No, edgy
> again. No, safe again. No, edgy, edgy! Get the hell out!

There are riffs on almost everything: therapy, self-help books, bomb-making equipment, noises, footsteps, suits of armour. Spatial Fragmentation Hallucination Syndrome makes an appearance, as do Jumbled Time Syndrome and Knowing and not knowing [sic]. The narrator's irony is a tonal equivalent of the narrative line for which we are often scrabbling about. Needless to say, we can't trust a word of what we're told.

> At this point I have to own up and admit that I was
> wrong, for I thought she [Jetty] was going to two places.
> I thought she was going to shoot John Doe first, to shoot
> him at his headquarters, then going to the Almost
> Chemist of the Year to shoot Janet, the sister, the wife...
> I'm reporting this faithfully, and that's why it's compli-
> cated, but I know you wouldn't want me to be making
> these things up.

Beneath it all, as with all satire, is a terrible anger. Burns uses black comedy to expose and give a grotesquely exaggerated version of women's suffering at the hands of men, and men's suffering at the hands of one another. Both, far from being made up, are all too close to truth.

'Ordinary murders were eerie, unfathomable...only political murders happened in this place.' 'This place' is Belfast, but it's never named. *Milkman* is set in 'our area, our district': its parks and reservoirs where the narrator and third brother-in-law go running; its streets and entries; its churches. It is 'a district that thrived on suspicion, supposition and imprecision'. The novel is, said Anna Burns on winning the Booker, 'about a whole community'.

'And with the characters in *Milkman*,' she tells me, 'they just had those names, I never saw any others. Maybe-boyfriend's a name. Tablets girl, she's a name, and of course Milkman is a name.'

In other words, there are names, but not, perhaps, as we know them. Beckett's bleak absurdities come to mind, not for the first time in reading Anna Burns. One critic of *Milkman* said that if Beckett had written a prose poem about the Troubles 'it would read a lot like this'.

To discard names-as-we-know-them is in truth a powerful technique. The effect of using 'Somebody McSomebody', 'third brother-in-law', 'real milkman', 'wee sisters', 'maybe-boyfriend', 'tablets girl', 'longest friend', or any of the other occluded, lower-case personae in the novel is to universalise. The world becomes nameless. 'Nothing must be named, not the city of Belfast, not the IRA, not even the narrator,' said the *Telegraph* review. The narrator could be any woman who has attracted the attention of a sexual predator and is in danger. We are in Belfast, but we could be in Syria, in Somalia, in Gaza or Myanmar: trapped inside any community caught up in sectarian violence, or within a war zone, or under military or despotic rule.

Within the novel, the question of names is, however, scrutinised many times.

> After they shot him, and the six unfortunates who got in the way of him, it was revealed, along with his age, abode, 'husband to', 'father of', that Milkman's name really was Milkman. This was shocking. 'Can't be right,' cried people.

> 'Far-fetched. Weird...' But when you think about it, why was that weird? Butcher's a name. Sexton's a name.... 'It broke bounds of credibility,' said the news, but lots of things in life break bounds of credibility. Breaking credibility, I was coming to understand, seemed to be what life was about.

Elsewhere, when Somebody McSomebody, a fervent supporter of the renouncers, uses 'my name, my forename', the effect is to make it transgressively and disgustingly intimate. The name becomes one of the most private parts of the self. 'They said my name then, my first name', the narrator writes of threatening girls in drinking club toilets, 'thereby crossing over and shunning the interface'.

We know we are deep, once again, in the Troubles – 'there were beatings, brandings, tar-and-featherings, disappearances, black-eyed, multi-bruised people walking around with missing digits who most certainly had those digits the day before... impromptu courts' – but neither side is given its known, or formal name. They are 'renouncers of the state', or 'defenders of the state'. Again, the effect of this is to charge shadowy, unnamed figures with menace.

The novel is unsparing in the light it casts on both sides. As in *No Bones*, each is as dangerous as the other, each commits atrocities, and 'the renouncers thought nothing of now and then disappearing each other'.

'Even I knew, though,' says the narrator, 'that people with ideological causes didn't always act in the name of their cause.

Personal slants happened, singular irregularities, subjective interpretations. Crazy people.'

One such is tablets girl [sic]. She has poisoned and almost killed her own sister; she poisons and almost kills the narrator. She is perhaps the individual, psychotic embodiment of the violence which is everywhere: offstage, in the past, or about to erupt. Or she is the embodiment of the damage wrought upon individuals in this place, where going crazy is all you can do.

> 'I tried to elicit the wherefore of her poisoning,' [her now blinded sister tells Middle Sister] 'unravel the distortions, have her right mind restored to her. She said it was impossible, that it was perilous to focus on good things when there were bad things... She said old dark things had to be remembered, had to be acknowledged because otherwise everything that had gone before would have been in vain.

There are many other 'old dark things' in the novel, and in the narrator's own family. Ma has married the wrong man. 'I never understood your father. When all was said and done, daughter, what had *he* got to be psychological about?'

> She meant depressions, for da had them: big, massive, scudding, whopping, black-cloud, infectious, crow, raven, jackdaw, coffin-upon-coffin, catacomb-upon-catacomb, skeletons-upon-skulls-upon-bones, crawling along the ground to the grave-type depressions.

Da spends much time in a mental hospital. 'Males and mental hospitals went together far less than females and mental hospitals went together,' reflects the narrator, when she finds out where he's been. She is one of a family of ten. When she is poisoned, and her mother insists on taking her to hospital – something which immediately risks being labelled an informer – neighbours sum up the family thus:

Poor widow, household of girls, husband dead, one son
dead, another son on the run, another son gone errant
and yet another son creeping in and out of the area as if
he was up to something. Then there's your eldest daughter in unspeakable grief [her lover has been blown up by
a car bomb], your second daughter banished by the
renouncers, your third daughter perfectly perfect apart
from her French, which officially is the bluest in the area.
And now there's this daughter possibly to be had up for
traitorship [if taken to hospital]. Consider the wee ones...
No... No hospital. This one will have to pull through.

The 'wee ones' are the wee sisters, who are brilliantly done: precocious, demanding, adorable. In addition to the family and its
in-laws are the narrator's maybe-boyfriend, a car mechanic and
hoarder of car parts who has won a 'supercharger' from over the
water, and whose life is therefore at risk from the renouncers. His
parents are 'the international couple': world-class dancers offering
a rare glimpse of glamour and hope as they pirouette out in the
street, whom the wee sisters and all the children long to be. Many,
many others populate the novel: 'the women with issues', the
feminists who meet in a hut plastered with posters; the girls in the
drinking clubs; the women of the district who, like ma, have always
loved real milkman, a character quite distinct from Milkman.

But centrally there is the narrator. We never know what work
she does, only that she has a job, goes running, and is attending
a French class. 'Le ciel n'est pas bleu', the tutor tells her astonished class, opening their eyes to the possibility of sunsets, and a
different way of seeing the world. The narrator's real distinguish-
ing characteristic is that she reads while walking, something
which sets her apart. 'This would be a nineteenth-century book
because I did not like twentieth-century books because I did not
like the twentieth century.'

And there is Milkman, a paramilitary who 'appeared one day,

driving up in one of his cars as I was walking along reading *Ivanhoe...*'

> 'You're one of the who's it girls, aren't you? So-and-so was your father, wasn't he? Your brothers, thingy, thingy, thingy and thingy used to play in the hurley team, didn't they? Hop in, I'll give you a lift.'

He is the novel's psychological poison, corroding everything in her life. He knows her routine, he follows her. 'Before the milkman, maybe-boyfriend's touch, those fingers, his hands, had been the best, the most, the absolute of lovely. But now, since the milkman, any part of maybe-boyfriend coming towards me brought up in me mounting bouts of revulsion...'

And his apparent involvement with her, this strange girl who reads while walking, leads those watching – and there is always somebody watching, surveillance is one of the novel's themes – to grow suspicious, to blame, to point the finger. The effect is to cauterise this young woman's identity. Her face freezes, she finds it hard to speak. 'I, too, came to find me inaccessible. My inner world, it seemed, had gone away.'

It is only with Milkman's death – there are plenty of people who want him dead, and a good many who will die before they find him – and with her recovery from tablets girl's assault, that this young woman is able to start running again, out in the evening air, and come to some sort of recovery. As with *No Bones*, the ending offers the most cautious note of hope.

'Somethin' happened political. Now what was it? Was it the hunger-strikers? No, not yet. Was it a Butcher killing? No, not this time. Was it someone shot in the area? Oh, that's right. It was someone shot in the area. She was a past pupil and she was shot in the area and that's what started it.'

Within months of receiving the Booker, Anna Burns was awarded the inaugural 2019 Orwell Prize for Political Fiction.

The award was for *Milkman*, but this and *No Bones* are sister novels. In both, the political situation of Northern Ireland, in 'the great hatred' of the Seventies, as she describes it in *Milkman*, stands behind or blood-spatters every page, and the fall-out is disintegration and despair.

Anna was thrilled to have won this award – 'It was fantastic.' But when a journalist asked her if writing was a political act she didn't know how to answer. 'It's not how my brain works.' This was the starting point for a *Guardian* article in 2019 which looked at the competing claims of art and politics in the contemporary novel.

Perhaps it is true to say that while Anna doesn't connect with the notion of writing as a political act, her work itself is – perforce – political. She has made it clear that she never writes to make a point, or explore an issue. 'I write it and then I see – oh, yes, this is sexual abuse, this is sexual scandal, this is a book about rumours, gossip, the power of gossip, the power of history and also the power of fabricated history, when rumours become the history.'

To date, although this will change very rapidly now, her work has not attracted much scholarly attention. An interesting start has been made by an American academic, Maureen E. Ruprecht Fadem, who describes *No Bones* as 'a post-partition, post-colonial, post-1969, post-modern novel' and makes it the subject of a chapter in *The Literature of Northern Ireland: Spectral Borderlands* (2015).

Her thesis is that the partition of Ireland in 1921 fractured self and society in the North, and resulted in poetry and prose which is haunted by spectral presences from the past. She sees the twenty-five years of the Troubles as 'a veritable disaster zone', and the novel 'peopled by mad militants for whom brutality is an addictive drug'.

Much of this chapter is eloquent and insightful. Some is less so. Ruprecht Fadem positions Anna Burns as historian, rather than novelist, and it would seem that much of the comedy and satire in the novelist's voice escapes her.

However, she valuably points to the way in which *No Bones* is mapped onto huge historical figures and events: the revolutionary Wolfe Tone; the Glens where the mid-nineteenth century victims of the Irish famine were buried, and which Amelia's tormented mind visits during her breakdown; the massacre on Rathlin Island from which past horror springs the furious giant who bears down on the anxious little party on their day out. She also points to the way in which the ghosts of those who died in the Troubles haunt the narrative, mediated by Roberta McKeown, Amelia's childhood friend, 'blown up by a car-bomb in 1975', who appears in a London street as she collapses into breakdown.

Anna doesn't talk about her fiction as haunted by the ghosts of the past, but of *No Bones* she has spoken of 'how hard it is for...people to let go of pain...of something that is familiar, even if it is killing them', a remark that reminds the reader of that comfortable cliff edge. She has said that she sees that novel 'as one big giant fight: voices out there, voices in here. The fact that so many people died reflects the reality of that particular period of time. It's both about a specific historical period and about people and their relationships and how violence can emerge and be passed on.'

All this perhaps places her as much within a psychoanalytical as a political framework. Essentially, she has not set out to campaign. She has set out to show.

This essay has tried to show something of how Anna's brain does work. Although her novels are drawn from her own life and the community within which she grew up, and although she is seeking to show the damage that was done to that community, her commitment is to the art of fiction. She is vessel and artist and wordsmith: I do not like this word, which feels lazy, but her prose is as powerful, hammered and meticulous as any piece of material wrought into shape.

'That does seem important to me – the rhythm, and where the word goes, and whether the syllable is too long,' she says when we talk. 'Even if I like the word, it might not work. Sometimes reading out loud, saying a word that isn't there – you realise it's a better word... And I can tell what's bedded in, and what needs more time.'

She is inspired and sustained by something quite otherworldly. 'I write down what comes.' Her relationship with her characters is as personal as if she had grown up alongside them, and this is as true of the mad horde of Does in *Little Constructions* as it is of sociopathic Bronagh McCabe in *No Bones* and the deranged tablets girl in *Milkman*.

Anna Burns is a philosopher, with a great deal of accrued wisdom, who mocks pieties without a blink. 'Funny little thing, therapy, isn't it now?' she says in *Little Constructions*. She is asking not only what it means to be human, but what it means to be alive. 'A life which had never worked in the first place,' is how she describes the existence of a terrified man in *No Bones*, who hangs himself. She has, in truth, been close to many dark things, has suffered and been saved and fulfilled by writing. It is her work which has enabled her to look at everything she turned away from in her youth, in one of the darkest political periods of twentieth-century history, right in the face.

There is writing, and there is 'the other writing'. In our conversation Anna frequently made this distinction. 'The other writing' is the raw, unshaped outpouring of experience with which her recovery began. Writing is that which now engages her, professionally and artistically. I know no one else who speaks of 'my writing' in quite the way that Anna does, as if it were a friend, or at least another person.

'What shaped me as a writer?' she reflects, as our conversation comes to an end. 'Getting sober and getting all the other writing out, and creating a space. Anything could have come, but writing came, and I don't really know why, except that I really do like words.' And she quotes the Irish writer Eoin McNamee, whose work she much admires. '[He] said "I do my thinking on the page," and I thought: that's exactly what I do. And I know... I need patience, not to rush things, and I do have that with writing. I'm prepared to let things take their time, and not finish until they want to finish.'

The Nature Writer

RUTH PAVEY

'I had the thought that if I was good at anything, it was with words. I always felt that words were my friends. But writing can be hard: you do need encouragement.'

The first time I became aware of the name Ruth Pavey was a very long time ago, when I was visiting the vet. Waiting to pay for some feline procedure, I found my eye caught by a petition on the counter. It was against bear baiting, in a country I have now forgotten. There was her signature: I thought it a strong name, and it also rang a bell. Eventually I realised that this was the Ruth Pavey whose literary reviews I had read over the years in the *Observer* and *Independent*. I conjured an interesting person, paid the exorbitant bill and left, with my feline in tow.

Some years later, I met Ruth at a party. If I say that her clear blue gaze had me spellbound it will sound absurd, so I won't say that, but I did think her beautiful and distinctive. We had sons the same age – nine – and we talked about them, among book-related matters. Later still, it transpired that we had attended Surrey schools which played hockey against each other – Ruth was in the team, I was nowhere near it. One of the less sporty things which Ruth's school taught her was the art of sitting down, an accomplishment which on occasion she demonstrates to her friends, to the accompaniment of some mirth.

She has other accomplishments, few of them fostered by that school. Over a long lunch in Warsaw in 2008, when we went travelling to the Baltic States together, we bemoaned the narrowness of our education, but Ruth has certainly made up for lost time. She plays the cello, cultivates four pieces of land, writes the garden column in the *Ham & High* (*Hampstead and Highgate Express*) and after a long career in reviewing has now published books. She is also the only writer in this one who practises drawing.

After that lunch we took ourselves to the Lazienki Park, and sat on the sun-warmed grass among Polish families relaxing on a Sunday afternoon, listening to Chopin broadcast from loudspeakers across the lake. A huge romantic sculpture of the composer is set within it. Ruth had her little notebook with her, as always on holiday, and made pencil sketches of trees and those about us.

Now, her loose, airy drawings of wild plants, cows grazing by a river, an apple tree with too much mistletoe and more illustrate *A Wood of One's Own* (2017), together with hand-drawn maps of where the wood lies and what is in it.

It lies on the Somerset Levels, an area of the county in which Ruth was born, but of whose watery existence she had known little except when from time to time they were flooded, and appeared in the national press, fields become a glassy sea. But in the late 1990s family reasons were drawing her back from London, where she had long been settled. She was taking a route which led her

> across a landscape I had never seen before, of willow, water, grass, cattle, swans, ditches, distant hills...the Somerset Levels. With their soft, painterly light, spacious skies and melancholy, their feeling of not quite belonging in the present, or at least part of the past still being present, I fell for them...in general, neither expecting nor receiving much attention, they persist in their half-dreaming, vegetative way, a silted place of slow waters, eels, reeds, drainage engineers, buttercups, church towers, quiet.

Although *A Wood of One's Own* is Ruth Pavey's first book, it has brought her some attention, both for her beguiling prose, and the project she describes. In 1999 she acquired at auction a four-acre piece of scrubland on the Levels, and gradually planted within it some 150 trees. She has now been working on this little piece of land for over twenty years, an enterprise which might be said to be the culmination of her long-held interest in the natural world – trees, gardens, cultivated and wild plants, wild creatures – as well as in writing itself.

Her style, which moves from the lyrical to the dry, has been shaped by a lifetime's reading, and the book is adorned with epigraphs from Thomas Browne, Yeats, Ruth Pitter, Shakespeare, and traditional song. It is also honed from decades of literary and garden journalism, something she fell into during the 1980s while teaching in inner-London schools.

Ruth is modest about her teaching – 'I never felt I was very good at it, at least not at the discipline side,' but the activities with which she involved the children in after-school hours were delightful, mostly involving making things: pots, pictures, gardens. Many city children live in flats: to create a little garden in a corner of the school playground is invaluable.

She makes one fleeting but potent reference to the classroom in her book. This is to a refugee Bosnian woman and her seven-year-old niece, who arrived at the school where Ruth was teaching not long after she had bought the wood and was making cautious but happy inroads through the brambles on her first day. Having lunch over a home-made fire as the rain eased off, looking about her and listening to the birds, she thought of this woman, and the nightmare she had endured to reach the United Kingdom. Soon afterwards, she and her niece disap-peared, no doubt relocated. 'With so many people like them, rootless across the world, it seemed to me all the luckier that there was I, about to start planting trees in the county where I had been born.'

> There is a lot of hope involved in planting a tree. First
> that the sapling will grow at all, then that you will live
> long enough to see it becoming a real tree. But beyond
> that stretch years, perhaps even centuries, for the tree to
> go on growing and living, till people with no idea who

planted it will love that old tree for its beauty, girth, the
roughness of its fissured trunk, its long endurance.

There is a lot of hope involved in beginning a book, particularly
your first. This essay looks at how the purchase of the wood, and
the composing of the book began, and at a life in which reading,
writing, drawing and planting have all been central – with diver-
sions along the way.

Ruth describes to me the way in which the different parts of her
life connect as 'a nexus of painting, gardening and literature',
and then remembers music. She is someone who could have
gone in several directions – at seven her teacher suggested she
should go to a specialist music school –– but in fact has managed
to combine all of them. Her London house, bought with friends
in 1972, reflects this.

'My house is quiet, plant-filled, veering towards the bookish
and shabby,' she wrote in a *Guardian* article in 1989. By that time
she had bought out her co-owners, remaining friends with most
of them to this day. To this day that description of her house fits
well, but omits various things, including cats and a piano.

As in many Victorian London houses, a long ground-floor
room runs from front to back. A vast ficus in a pot stands in the
bay window, but in summer is banished to the front garden,
letting the light flood in on to ancient sofa, rugs on a wooden
floor, the fireplace. On festive occasions there is very often a fire,
and a cat before it. This might be Sweet Rocket (slender tabby
with white socks), or it could be her son, The Otter (large and
dark). The walls are painted a faded blue, hung here and there
with family watercolours and with a wall of books. Cards, invitations, and photographs of earlier cats all poke out between the
spines.

The table beneath is piled with books, letters, tea cups (Ruth's
china is always interesting,) bowls of apples or pears from the

wood, at least one jug of flowers, and notes about this and that. I mention in passing that many outgoing letters, or notes to lodgers, are pinned in mousetraps, hung from the dado rail in the hall. The piano across the room is heaped with scores and candlesticks, the cello in its case alongside, and in the opposite corner is a desk of sorts, with laptop and a mountain of stuff upon it. Also, generally, a cat, generally George Herbert – long-haired, black with white chest and socks, amazing whiskers; a creature in whom the magnificent and the adorable combine to render his admirers helpless.

Nothing in this room, or the light-filled new annexe built out into the garden, or the garden itself, is neat. Everywhere, there is something good to look at: pots, cuttings, boxes of fruit or collected kindling, cards from friends, back numbers of the *London Review of Books*, bags of cat food, books and bulbs. Hung here and there are home-made calendars, often adorned with the picture of a hen or two (see below). The impression of the whole is of a full, appealing and creative life. I did once describe it as a creative muddle, but was reproached. 'I try so hard to keep it organised!'

On the other side of George Herbert and a glass half-partition the room culminates in a tiny kitchen overlooking the long and tangled garden. White *Alberic Barbier* roses clamber in profusion over the wall, to join the neighbour's Rambling Rector; there are plants in pots and plants in loosely bordered beds: hydrangeas, jasmine, snapdragons, fuschias, nasturtiums. A path leads through it all, down past an old table and chairs set beneath a laburnum, at which many a glass has been raised at many a summer party. At the far end is a run which once held bantams, each with a name; their slaughter by a fox some years ago was a dreadful thing. Another fox and her family now make a comfortable home beneath what is in theory a writing hut but in fact the repository of tools, chairs, boxes and spiders. Next door, the birds of a pigeon-fancier used to rise each evening into the air and return in a clapping cloud.

This is Ruth's London garden. She also has an allotment, a few miles up the Holloway Road in a turning off Highgate Village, acquired in 1989.

'Allotment sites have the power to create magical enclosures,' she wrote in the *Ham & High* that year. 'There's a kind of quiet sprightliness to it all... All around are shining scenes of industry.'

Ruth herself is nothing if not industrious, although she describes her way of going about things as proceeding in a looping, haphazard fashion. As she understands it, this is also characteristic of the mother she lost when she was six. This event, which left her father heartbroken, and she and her two brothers without a family home, perhaps lies behind her project with the wood.

'Somerset was where we had been happy,' she writes in the book. 'I am not saying that I took on this venture because of a subterranean feeling that my mother would have loved it, but perhaps that played into it. Losing my mother so young, surrounded by private grief but not much communication, I am aware of having created in her image an invisible guide and companion.'

With her mother's death, Ruth and her brothers went to live with their aunt, the widowed sister who had never wanted children but who did her very best by them. The brothers were already at boarding school, returning in the holidays. A musical child, Ruth pushed away that suggestion of a place at a specialist school, saying her father would not like it. Whether he would have done or not, she does not know. He himself, a veteran of Gallipoli who never quite recovered from the experience, nor from the loss of his wife, died in 1976.

But this, as they say, is to look ahead. Meanwhile, the six-year-old Ruth took up residence with her aunt, and went to school.

'Because my mother died, which I now realise was far more traumatic than was given credit for at the time, I think that put me off my stride for a while,' she tells me. 'From six, seven, eight, I was much better at maths than reading or writing – I was really quite slow with them both.'

But she loved being read to. The small square *Little Grey Rabbit* books were already in the house, from her brothers' time of being read to. Her father liked quoting from them. She fell under the spell cast by Alison Uttley and her illustrator Margaret W. Tarrant, whose gentle watercolours perfectly complement the stories of country life and country doings: the making of primrose wine, the finding of a home for Wise Owl when his tree blows down in a storm, Old Man Hedgehog tramping across the frosty fields to collect milk from a cow.

'These books have exercised far too great an influence over me,' she writes in *A Wood of One's Own*. 'How is one to embrace modernity with Little Grey Rabbit still pattering through the imagination making cowslip balls?' She also enjoyed Kenneth Grahame but shied away from terrifying Grimm, and a grisly tale of how Robin Hood met his end. 'I really didn't like books where bad things happened,' she says now.

It was *The Famous Five* who eventually unlocked the pleasure of reading. After their terrific adventures, 'They were all home in time for tea.' From then on, 'I found reading absolutely wonderful – an escape from life, really, to be able to enter different worlds.'

When she was ten, Ruth went to boarding school, at first excited by the idea that she would be entering the big brave world away from home which her brothers knew. But although she began there to develop as a writer, through essays and especially through letters to her aunt and father, and to her friends, overall she now knows she would have been much better off going to the local grammar school. The curriculum the girls followed was taught so narrowly – 'In English I'd just copy down the word "vivid" from the board' – that a notion such as reading round the subject felt outlandish. 'I had a very air-heady attitude, really. I had no idea how to be scholarly, or look things up on my own.'

But at A-level she made one important discovery: Virginia Woolf. 'We were also doing Wordsworth, and I couldn't abide him then, with his Duty: "stern daughter of the voice of God" – he was the sort of thing I was in rebellion against in my heart, very stodgy and old. But *To the Lighthouse* was on the syllabus and I read it. At first I hadn't got a clue what was going on. Then I read it again and thought it was absolutely marvellous. There's a lot about gardens, and the painter, Lily Briscoe, a very observant, interesting character.' So she threw out Wordsworth and wrote about Woolf – entirely untutored, since her teacher seemed not to have read her.

Meanwhile, she was discovering gardens. When I ask her about which ones might have been an early influence, she is very clear. Both her parents had been keen on gardening, and she knows that her mother made a pond. 'We certainly used to look at gardens and go to historic houses.'

But individual gardens which made an impact? The first was in a village not far from Yeovil, where her godmother took her twice, when she was visiting in her teens. 'It was like an allotment, separate from any cottage, with an old man cultivating it. There were paths, but they didn't show – it looked like a field full of interesting flowers, and I thought, This is the sort of garden I like. It seemed so uninterrupted by human intervention.'

The second was Sissinghurst, where she went on a painting trip with a sixth-form school friend. Looking back on that day, Ruth realises that the figure they could see in a distant deck-chair was Harold Nicolson – she knew about Vita Sackville-West through Virginia Woolf, and had read and admired her long four-seasons poem 'The Land'. 'I thought the whole place was enchanting. It felt very lost in time, not many visitors, very beautiful.'

She also continues to love and admire the classical garden at

Stourhead, on the Wiltshire/Somerset border. 'Lakes, temples, an early example of the whole eighteenth-century English landscape movement, laid out by the Hoares, a banking family. A later nineteenth-century Hoare planted rhododendrons – purists disapprove, but they look fantastic when they're out.'

In sum: 'It was those three which set me up.'

At A-level, Ruth managed to fail Art. 'I suspect at that time I was doing things which were very nervous and tight.' As for Woolf: 'Heaven knows what I wrote.'

She set off for university interviews without any preparation. 'Having gone to this blinkered school, I had no idea how well-educated other people were.' Nowhere offered her a place, and she was devastated. Like most young women then, she took a secretarial course, 'which made me realise how ghastly it would be to be a secretary, which I'd suspected already.'

Then one evening her older brother, by now working in the City, brought home the evening paper, with a scandal in it. 'A beautiful young woman had been asked to leave the Ruskin School of Drawing because she did no work – she was just having a good time in Oxford and taking part in plays. And I thought: That sounds good!'

She applied, was offered an interview, and set off with a portfolio of drawings. The then head, Richard Naish, liked a drawing of a workman in overalls, and to her astonishment gave her a place. It was 1966.

The Ruskin, like Oxford itself, was a revelation, a wake-up call, a place of happiness. 'I had a lot to learn when I got there.' Housed then within the Ashmolean Museum, it offered the twenty or so students of that year free run of the galleries and a three-year course covering drawing, painting and printmaking. One of the tutors had been at the Slade, in the rigorous era of Henry Tonks and Philip Wilson Steer, and Sir Joshua Reynolds might have recognised the curriculum. Ruth did not enjoy time spent in the Cast Gallery – 'what a bore, dusty plaster casts' – but appreciates that the students were being given an education in how to draw. Now, she says that what she likes about drawing is that it makes you look at things in far more depth.

But away from the Cast Gallery they all wandered around and got to know a lot of things. There was a wonderful collection of Dutch flower paintings, which nobody took seriously. Required to write an essay, Ruth felt too uncertain in herself to write about them, choosing instead the more conventional Samuel Palmer and his trees.

'If I were writing about the Dutch flowers now I'd be wanting to find out about the importation of those plants, who was painting, who was buying. But I didn't know how to approach anything, because I wasn't educated.'

This began to change. 'That whole time of being at the Ruskin was an education to me. Many of the people I became friendly with – on and off the course – they just knew stuff, they had so much more of a grip on the world. And they had a competitive worldliness which I was completely unused to. Drama, debating, writing for *Isis*…'

And singing. Ruth considers her audition for Scuola Cantorum, Oxford's premier chamber choir, one of the luckiest moments of her life – not because she got in, but because of whom she met while waiting to be called. This was a young woman called Emma Kirkby, who was up reading Greats (Classics) at Somerville, and who had been singing parts in madrigals since she was fourteen. 'I didn't even know what a madrigal *was*.'

Neither of them was offered a place, something Ruth has been dining out on for years, although it has since transpired that there were other, non-musical reasons for the oversight with Emma. But they struck up a friendship which endures until this day.

'She opened up a whole window that was only just coming open anyway, about early music. She was part of that movement: happened to have a wonderful voice and be extremely intelligent, and was able to fill a space, with all the interest in early instruments.'

Other, long-lasting friendships were made in those Oxford days, where women were in short supply, and at a premium. One of the young men Ruth got to know – 'brilliant, attractive, but not altogether reliable' is how she describes him in her book – became, in 1970, her husband. In 1972, with two other friends, they bought the London house. The house has lasted; the marriage did not.

'All the children's books we read were set in the countryside,' Ruth writes in *A Wood of One's Own*, 'so I concluded that people were only allowed to live in London once they were grown up, which may explain why moving there in my twenties was such a thrill.'

She had left the Ruskin with a qualification 'which had more words than weight': an Oxford University Certificate of Drawing and Fine Art. She did not feel in any way good enough to pursue a career as an artist, but had garden design in her sights. She worked for one summer in the Oxford Botanic Gardens, and then for a year in the garden of Rhodes House, 'a pompous place built in the twenties when the British Empire was still riding high', she informs me. 'The idea was that Prime Ministers and so on would come down at weekends to meet the Rhodes Scholars: bright young people of the colonies who were going to be the next leaders of the empire. I thought the house ugly, but liked the long herbaceous border.'

From here she applied to do a landscape architecture course – there were very few then – at Hammersmith College of Art and Building. As with her university interviews, this was a dispiriting experience: she went up with plans for redesigning the Rhodes House garden and showed them to two male tutors who were into modernist architecture. They sniggered at her planting plans, and 'I came out feeling absolutely crushed.' She was in fact offered a place, but turned it down, later realising that in truth she was more of a responder than a designer.

One of those jobs followed of the kind which most of us have done at some time, for want of anything better. Ruth took it, thinking she might learn the technical drawing skills needed for making garden plans. But retracing the underground cable maps of the Southern Electricity Board, who were converting all their measurements to metric, only taught her how to hold the appropriate pen.

Meanwhile, her husband, immersed in post-graduate studies, had ideas about changing the world through trades unions. Ruth decided to change it through education.

As London seemed the most likely place for them to start, she applied to what was then the Polytechnic of North London to train as a primary school teacher. But before they moved to London her husband took a research job in Geneva. With Ruth enrolled on her teaching course, a semi-detached marriage now began. Besides teaching, by this time she had another direction, which had begun to creep up years before: writing fiction.

In her first long summer holiday, out in Switzerland, with her husband at work, Ruth began her first novel. The early hand-written pages blew out of the window in a draught, but she retrieved them and continued, completing, with much rubbing out and typing up, a story about her schooldays. It did not cross her mind that this was what we call a draft, and she was hurt and bemused to find it rejected.

She followed it with a novel about a community centre set in an old piano factory: 'about how you don't need to be a bad person to do harm' – something which reflected her by now troubled marriage. The third had a lovely title, *Light in Distant*

Rooms, a line from an Indian poem, and was about wartime evacuation, dislocation of class and place. By now, she and her husband had parted.

Ruth's career in fiction was not without its possibilities. On the strength of some short stories, a literary agent who was to become prestigious took her on and encouraged her in the writing of her second novel. She then rejected it. 'The general view of my novels by kindly people was "sensitive, perceptive, uncommercial".'

At one point, when an agent expressed real interest, 'I felt as if I was taken up a high mountain and told, "All this could be yours".' 'All this' included money, tie-ins, general excitement. Another time, an agent appeared to be probing to find out how well connected she was. Ruth didn't want any of it. 'Now I realise they were just trying to do their job, but at that time I think I must have had an old-fashioned, lofty distaste for networking or commercial success, maybe for any success at all. In which case it would have been more realistic to stop bothering the publishers.'

She had also realised that 'there was always a lonely little girl or young woman in my books. I knew she was me, and why she was there, but I got fed up with her. I didn't want to write about her, I wanted to get on with other stuff.'

Eventually, late in the 1980s, a friend said, 'Of course you're not getting published, no one's heard of you.' She put her in touch with the literary editor of the *New Statesman*, and a whole new writing life and direction began to open up.

'I loved reviewing,' she says. 'The journalists were so nice. You could talk to them on the phone!' The dread words 'she's in a meeting' flew away in this new milieu. 'I found it refreshing, easy to get into, and you went to see wonderful things or read wonderful things.'

So began years of reviewing garden books, fiction, fiction in translation; of visiting and writing about gardens and exhibitions – all this combined with teaching, so she was working hard. From the *New Statesman* she branched out to the *Ham & High* and, through a helpful word, got a toe in at the *Observer*, where she began to review fiction and garden literature. Later, when Boyd Tonkin was at the *Independent*, nurturing literature in translation, Ruth says it was thrilling to be sent novels translated from a host of languages and cultures. 'I may have been a fool rushing in where others might have been more circumspect, but I loved it.'

Had she wanted to pursue her own career as a novelist at this point, the opportunity to make herself known was there in principle, with plenty of literary parties. 'Somehow I always found myself talking to the second bottle-washer. I think the only chance I got to join the enchanted circle was when I was invited to meet a famous novelist on Christmas Day. And I said, "*Christmas Day?* I've got my family with me!"'

Like all the best literary journalism, Ruth's reviews are inform-ative and astute, with a colloquial and engaging tone. She has an ability to see the best and nose-dive on the worst: 'Matters close to the heart are tackled from the head' is how she dismisses one novel, and of Ben Okri she murmurs that 'his voice does take a bit of tuning into, and staying with.' She has – unsurprisingly – a novelistic eye for detail, and is good with lists.

'He is a master of incidentals: the weather, light, noises off, snatches of conversation, incongruities, smells.'

'What the book [about the road to Santiago] really dwells on is churches, monasteries, empty roads, quiet villages, images of saints and kings.'

The subject of one biography is summed up thus: 'She liked men, cigarettes and cats.'

Ruth was given many round-ups of first novels to review, but also new work from Claudio Magris, Maureen Duffy, J.M. Coetzee, Tatyana Tolstaya, early E. Annie Proulx, Deborah Levy and Anne Tyler – 'a quirky, dancing sort of writer'. Work in translation included novels from the Hungarian, Portuguese, Spanish, Swedish and Russian. Of Shusako Endo, 'the great Japanese Catholic novelist' (there can't be many of those) she writes that 'his limpid, unassuming style makes airy work of his heavyweight content.' 'Limpid' and 'unassuming' well describe aspects of her own style in her own first book.

Her non-fiction reviews include memoir and biography, as well as art books and books on particular gardens and houses. She reviewed books on Manet, da Vinci, cave painting; on Kew Gardens and Humphrey Repton, and did plenty of seasonal round-ups of garden books. 'Like love, gardens are lucky if they last,' she wrote once, and 'Garden books had better feed the imagination.' There is a nice review of a selection of Christopher Lloyd's old *Country Life* columns, full of his friends, as well as flowers, of which she says: 'Together they build up a welcome sense of gardening as a part of social and cultural life, rather than an escapist annexe.'

As for the *Ham & High*: she has been writing for this much-loved paper for a good three decades. In 2001, when the garden column had lapsed, she became its gardening correspondent, and is so still.

Each of her pages has a feature and a sidebar: Things to Do. These might include Treasure your Tadpoles, Cut Back Your Lavender, or an invitation to go and look at the cherry blossom in Regent's Park. The features cover the usual flower and produce shows, festivals and open gardens, clubs and societies, but include engaging profiles: the woman who plants the roundabout in Highgate village; Ruth's Greek Cypriot garage mechanic, planting Mediterranean fruit and herbs on his allotment just off the North Circular; the new head gardener at Fenton House, a seventeenth-century merchant house now belonging to the National Trust.

There is also the occasional obituary: of a renowned dahlia

grower, and, recently and sadly, of her friend Margaret, who cultivated the allotment adjoining her own, and who in 1999 came to give moral support on a wet spring day at the auction of that wood on the Somerset Levels.

'It was still raining. Great clods of clay attached themselves to our boots as we struggled up the ploughed field at the end of the grassy track. Nettles at the edge had grown enormously... It looked very dense, very wet, but very beautifully green.'

Thus, the purchase at auction concluded, Ruth and Margaret made their way towards this overgrown patch of land. Ruth had seen it before, 'in the last glow of a sunny spring evening' a few weeks earlier, when looking through an agent for somewhere to buy in this for her newly-discovered area. She'd rather dismissed it, having her eye on three quiet fields with open views across the Levels and perhaps within her budget, but, in the way of auctions, these went swiftly for almost twenty thousand pounds, and that was the end of that. Then came a farmhouse, neglected and gloomy, which also went under the hammer fast.

And then, with the auctioneer making half-hearted noises about scrubland of possible interest to conservationists, and with a friendly solicitor doing the bidding, she found herself, within a few minutes, its owner. Well under £3000 for four acres, and here these acres were, sloping up and away at the top of a long track from the road to Aller and proving hard to get into.

A wheat field lay along the left-hand side of the track; field maples were coming into 'delicate bronzy leaf' along the border. On the other side stretched an orchard, also coming into the fresh new leaf of spring. They could see 'the pale, shapely spathes' of lords-and-ladies under a hazel tree, and standing on tiptoe made out nettles and weeds and brambles smothering a heap of fallen willows in a ditch. The auctioneer had mentioned that clearing these was a requirement, and Ruth found it comforting to know what her first task would be, but wondered if clearing the ditch would mean that the land would then dry out. 'I was already getting keen on being the owner of a marsh.'

But whatever lay ahead, she now had a little piece of the county where she had been born, albeit in quite a different part of it, and a new double life was about to begin: moving between the London world of teaching, book reviews, friends and music, and quiet time in Somerset: out of doors in all weathers, giving something neglected and half-forgotten the possibilities of recovery and growth. 'The tilt of my life was changing.'

Eventually, she would write about it all.

A Wood of One's Own is a lovely and inspiring book. It began with the diaries Ruth kept over fifteen years, recording her progress. She then shaped them thematically – whole chapters on Tree Planting, Wild life, Equipment, etc., but readers tended to get a bit overwhelmed by this. Then, with the support of a helpful agent, she worked with an editor to give it the structure it now has: a chronological story in ten chapters, each with a facing illustration, each with an epigraph and inviting title.

Opening with Searching for the Place, it moves to Searching for the Genius, with a nice quotation from Pope: '...all must be adapted to the Genius and Use of the Place...' something to which she was alert. There are chapters entitled Apples, and Other Early Encounters; Mowers, Hooves, Teeth; The Rollalong. Ah, the Rollalong. I shall come to that.

She drew two airy maps of the place, which serve as end-papers. One shows the wood's location: lying on a stretch of land between the village of Aller and the town of Langport (site of a Civil War battle), through which the River Parret makes its way. You can see the Parret from the wood, its broad banks grazed by cattle. She drew the cattle, too, in outlines reminiscent of E.H. Shepard. The other map shows the wood as it now stands: the old and new fruit trees, a hazel wood, an ash wood where raucous rooks build their nests in spring, the butterfly garden, the pond and new hedge.

Thoughtfully designed, and enhanced by her maps and illustrations, *A Wood of One's Own* is not just distinctively written but looks good, immediately pickupable; with Duckworth, her publisher, right behind her, it attracted attention from the beginning. Ruth has found herself now part of a genre, the Nature Writer, which, as things stand, seems to be more associated with male writers. She didn't set out to strike a blow here, but what does she think about this?

'Nature Writing is on the up precisely because the flora and fauna around us are very much on the down – ironic, isn't it?' she says. 'I don't think many of those loosely connected with the label "New Nature Writing" are happy with it, but publishers and booksellers need to categorise, so Memoir/Nature is the slot.

'When I started work on my patch of land, the few books I could consult were all written by tireless-sounding men, skilled with the chainsaw, the billhook, the axe, and all keen on coppicing. Then came the memorable literary triumphs of those whom Kathleen Jamie so memorably skewered as "enraptured, lone and male". When it occurred to me to write about my experiences in the wood, neither of these models was much help.

'I suppose if I've fallen back on any model, it's the self-deprecation, with a touch of rapture woven in. There are more women "nature writers" around now, but with the exception of Helen Macdonald [author of *H is for Hawk*] the winners still tend to be men.'

'The chainsaw, the billhook, the axe' – throughout the book, there is in fact much about the practicalities of the enterprise. But there is also a great joy in light let in, and in the soaring skies above the watery Levels. 'Light is a magician,' Ruth writes, and when we talk in my Herefordshire kitchen about the whole act of looking she says simply, 'Colour is one of the best things about being alive.'

Her pages are filled with varied greens of moorland, hedgerow, trees, with the reds and browns of butterflies, the startling blues, pinks and yellows of wild flowers: the knapweed, moon daisies, campion and yarrow she introduces, as well as the more domestic daffodils. There are disquisitions on moss, snowdrops, nettles, bluebells; she writes of the traces and tracks of animals, and the 'flustering about' of duck and moorhen down on the river bank.

Her descriptions of landscape, sky and weather are those of a painter: a 'watercolour sky', 'the felty evening greyness', 'the wind whipping clouds across the spacious sky', 'the billowing cow parsley and wide, breezy skies'; 'a mild morning, with sunshine coming and going and birds swooping in and out of the hedges', 'the reedy suggestion of a ditch'; 'the sweep of the open grassy landscape... A few cows, one swan, miles and miles of open land'.

This quiet, observant voice is laced with a gentle humour and understatement, and the diction is sometimes reminiscent of an earlier, perhaps more civilised time: words like 'amiable' and 'agreeable' quite often make an appearance, together with phrases used with a suggestion of a smile: 'inclined to think', 'one might consider', 'I concluded that...'

But the pleasures of this book lie not only in the limpid prose, and the accounts of digging, planting, pruning, mowing, but in the author's sensibility. There are some people, making such a purchase, whose immediate ambition would be to clear. Hacking and slashing away, bringing in machinery, they would see a constant battle against weeds and predators. But Ruth notes that in the early days 'the place felt secretive, mossy, withdrawn, intent on its own business', and what she describes is her co-operation with those who were there before her, those who live within it or alongside.

'I felt the presence of the many unseen creatures for which this was their place, the only place they had,' she writes of her first day there on her own, when she remembers the Bosnian refugees. And her feeling for animals – expressed in London through those beloved cats, and the fox she has let make a home beneath her garden shed – runs throughout her account of owls, partridge in frosty winter 'fluffed up round as rabbits', 'lapwing flying over the moor', 'the deer's rough voices', 'the occasional scuffle or cry'.

She does, of course, have to do some clearing: 'Guessing that the Genius of the Place might be shy, I started with secateurs.' But those willows in the ditch have to be uncovered and pollarded; the brambles have to go, making a space for new tree planting. To help her, she enlists Andrew David, a local contractor whose practicality sustains her. After she has tried to settle in native hedge plants, she notes that, 'Nothing I plant is unobserved by rabbits, deer or mice, and very little is not to their taste.' And she does, of course, have to protect new young trees against the depredations of all three, putting up tree guards, though when it comes to making a puddle into a pond she does not line it, fearing for the life of the water voles whose holes she has noticed here and there.

Andrew is just one of those who become important over the years: people dot the narrative like trees in a field. Some are from the past: the historian in Ruth writes of King Alfred and his encounter with the Danes; of the Civil War and the Royalists whose horses drowned in ditches as they fled across the moor; of William Pitt, who a few miles away planted cedars still standing; of Cecil Sharp. The descendant of one of the folk singers whose songs Sharp recorded still sings now and then in the local church.

Present-day people include, most importantly, Ted Knight, who owns the orchard which borders her land. With him, until he falls ill, she is in constant dialogue about willows, water, sheep (she wants them), cows (not a good idea) and fencing. Her brothers and her farming cousins all come to visit, offer help and advice, bring and, more rarely, plant saplings. And then there are the country people from whom she buys tools: a strimmer, a scythe and a mower. There are the nurserymen she visits to buy 'maiden' apple trees, as well as, over the years, young cedar, larch, spruce, oak, beech, poplar, birch, walnut, field maple, holly, horse chestnut... The list goes on.

> I had not thought of being an orchard-owner, of growing fruit trees. Oak, beech, cedar, walnut were more in my mind, trees that could still be here in a hundred years time. But there was no mistaking that the Genius of this Place was less pretentious, a good, everyday apple sprite...I did not abandon my hope of noble trees, just tempered them, so that the four acres became shared between orchard and woodland.

Existing trees include old apple, hazel, ash, hawthorn, sloe, elder, field maple and wild plum, with 'one good straight oak'. She takes herself on courses: more people enter the story, one teaching the art of grafting, the complexities of which even she, an experienced gardener, finds mystifying. She learns about scions and rootstock, remarking that: 'so many ways there are, of getting things wrong...'

Where was Ruth to stay overnight, when she came down from London? For the first six months or so, she stayed in local B&Bs, but: 'Staying in a B&B has its awkward side. The hosts have to appear to welcome strangers when really it is the money they most welcome, the guests have to tiptoe about, trying not to derange the dried flowers or plumbing, then look grateful at breakfast.'

She cast about her, wondering if she could put up a shed, but was quickly dissuaded from this by Planning. Then Ted, he of the orchard, offered a solution, currently parked outside his ponies' stable. Ruth had grown fond of the ponies, giving them apples when she arrived, but had barely noticed the large grey container thing in the yard. Apparently it was a Rollalong. This,

Ted explained, 'as though to a learner of English', was a mobile site cabin: a place for workmen to take their rest on big projects, with – he put up a small step ladder and took her inside – a window, sink and stove, fitted table and bench, a wall-mounted gas fire and two gas lights. There was also a chemical toilet, or could be. 'You'd have to put one in.'

'To say that the Rollalong was heaven would be to exaggerate. It was dingy and smelt of damp, but for my purposes it looked perfect.' Furthermore, it was on wheels, something which would please Planning, and thus could be moved up onto a suitable place in the wood. A short while later, it was hers, for £600.

Ruth's account of how this new home was hauled up into a clearing, of her cleaning and furnishing, painting and settling into it is one of the highlights of the book. It also shows her courage. Not many of us would be up to spending nights alone in such a thing, out in the middle of winter, out in a dark, dark wood (shades of *Wind in the Willows*) with no one around for miles. Her elder brother was horrified by the idea, and Ruth herself was fearful on her first February night. As a small child she had been terrified by a thriller she once saw with her brothers in the local cinema. For a long time afterwards she had trembled in bed, awaiting the arrival of murderers, and it was the thought of murderers which troubled her now, enough to get into her sleeping bag on the lilo not just with extra blankets but with a hammer at her side.

> Actually, the only trouble in the night was cold... The old habit of wearing nightcaps began to make sense. I wound a scarf round my head and wondered, however do people manage to sleep rough? There was the sound of deer trumpeting, far off, and rain on the roof. All in all, I loved it.

After some time, having paid off the mortgage on her London house, she was able to take out another on 'a ruin of a cottage' in Langport – another project, and another garden to cultivate, this one leading down to the edge of the moor and visited by badgers. But even so, these days, 'The Rollalong remains the nerve-centre of everything I do in the wood, the place where teas and coffees are made, the wine poured, the books, outdoor chairs and binoculars live, the retreat when it rains.'

In 2007, it was the centre of a tremendous party, given to celebrate many things, not least a birthday. Friends from London and new local friends all climbed the track, past the wheat field golden in the summer sun and Ted's orchard filled with ripening apples. The party lasted from lunchtime – we all took picnics – until well into the evening, and included dancing to a tango trio; a clue-led hunt for the Hermit's Hut (there was a certain amount of male competition between the various Hermits); meringues put together with clotted cream inside the Rollalong and munched amidst the trees by lantern light. It concluded with a lovely thing: a cellist and violinist perched above the pond, playing duets at dusk. Even with lanterns, they could not see the scores, so they had tiny torches strapped to their heads. This was really all we could see: it was like watching large, luminous insects bobbing about in the dark.

Ruth Pavey's last chapter is entitled 'As Things Stand', and here, as in our conversation, she reflects on many things. One is what will become of the wood when she's gone: 'the work that this patch requires to keep it open, sunny and hospitable to its trees and varied wild life...the wish to ensure that the plant and animal life of a particular patch of the earth will continue to flourish, safe from domineering humans.' She has begun to question the whole idea of nature reserves: are they for us, or the creatures within them?

And since she bought the wood the realities of climate change have been borne upon us all, and she has noticed changes there which perhaps reflect this. The fissures in the clay soil have grown larger as the temperature has risen. There are fewer butterflies and fewer insects generally. Although she cannot be sure, it feels as if there are fewer birds, and certainly it's a long time since she heard a thrush. Saddest of all, the rabbits who were everywhere when she arrived have simply vanished.

'About two [three now] years ago, when the book was coming out, I was sounding extremely confident that the wildlife in the wood would just go on without me when I was gone,' she told me. 'But one day soon after that I walked up on a visit and blow me, the rabbits had disappeared. It was really shocking: I couldn't believe it at first.'

They had, she learned later from a radio programme, fallen victim to Rabbit Haemorrhagic disease, something brought into this country through importing domestic rabbits from China. 'I mean, why do we need to import domestic rabbits from China? And it isn't only climate change, it's international trade which is causing such problems – we introduced Ash Die-back disease by importing ash saplings, when we can perfectly well grow our own.'

Overall, she is simply concerned about 'our assault on the natural world'. She is about to publish a new book, *Deeper into the Wood*, which covers a single year in its life and includes research on 'what cause is having what effect'.

The wood, she says, will always be a work in progress, 'and maintenance is never as much fun as doing in the first place.' But her visits there are still uplifting.

'I am not sure why we humans should take comfort from the natural world,' she writes, but though the natural world is 'harsh and implacable' she also finds 'there is something very buoyant about the company of trees, plants, animals, birds, insects, all intent upon their own lives.'

As far as we know, they just get on with it, having offspring, trying not to starve, not to be eaten, without asking *why*. Perhaps some of this buoyancy transmits itself, helps keep us afloat, too. My oldest friend from schooldays touched my heart recently when she exclaimed that she loves being in the wood, how it makes her happy just to be there. That is how I feel, too.

The Writer in Exile

AFRA

Black Stone, Iran

It was pain which made me write – a light inside me which nothing can turn off.

The first time I saw her, she was running from the room in tears. We were in a workshop run by Write to Life, a long-standing group within the charity Freedom from Torture. I was one of the volunteer writing mentors, working with survivors and asylum seekers from all over the world. Afra was from Iran.

'In the evening of an autumn day [she writes] the wind blew me and all my belongings to a land called "home country". It was a forced journey, made to save my life. I passed through mountains and valleys, cities and villages. Finally, I got to the border. The soil was red, and hidden under frosty furrows, witness to a cruel history made by human beings: the military owned the land and were on watch with guns for any passerby. I was surrounded by endless dim desert: nothing could fill up my emptiness.

An inner voice was the only sparkle within me and the endless freezing air became a giant to swallow me and my inner hopes. I thought I would perish, struggling between breathing in and becoming the icy statue of a human being. Then a tiny ray of sunlight gave me some warmth. I opened my eyes and saw verdant fields beyond the river. I gazed at them and their beauty, but I was afraid of dying.

The day passed, and the sun accompanied my journey. When night came, I became the guest of a stranger, a host who spoke in a familiar language. I still had to continue my journey, but who knew where it would take me?'

In his great essay 'Reflections on Exile' (1984) Edward Said writes: 'Exile is strangely compelling to think about but terrible to experience. It is the unbearable rift between a human being and a native place, between the self and its true home: its essential sadness can never be surmounted. And while it is true that literature and history contain heroic, romantic, glorious, even triumphant episodes in an exile's life, these are no more than efforts meant to overcome the crippling sorrow of estrangement. The achievements of exile are permanently undermined by the loss of something left behind forever.'

Afra left everything behind. She is Kurdish, the fourth of five children. They grew up in a city in the west of Iran which once, she says, was called a mini-Paris – cultured, with classical music concerts. She now describes it as 'a mixture of everything: love, happiness, pain, poverty, care, family bonds and a lot of political issues'. Her family was working-class, her father a plumber, her mother a housewife, and she felt her home to be a microcosm of whatever was happening outside: 'I could see the echo inside.'

Outside were the terrible workings of a new regime: the first years of the Iranian Revolution which in 1979 overthrew the Shah, for a decade gave power to Ayatollah Khomeini, and established Sharia law. 'They used execution as a tool to survive and get set up – whoever did anything wrong they were killed, just like turning a light on and off.'

A woman's life had half the value of a man's: in matters of crime and punishment, or of inheritance. *Girl with A Gun: Love, loss and the fight for freedom in Iran,* by Dianna Nammi and Maren Attwood, is a recently published account of those days in a terror state, and of the courageous Kurdish women who joined the resistance.

'I was aware from a very early age that I had to be careful,' Afra tells me, 'because the punishment for a mistake was to get married, and I was determined that that shouldn't happen. We had to wear a scarf in my teenage years, and I wore it so that my face could not be seen, because I didn't want to be told off. I didn't want to be made to marry. I was mindful not to do anything that would spoil my dream – to look after others, to make a change.'

Within the home, 'My family were not religious, but I had to be careful. My father was quite rigid – against any new thing. Sometimes he was so harsh...' None the less, she loved and respected him, and perhaps they had a special bond, 'a kind of sensitivity' to one another. When we talk, in our long interview for this book, she opens her hands, and shows me how his own hands were covered in callouses, from constant manual labour. 'I understood that what money I had came from those hands, and I needed to be sensible about it.'

Although her parents were uneducated, and her mother 'an innocent person, quiet and passive', they believed in education, especially for girls. 'We were all bright, clever children. But it's like a garden: where there is not much water or sunshine, it is quite hard for the seed to grow, and grow up, and for buds to appear. Even now, talking about that period is not easy...'

And in describing her background Afra evokes a home not without love or ambition for the children, but – as in the world outside – full of what could not be done, or said. There was a seven-year gap between her and her sister, the oldest in the family, but even as a little girl she felt as if she were the mother – to her father, and to her siblings. 'From a very young age I felt I needed to hold all their hands and look after them.' She also felt helpless: because she was so young, and because, as they grew up, her brothers took on the strong male roles of a patriarchal society. 'The situation was really difficult, and I stepped back.' And she adds: 'I didn't want to go through what my sister went through.'

This older sister, whose name I still do not know, became what Afra describes as the pioneer of the family. 'She was a radical, completely against the family system, the religious system, the whole society-system. She was at so much risk, and nobody could help her. There was always a regret that I couldn't do enough, but the age gap was so big – it wasn't easy for me to do anything.'

It was writing which became a release for her feelings of sadness and frustration. 'I can remember the first time I started to write: I was maybe ten or eleven or twelve, and it was the first time I couldn't talk to anyone. I wrote, and then I crossed out; I wrote, and crossed out, because I was so scared that someone might read it.'

As Afra grew older, she began to overcome this self-censorship.

'I became a bit braver and I had diaries – when I was in secondary school, and when I was a student, and a teacher. I allowed myself to leave it, not to cross out, and I was writing more and more about the pain: how I felt sad, unheard, unseen, and also much more about what was happening outside – in the school, in the street, with families, my family, my father.

'It was like he was a small window for me to see the reality of what was happening outside. He was being exploited, working for people who didn't pay him well...I was so angry. And this is what I mainly wrote about in my diaries, as well as my own feelings. And all I was writing had a sense of pain and sadness and objection: I don't want this.'

By the time she fled from Iran, she had accumulated about ten small diaries, recording everything that had happened in her world as she grew up. 'They are the only things I left back home, and I felt so bad: I asked my mum to destroy them, no matter what happened. And this is a treasure I have lost in my life.'

Ever since she was at primary school, Afra had wanted to be a teacher. She would come home with a piece of chalk, put on her mother's low heels, like the ones her teacher wore, and act out giving lessons in front of a mirror. She laughs as she describes this, but she adds, 'Sometimes I talked [to myself] and cried. Since a very young age I was so familiar with pain. I was old for my age, not just because I was clever, but because I had experienced pain. Reality.'

The system allowed students to begin teacher-training as soon as they started secondary school: a kind of apprenticeship, perhaps, but with specific requirements. In her application interview, she was asked if she prayed. This would mean leaning forward for a long time. 'I said no, because it made me feel faint and dizzy, and they knew I was lying, and they refused me.' But she applied again, after taking final school exams – the equivalent of A-levels – and this time was accepted.

Conditions were arduous, even dangerous: students were sent out of the city, travelling to distant mountain villages, impoverished places where to be an unaccompanied young woman risked bullying, sexual assault, even rape.

'My father wanted my brother to accompany me, but I wanted to be independent.'

And in the bitter cold of winter she would get up in the small hours, and with fellow students take a bus, and then walk a long way up the mountain in the dark, to the village where they were to teach. 'We were just young girls, and anything could happen to us. It was really scary. Sometimes we had to wait in the cold for hours for the bus.' Once or twice they asked a passing motorist for a lift, something she found terrifying. But although Afra knew of young women who were indeed attacked, she survived three years of this, returning to visit her family once a week. 'It was a really difficult time, not just because I missed them, but because I was worried about them.'

At the end of these three years she began a two-year teacher training course, studying to teach literature at a college in another city, a few hours journey away. In that three-year period she shared a rented house with four other young women, all of whom, like her, were beginning to get involved with what were essentially the politics of resistance.

'Everything started from there, informally, and when we had finished our training, we started an NGO.' To organise in this way was both courageous and dangerous. 'I had difficulties with my father, but I thought, I have done what he wanted all these years, I have considered him, and okay, I love him, but he is not going to stop me from being what I want to be.'

Nothing had stopped her radical sister. The exact circumstances of her activity and of that time are still too painful for Afra to talk to me about, but in the summer of 1991, at the end of her own first year at college, this young woman was arrested and taken for execution. Though Khomeini had long been gone, the regime, now under Ayatollah Khamenei, was still in power, and if anything more brutal. 'We lost her,' Afra says simply.

It took her ten years to recover from this terrible event. In the second year of her training, 'I was truly grieving. But meanwhile I was doing what I was doing – I was like a machine. I worked, I came home, I cooked, I taught two students, I looked after my family and mainly my nephew.' And where in the past she had written in secret, kept quiet, felt helpless; where now she might have been terrified into submitting to an ordinary, safer life, instead, in her grief and mourning, she became radicalised.

'Being involved with politics gradually allowed me to come out from that darkness. It was a route for me to bloom, to begin my dream, to make a change for a better world, and also to heal the pain I had for the loss of my sister. I think I learned a lot from her life. She was very innocent, very young in a way. I am sure she would be alive now, if I had been the first child. But getting involved with politics gave me my identity: This is how I want to be.

'It was like challenging everything that said: Be a good girl, clean the house...I still did this, but I cared less for what my parents wanted me to be. And I was angry: I had a very hard-working brain and I wanted to study, to go to the gym, and I wasn't allowed to. But when I opened that door to step out – it was the time when I started everything.'

She got a driving licence. She started to go to the gym. She began to learn English.

'It was like seven days a week wasn't enough, and twenty-four hours wasn't enough at all. And I faced a lot of challenges, blame from my father especially: "What are you doing? You are a girl. People are saying bad things about us." To me, being bad was to get engaged to a man. I never did that. I suppressed all that – I had no time for my personal interests – it wasn't the right time. I started to let my mind lead my emotions, and I didn't want to waste the opportunity to live fully.'

And at a very dangerous time, she and few other teachers who were now her political colleagues established a teachers' union, and went on a national strike. 'I was one of the first few members. I was the only woman among three hundred men from different provinces attending the national strike in front of the Parliament.' Although it had been women who founded the new union, most were too afraid to attend the strike: making yourself a target could mean losing your job, with many consequences. 'I was just wearing a scarf,' Afra says, 'not fully covered, and I was so scared: it was the risk of everything and we could not predict what was going to happen. I gave my other sister my money and my bank card, in case I couldn't go back.'

But she survived this first real encounter with the authorities, and began to develop the NGO she had founded with her friends. As I understand it, such non-governmental organisations had been accepted in Iran for some time, and are tolerated to this day. However, when Afra's group began to get going, a women's NGO would usually be operating within the domestic arena: sewing groups, cookery classes. Afra's had a radical women's rights agenda.

'We women were second-class, worth half a human being. An NGO was the only option for us to start from somewhere. We ran workshops where lawyers came to talk about rights, divorce, custody of children. In 2003 we celebrated 8th March, International Women's Day for the first time for more than eighteen years [since] the regime came to power. After that, every year we celebrated 25th November: International Day for the Elimination of Violence Against Women, and May Day also. And all those things were crossing a red line: we should not be doing any of it."

Many years later, living in London and attending the Write to Life group, Afra wrote dramatically about the fear and exhilaration involved in crossing that red line, and the courage these women needed.

THE VOICE THAT CHANGED MY WORLD

There is a sports stadium full of people. There must be about four thousand: young boys and girls, men, women, parents, teachers, workers...

All are paying full attention, waiting, curious to hear more. On all sides are red banners and placards, with 8TH MARCH 2003: INTERNATIONAL WOMEN'S DAY in large letters.

It's my turn. The programme presenter calls me by name on the microphone. I am in black, my head covered with the horrible black shawl that I am forced to wear. I feel its heaviness on my head, but you can be sure I will just use it as a weapon against them. However much they want us to be invisible by it, they can never stop me from voicing my beliefs. I step towards the stage: light, heavy, anxious, proud, tall, straight and firm. For a second I glance around, scanning all the eyes and ears waiting to hear from me. Wow, this is amazing, and exactly what we wanted. I know I need to speak with my biggest voice to be heard by the world. I start loudly, saying, 'Happy 8th of March, the symbol of freedom and equality, to you, all great comrades, and to the world.'

I really want the world to hear me. I am sure it is my loudest voice – but not sure if it is loud enough. But I am certain that it will be heard again, on five continents through satellite and social media networks, by tonight at the latest.

I am quite anxious to let people hear all I want them to hear before I'm forced to stop. I carry on, loudly announcing that the execution of prisoners by the Islamic regime is systematic murder, enforced by a system that is supposed to be in power to protect citizens' lives. It's against human rights law, which condemns execution.

I feel, and hear, such strong power in me and my voice. I feel strong as a mountain and loud as a waterfall. Such an amazing moment.

That day passed, and we said what the public needed to know, before the darkness returned to overpower the daylight. My comrades and I wanted our voices and strength to stir up a storm that would disturb the oppressors' sweet dreams. And before we were crushed back into silence, at least we had broken the icy wall of fear that had locked the voices in our chests over more than twenty years of the regime's power.

We still have a hard battle.

But WE ARE STILL ALIVE...

Afra and her group were called up by the city authorities and interrogated. Who were they? Why were they doing these things? What was their background?

'I just kept quiet about my sister when they asked me – I was so scared. They started to swear at me, using bad words and intimidating me: If I carried on, they would tell people, and my family, that they had seen me with a man... They tried to scare us, and I was scared. For a while we had to keep quiet.

'But in the end we would not be silenced. For about eight to twelve years we attacked and retreated, attacked and retreated: teachers, women and workers, we all came together. At one point they said we were spying for Israel, which was funny, because we were against them. They did everything to try to keep us quiet.'

After five years of this, Afra began to feel in real danger, and moved to Tehran. There, she managed to complete an MA in Sociology, a few years after completing a degree in Farsi literature.

'It was a bit safer, a big city, I could disappear, but I had to go back to my home city sometimes. In the end, even Tehran wasn't safe. I lost my job, and then it was more difficult to manage. I was well known to the authorities, and it was a very risky situation, risking arrest, imprisonment, detention, execution. And I couldn't trust anyone. Even my family couldn't accommodate me – they were so panicky, they felt so unsafe. I decided it was better not to put myself or anyone else in danger.'

Finally, she made contact with an undercover agency. They would get her out of the country to safety.

'The journey was awful. Every moment of it was full of uncertainty and unknowing. We were a group of people, we didn't know each other. We didn't know if we were going to be alive in the next minutes, the next hour, the next day. It was winter, it was very cold.'

Afra doesn't specify the details of this journey, the starting point, or the river they crossed, but they were packed into a small inflatable boat. Its capacity was five; there were twelve of them. She and another young woman had to crouch on the floor, awash with oil and water. Her jeans were soaked through; she was shivering.

'I didn't open my eyes. I didn't know where the tears were coming from, I just kept crying and wiping my eyes and the other girl and I just hugged each other, and I was begging nature, the universe, "Please help us – the trees, the sky, the ocean, the rocks – please help us, just for the hearts of our parents. I cried and cried."

'And then I opened my eyes and it was just wonderful – beautiful blue sky, very green fields, trees and bushes on the other side. And I told my friend, Open your eyes. Even if we die it is worth it, just to see this. The river was blue with the reflection of the sky. I had never seen a green like that, that blue river.'

They were out of Iran, over the Greek/Turkish border. Cold

and very hungry – they hadn't eaten for twenty-four hours – they were given olives and cheese when they got out on the opposite bank. ''It felt so good: we had survived, we were alive. Every blink I had felt under the arm of death – I had never experienced anything like that, not then, not since. But when we got to the other side we were happy.'

But their escape had only just begun. They had to wade through wet mud, pushed and shoved by minders who were as afraid as they were of getting caught. Then came a ten-hour car journey: they had to crouch down in hiding, in such discomfort that even a later operation has not fully relieved the pain in Afra's feet and lower back. Eventually, after a flight, she arrived in London. She was wearing trainers too small for her, which hurt. She had just £1.

HEY, PASSENGER!

Hey, passenger!
Show me your hands!
Where have you come from?
You smell dirty.
You look guilty.
Show me your hands.
Give me your ID.
Not back, not further, just stop here.

Let me draw breath.
Don't shout at me.
I am just a passenger.
No departure, no destination,
Not even gloves to cover my hands.
I have left my hands somewhere, I don't know the name.
They are in a land with a strange language, but familiar
people.

They should sow my hands in the field there,
To harvest freedom.

I am from homelessness,
from terror, from chains,
from a life sentence for demanding a life.
I am guilty
of rising up
and breathing freely.
I am guilty
I am exiled from a piece of the world where you are not
allowed to sing
even with the music of the wind.
I am the gagged voice of freedom.

I know you, I know you, I know your type.
You will be a nuisance,
so better to detain...

There is nowhere for me to rest.
It doesn't matter where I am:
I need to fight again.

It was in London that Afra began to write once more. Her first months in this country, as for many asylum seekers, were very difficult: she felt lost and afraid, struggling with interpreters and minimal English to account for herself. 'Hey, Passenger!' is one response to her reception here. She made it to Lunar House, the headquarters of UK Visas and Immigration in Croydon, where she underwent the preliminaries of body search, basic screen interview and fingerprinting. From there she was sent first to temporary accommodation in a hostel in Wakefield, and then, for three months, to a longer-term hostel in Stockton-on-Tees.

'The only thing that was important was that I was alive. I didn't have any hope, couldn't imagine anything. The only thing I felt was I was healthy because I had survived. Gradually all the pain came back into my body. Life was completely complex and difficult. Everything was hard – the weather, the language, my feelings of pain, regret, sadness, guilt – all were difficulties I had to go through.'

Being granted asylum here can take years, the long, lonely waiting for a decision only adding to the trauma of the past. 'Exiles are cut off from their roots, their land, their past,' writes Said, but that is to assume that the past is something to be cherished. Many of those seeking asylum here and in other European countries are caught between a place to which they dare not return and a place which, whether welcoming or hostile, is, as Afra says, hard, strange and full of barriers.

But her case was strong: within a few months she was granted leave to remain. The decision shows this country at its best. She was safe, housed in a bare little flat in north London; she had survived. But, as she says, she was flooded – often overcome – with pain and grief. Her anguish expressed itself in her body: headaches, sleeplessness and anxiety began to torment her. It was her GP who in 2011 encouraged her to refer herself to Freedom from Torture.

This British-registered charity, founded by Helen Bamber in 1985 and based in north London, offers medical, legal and psychotherapeutic support to survivors, and campaigns for an end to torture world-wide. Those who arrive here are by definition suffering from post-traumatic stress disorder, and their needs are great. They are helped not only by doctors, lawyers and psychotherapists, but by supportive groups and activities. The purpose-built building itself is large, light and airy, with a spacious garden; there is a studio for painting and pottery; there is a choir; there are gardening and baking groups. A long-established writing group is run by the writer and journalist Sheila Hayman.

Members of Write to Life are generally referred by their therapists. Some have a writing background, as journalists or teachers; all have expressed a desire to write, both about their past experiences and the demands of a new life in a new country. Meeting once a fortnight, the group offers a safe, creative space in which to do so, working with mentors – all of whom have writing and/or teaching backgrounds – in one-to-one sessions and within workshops. It was in one of these workshops – I cannot remember the theme – that at the end of 2012 I first took notice of Afra, running from the room in tears, not so very long after her arrival. A few weeks later, we began to work together. We continued to do so for seven years.

When we met for our afternoon appointments I always noticed her impeccable politeness. Afra is tall, and I had to reach up a little for the three kisses on the cheeks with which she greeted me. She was smiling, charming, apologetic if even a couple of minutes late; she stepped aside for me to go through a door first, as we made our way down a corridor to our meeting room. Once inside, in those early days, she allowed her exhaustion and distress to show. She was on medication for headaches, for unidentified pains, for insomnia, depression and anxiety. Sometimes she wept. Though her spoken English was getting better all the time, she was still struggling with it on the page. Despite all this, she was writing, both poetry and prose, and we worked together to try to find the right English words for the events of the past, and the powerful feelings she wanted to express.

Quite early on, she wrote about a dream. She was walking in a forest, which at first she found beautiful, but where, as it grew dark, she began to be afraid. An owl hooted, it began to rain; she was very cold.

> A flicker of moonlight helped me to see a high building. I went closer. The building had a big green half-open door. I peered round it. Then I stepped in, and saw a huge, beautiful hall, illuminated by a little candle. A big ancient mirror reflected the little light... I started to move towards the stairs: first, second, third...all was calm and quiet. I was stuck, wishing to find the energy to go on... I took a deep breath when I reached the top.

An orange door, carved in relief, took my attention. I pressed my ear to the door. At last I could hear sounds from inside. It seemed as if [people] were dancing, and a soft voice like the voice of a tiny girl talking to her mummy to make her laughing and happy. I could smell roses. Was it Spanish music? Intrigued, I knocked on the door and went in.

Wow. Everywhere was full of flowers and great big lights, and everybody was happy and waiting for someone to come through. As I stepped in, I was surrounded by cheers and laughing and smiling faces and open arms. I was thirsting to hug them – I didn't know who to hug first, my mum, my sisters...

And here it all ended, and she woke in tears. This dream, with its longing for her family, its imagery of light amidst darkness, a long and difficult stairway, a little girl making her mother laugh, everyone greeting her return, could not have been more poignant. For much of the time, living alone in a cold, barely-furnished flat, attending English classes but with little else to occupy her, Afra's life at this time was very hard. But she had a therapist at Freedom from Torture, and she had the writing group.

Gradually she began to open up within the workshops; she became an important voice there. And in our one-to-one sessions her work was developing into something very powerful. We spent a long time on a bleak, bitter poem which I still admire greatly. It describes a visit to a cemetery in Tehran full of the graves of those who, like her beloved elder sister, had been executed by the regime.

CITY OF THE DEAD

Friday morning. A rest day.
I am full of anxiety and persecution from the past week.
Full of a heavy silence,
A lost calm.
Looking for someone to open up with.

I want to go somewhere not too far away,

I want to go to the city of the dead.

I am full of questions.
Why? Why?
My heavy hands
are full of the effort of everything.
My eyes are full of the dust of cruelty,
of watching someone forced to die.
But in this concrete field everyone is free...

No need for a passport or full bank account here.
There is nothing to worry about
In this grey ground.
The residents have already paid lots for nothing.
There was a high price of brutality: blows, bullets.

And now they are free not to breathe.
Free to be speechless,
free to keep quiet,
free to witness nothing...

Here is where they are free to say nothing about their
                                            rights to life
– love, freedom, happiness –
And not a single child is homeless.
Not a mother is screaming
for the pain of losing her young children.
How good to have somewhere to experience all nothings.
Here is a symbol of forbidden love and forced death.

Here is the graveyard of my comrades.

Carrying all the trauma of the past within her, Afra was also alert to what was going on in the world. In 2013 came the first of the drownings in the Mediterranean as desperate refugees from North Africa attempted the perilous crossing to Italy. They were crammed into a small ship whose engine all at once caught fire. It went down off the coast of a Sicilian island, with the loss of hundreds; with this tragedy, Lampedusa was suddenly headline news. Afra responded with this poem.

LAMPEDUSA

To the Africans shipwrecked off the coast of Lampedusa, October 2013

For you, stranger, passenger
who trusted the sea
and lent your breath to the sea:*
when you gasp for air
our own breath begins to die.

Your eyes were full of the endless sea
the sky turned so grey
and the water turned black
when it became a grave for your dreams.

I touch your pain
I wish you had not trusted the sea
Even though I did trust it myself.

Shame on the world!

Do not imagine I don't understand your language
without any word or syllable.
Your language is every single syllable
of hidden voices: from me, and all the women of my
motherland,

Even though now, today,
I have chosen exile.

Your groans become screams
Your cries are the screams of our daughters being raped,
buried alive, stifled, murdered.

I am so sick of these bleeding wounds.
Why does the sky not weep to quench the pain?
Why does the sky not weep to quench the pain?

★ 'lent your breath' is a colloquial Iranian phrase
meaning deeply trusting, risk-taking.

The poem was published both on the Freedom from Torture website and in the *Guardian* Online. It was read at the Edinburgh Festival. I think all this pleased Afra, but she had not written for publication, and although by now she was beginning to think about work, and qualifications, it was not as a writer.

'I used to use my writing to make a change when I was back home,' she told me recently. 'But here – I find life is full of challenges, difficulties, so I'm saving energy for all these things.' Working with Write to Life was a powerful means of expression and release, but still very much for herself, even if her subjects were sometimes taken from world events.

Although she had taught literature for so many years in Iran, to teach here was something she knew she was not strong enough to do. For a while she considered retraining as a librarian, but eventually she settled on a degree in Counselling and Psychotherapy: by now a British citizen, she was able to take out a student loan. Academically and personally the course was very demanding, but she continued to attend our one-to-one sessions and the group. Individual lines in her poems shone out memorably.

'Bus Poem' describes a long journey through London: 'The 43 bus from Archway to my destroyed youth.' From an untitled poem: 'The pavement has recorded all the footprints of unwanted travellers as asylum seekers, no matter where their journey started from.'

'The cost of being a woman', written in 2013, could speak for the whole #Me Too generation.

I am not a doll to be played with by everyone.
That's how it used to be.
I have risen to my feet.
Look at my eyes. They have something to say to you.

The strength and determination in these four lines gives an insight into the kind of person Afra was in Iran at the height of her political activism there. It is who she has continued to be.

'The voice that changed my world' (2018) came out of a workshop run not by a regular mentor but by a guest, a therapist who ran a session in which members of the group were encouraged to exercise their voices – to whisper, to shout, to sing, to let themselves go.

'To me the workshop was as delicate as sowing a seed in the soil,' Afra wrote afterwards. 'In the beginning I thought I never had a voice in my life... It was the right time to go through finding something precious that I had lost in the journey of moving country, and also in exile.'

The following week Sheila Hayman asked the group to write about a voice that changed their lives.

'Amazingly,' Afra wrote, 'what I found was that my own voice was the voice that changed my world.' She has described that speaking out in Iran in 2003 as a real breakthrough: personal, social and political. It was vitally important then, and in describing it years later, safe in London, she writes, 'I am more able to own the voice I had lost. A voice that also was a big part of my identity. I am more able now to recognise that I do want to own it again.'

On International Women's Day 2015, twelve years after she took that stadium microphone, Afra took another, reading an account of her journey and new life here to a group of Freedom from Torture supporters, meeting at Ruskin College, Oxford.

'In the evening of an autumn day the wind blew me and all my belongings to a land called "home country"...'

It is a measure of how far she had travelled on this journey towards recovery that she was able to do this: writing and speaking in English; addressing a large public meeting in this country; showing how she had regained much of her strength; laughing and talking with people afterwards, enjoying being shown round Oxford, having tea. She had been a women's rights activist in a dangerous, deeply patriarchal society; she had been interrogated, tortured, threatened. Here, she was continuing to speak out.

'It was a forced journey, made to save my life...'

She called this piece of memoir, which I quote at the start of this essay, 'Journey from my past self to my current self', speaking of her flight, her arrival and her early days in this country. And at Ruskin she concluded:

'The main character in this story is a fighter against discrimination and for equality. She is a lover of freedom. She is here with you now.' She looked out over the audience. 'We might know each other, as people who have chosen to gather here are reminded of those who have crossed borders and risked their lives for freedom. Their stories are paralleled by the length of human history. Happy International Women's Day.'

So much better and stronger, Afra was still having dreams which made her weep. In 'I do have a home', written in this same year, she wrote about her dream of having her mother to stay in her little flat, by now furnished with a bed, a wardrobe, sofa, bookshelves and television, a rug.

> Every afternoon when my mum lies on the armchair I put the footstool under her legs, to help her rest. I go to the kitchen every night, wondering what I can cook, when I am waiting for my nephew to come back home and show his joy at the nice smell of food... My sister is back home around this time... At the weekend we're getting together for a walk to Highgate Woods. To enjoy my mum's

company, we make it short and slow. She is still recovering from the hard operation on her knees. It takes time, but we are here to look after her...

And with that poignant dream of reunion, she wakes. 'It's raining, and I am sunk in tears.'

By this time she had begun to teach again a little: in a traditional Iranian Sunday school run for young children and teenagers from other countries who wanted to learn Farsi. The unfinished poem she wrote about her time there expresses some of the tension and conflict between modernity and old Islam.

'I am against Islam whether old or modern,' she tells me. 'Both are anti-human rights.' She goes on to say that she is indeed against all religions. But both teacher and students have to attend this school, and in her poem the teacher conceals both her own frustration at giving up her time and her relief at being with her own people in a shared, but changing culture.

SUNDAY SCHOOL

In midday of an autumn day,
The sky is blue,
The city is bright and breezy.
One step forward and one back, I carry on going.
I really want to feed my eyes with this nice view of life.
No, I cannot.
My students are waiting.
They are forced to be there,
So am I, deep inside. It helps to heal me.
We get along well...
These young women are able to dress as they choose; the
teacher herself does not have to wear the veil.

They know what a cinema looks like.
They can find their way on the global map.
They can enjoy their own beauty and possessions...
They are not scared of opposite-sex classmates.

Their talk and laughter and joyfulness is not suppressed.
Everything is different from the other side of the world –
Apart from enslaving minds...

A pleasurable freedom in choosing words is wonderful.
The first discussion is about what they did in the past
                                                                    week.
The writing time is very calming: it slows down my own
                                                               pace, too.

But the difficulty in this place lies in the conversations she has
with her colleagues, still caught up in the old beliefs: 'Complex
collections of religion, dogmatism, the politics of oppression.'

There is a flashback to remind me
Of the left-behind country called home.

A homeless mind is arisen here...

Such a long way we have to go, even now, and here.

By 2019, a great deal had changed in Afra's life. She had a
degree, and a British passport; she had been able to meet her
mother for a reunion in Turkey. Her sister and nephew had made
it to London, and were living nearby. She was working in two
women's rights centres. For a time, until the project ended, she
was working with Grenfell survivors.

She looks, now, like a chic Londoner, in black leather jacket
and heels. She has, unquestionably, survived to make a place
here. But it is towards activism, more than writing, that her
energies are directed at present.

'I do write about politics and human rights issues, but I don't
actually publish anything. I am talking more than writing. But
I hope very much to go back to writing. The last time I
published was in 2014, on the Iranian Opposition website. I
attend meetings and protests and strikes. I take part in the May

Day strike every year, and I go on many more marches and strikes.'

In all these demonstrations she has been photographed many times. 'I have lots to say, and lots of photographers show how actively I attend strikes.'

But these images are unidentified: she is an eloquent but anonymous speaker; she is a face in the crowd. And although she has a British passport, and all the accoutrements of a legally settled life here, she does not want her photograph to appear in this book, and Afra is not her real name.

Why has she chosen it, the Persian name for Maple? 'I love this tree because its branches and leaves spread widely. It makes me think of freedom of choice, and space to protest against the overwhelming and brutal religious and patriarchal principles which have been an unbearable pressure on my whole existence.'

As for the photograph, this piece of Iranian landscape shows the Black Stone, symbol of the fight against the government, the oppressor. ''In folklore and songs the Black Stone is one of the beauties of the city. To me it is another symbol of resistance for the people who have been fighting against injustice and discrimination. And it is the name of one of the mountains overlooking my home city.'

The past and its terrors still lie within her; they still play out in sleeplessness and exhaustion.

And her writing? She has to do a great deal of report writing in her counselling work; it takes time and energy.

'It is not surprising,' writes Said, 'that so many exiles seem to be novelists, chess players, political activists, and intellectuals. Each of these occupations requires a minimal investment in objects and places a great premium on mobility and skill.' And towards the end of his essay he cites the German-Jewish philosopher Theodor Adorno, who believed that for an exile 'the only home truly available now, though fragile and vulnerable, is in writing.'

When is a writer not a writer? Afra's creative writing, expressed in the powerful poetry and memoir of the last few years, is now on hold. But is it still within her, if not on the page?

'In a way, yes.' She pauses, then is suddenly eloquent, 'It is inside me as a voice, all the time. It's flowing: I have that voice with me always, narrating things, describing everything I see. My mind is like a camera, the lens opening and closing all the time. It was pain which made me write – a light inside me which nothing can turn off.'

The Environmental Journalist

MAREK MAYER

Sue Gee

Marek Mayer in the Yorkshire Dales, 1982

'What would you say you stood for?'
Silence.
'Honesty and accountability?'
'Yes.'

Warsaw, October 1944

A long, long line of people is moving slowly through the ruins. Carrying their last possessions, they walk past sandbags, makeshift barricades, roofless buildings with gaping, blown-out windows. They walk past corpses. After two bitter months of street fighting; of crawling through the sewers; after weeks of hunger, exhaustion, field hospitals, relentless bombing, the uprising against the German occupation is over. Here and there, made from a torn sheet, a ripped-off cushion cover, a red and white flag hangs limply.

Warsaw has fallen.

On 2nd October, after five years of occupation, after fierce resistance in this desperate uprising, Poland has surrendered. Now these people, young and old, many of them resistance fighters, are making their way towards guarded exits from the city. From there, they will be taken to German camps, as prisoners of war.

Among them is Hanna Szamota, not quite eighteen, and without a family. She has served as a courier in the Home Army during the Uprising: I picture her keeping watch from observation posts, racing through the streets, running for cover, ducking down behind barricades made of sandbags, dustbins, furniture, sewing machines and saucepans – anything, anything. I see her in the family apartment, in a frantic search, gathering up every photograph she could find, cramming them into a suitcase with her clothes.

There is the lovely sepia portrait of her mother, who died when she was three. There is the sunlit picture of her father, his arms around her and her brother Marek, standing beneath a tree in a distant summer, long before the war. Dr Szamota had joined the army in the war's first months, was sent to the eastern front, the border with Russia. He had never returned. A few weeks ago, Marek, a combatant in the Uprising, had been shot and killed at a barricade by a German soldier. There are dozens of other photographs in that suitcase: the two of them as babies, as children, with cousins, aunts and uncles, grandparents. There are letters and documents, there is a scrap of paper with her father's signature, there is everything she could find.

They have reached an exit: orders are shouted out, the people are divided. Hanna will be sent to a camp near Sandbostel, in north-west Germany. Here, every one of those precious photographs will be stamped on the back: Stalag X-B.

Hanna Szamota was to belong to and create another family. In England, reached via Italy after the war, she married a young combatant in the Uprising, Jerzy Stanisław Mayer. From the age of sixteen he had killed many German soldiers in close combat. The vicious injury he sustained to his jaw, and other bullet wounds, would trouble him for the rest of his life. In London, the Polish Government in Exile was to award him the Virtuti Militari, the Polish equivalent of the Victoria Cross.

Like Hanna, Jerzy had been in a German POW camp. So had his parents: Brigadier General Stanisław Mayer, his father, had served with distinction in the First World War. At the beginning of World War Two he had been seriously wounded, captured and imprisoned, almost for the duration. Jerzy's mother, Irena, who had studied law, had taken part in the Warsaw Uprising and been arrested herself. In the chaotic movement of refugees, ex-combatants and displaced people to and fro across post-war

Europe, there was much searching, in Italy and Poland, until the three of them were reunited.

Finally, they arrived in England, where they were given political asylum. It was not until the Stalinist 1950s that Irena's mother, who had been living on the family estate in eastern Poland when the Russians swept in, managed to escape and join them all. Where Hanna and Jerzy met, we do not know. He trained as an electronics engineer; she, after time spent in a camp in Herefordshire, had begun training in Scotland as a nurse.

Finally, in the early 1950s, everyone was settled in a long street of mansion flats in Clapham, south London, which ran past a railway line. Jerzy's parents and grandmother had one flat; he, Hanna and their first three children, had another. The flats were owned by a private landlord who neglected to maintain them: rain dripped through the ceiling into saucepans; there was no hot water, and Hanna had to heat water for baths in a huge metal tub on the cooker. It wasn't until much later that the flats were taken over by a housing association. They were just about affordable for people beginning to make new lives, with new occupations. Another child was born here.

Hanna, who had lost everyone, now had a husband, a grandmother-in-law, parents-in-law. She had four children: Krystyna; then Marek, named after her brother; then Barbara and Danuta. Born within seven years of one another, growing up with Polish as their first language, enclosed within an uprooted family, they would all experience Poland and the war as being almost in the room. Through those cherished photographs; through endless stories, their early lives in England were lived almost entirely alongside, even within, the past.

They grew up in poverty; they grew up to cherish their childhood memories intensely. Each of them achieved distinction: Krystyna as a managing editor, Barbara as a photographer, Danuta as an artist. And Marek, with whom I lived for almost thirty years, and married six months before he died, became one of this country's most distinguished environmental journalists. If you haven't heard of him, that is because he wrote for and edited a specialist journal. It is also because he hid his light under a very large Polish bushel.

But those who read him, those who knew and worked with him in the rapidly developing green movement of the seventies and beyond, admired and respected him, almost held him in awe. The lines at the head of this essay come from a late conversation between us: they say it all.

And someone whom photographs show a two-year-old so frail that he looks almost boneless, grew into a tall, athletic, witty and irresistibly attractive man. Someone who took until his early forties to feel at home in English society had, by the end of his life, close friends everywhere. By those friends, and by his family, he was deeply loved.

Marek and his sisters started primary school knowing barely a word of the language spoken. Although they learned English quickly, at the end of the day they returned, effectively, to Poland. This was reinforced on Saturdays, when they attended Polish School, where maps of Poland, the Polish flag and the crowned Polish eagle, national symbol of Poland, hung on the wall. The school wasn't far away, and their military grandfather, now a divisional commandant in the Army in Exile, taught there. The children advanced their Polish grammar, learned history, and read poetry and stories, many of which their parents had read themselves, as children before the war.

On Sundays, they attended Mass, again with their grandfather; their grandmother came too, elegantly dressed as always. These two were very important, offering stability and affection, help with homework, a quiet place in the flat below where they could, as Danuta recalls, 'just sit and be'. Their mother was very busy running a household in difficult circumstances, but she loved drawing pictures for the children and with their grand-mother made theatre and ballet costumes: she was, they recall, 'incredibly creative' in that crowded flat. Marek had a room at the front, overlooking the street; the three girls shared a room in the middle. At the kitchen window, or on the balcony at the back, they all stood watching the trains which ran excitingly behind the mansion blocks; it was Marek who became a train-spotter.

Home was noisy. In good weather their mother took them out to Clapham Common, where they could run about. A photo-graph shows the three little girls sitting in a laughing row on the grass, Marek kneeling up behind them in the middle. They all look happy and secure, and they were, with two or three very happy holidays at the seaside.

But there was always anxiety about money. Their father worked long hours; their mother took on a job making jewellery at home, working late into the night. She was good at this, and also a fine needlewoman, who knitted jumpers, scarves and hats and toys for the children. A school photograph of Marek, aged about seven, shows a little boy in hand-knitted jumper and tie, looking gravely at the camera, hands clasped over the book on his desk.

By this time, his passion for trains, Dinky cars and Airfix models had begun: presents for birthdays and Christmas, which began with the first evening star, just visible in the sodium-lit London sky. Then Grandfather rang a little bell to say that Święty Mikołaj, Father Christmas, had arrived on his sleigh and the children were allowed into the living room to see the tree, with its pile of presents at the foot. This was on Wigilia, Christmas Eve.

In winter the flat was very cold. Marek and Krystyna took an oil can down to the paraffin seller, an elderly man who sat, day in, day out, in a cold and muddy alleyway off a nearby street. The children fell asleep to the warmth from the stoves in their bedrooms, gazing at the pattern of flowers on the ceiling made by the light shining through the stencilled metal top. I did the same, on a farm in Devon.

The girls went on to attend convent schools. Marek went to the Salesian College in Battersea, a Roman Catholic boys' school. The students were taught mainly by priests: overall, the teaching was of a high standard, and Marek was top of the class for a long time.

He joined the Polish Scouts, and went on trips; as he grew older, he went train-spotting alone. This was formative: travelling through the English countryside from station to rural station in pre-Beeching days, walking and observing fields, hills, rock formations, growing to understand and love the landscape. He began to get interested in geology, collected rocks and stones. He was working hard, and at home was helpful and affectionate. He made his sisters laugh a lot; they adored him.

In mid-adolescence, all this began to change. The gulf between his background and his English school friends began to yawn: he took a boy home once, was mocked for its peeling wallpaper, and never did so again. He retreated into himself, and his schoolwork suffered. A visit or two to a psychiatrist perplexed, even infuriated his mother. He retreated further, and the seeds were sown for a lifelong on-off relationship with depression, kept at bay by football, cricket, ferocious work and his own caustic wit.

But he did well at A-level, if not as well as had once been expected. In 1970 he was accepted at Wye College, a college of the University of London in Kent, to read for a BSc in Rural Environmental Studies. It was the first time he had been away from home for more than a few nights on a Polish Scout trip. When he left, his height was about five-foot ten. By the time he came home a year later, he was over six-foot one.

★

Wye College was set in the pretty village of Wye, close to the North Downs; hop fields and oast houses lay all around. It stood on a large estate, which included a farm, woodland, ancient grassland. A study and research centre in rural business and management, biological sciences, environment and agriculture, the college had glasshouses, specialist laboratories, climate-controlled rooms for growing plants and nurturing insects.

It was, in short, an excellent, highly regarded institution, attracting students from all over the world and offering MSc and PhD programmes, as well as first degrees. Students lived in halls and houses dotted around the village: it was in sharing such a house that Marek made his first lifelong friends. In those early-seventies summer holidays they gave him an entry into English family life – mostly, as it happened, in the countryside of Suffolk, where he helped with the harvest on a family farm and played cricket with the local team.

One of these Wye friends was Robert Paulley, who remembers him in the early days as 'a lugubrious Polish student who never said much, watched cricket all day and was clearly much cleverer than any of us'. Gradually he came out of his shell; there was a lot of larking about, including an occasion when he was handcuffed to the railings outside the refectory with a placard above his head: Support Gay Liberation.

'He forgave us after a few weeks... It was not all silly pranks. There were long periods when Marek stayed in his room with his head under a pillow in total depression. We would sit and give him potted versions of the various lectures he had missed.'

Over the three years they studied ecology, sociology, soil science, meteorology, agricultural economics, land use, rural and urban planning, climatology and much more: a thorough grounding. 'As might be expected,' Robert remarks, 'Marek generally only attended lectures that interested him – ecology, sociology and land use, if I remember correctly. However, his tenacity and dedication became very evident to all of us when he submitted 15,000 words for his library study on hedgerows: a very fine piece of work, but duly marked down, as it should have been 5,000.'

It was at Wye that he read a book which became centrally important to his thinking. This was *The Making of the English Landscape*, by W.G. Hoskins, first published in 1955, made a set text from day one of the course and now a classic. Hoskins set out 'to describe the manner in which the various landscapes of this country came to assume the shape and appearance they now have'. His elegant discussion of geology, woodland clearance, the creation of fields, settlements, enclosures, the Industrial Revolution and the modern world, spoke to Marek deeply. He had spent most of his life in an inner city, but through walking, through the field studies he did now, and a general soaking up of Kent and Suffolk, he came to cherish the English landscape. In his fifties, when he fell ill, Hoskins was the first author he took down from his shelves.

He graduated in 1973 with a 2.1. And what was he going to do now? For the next two years he did quite a lot, none of it related to his degree. He picked hops in Kent. He went up to Suffolk, played a huge amount of cricket, and spent at least one summer helping once more with the harvest. He came back to London and worked at Battersea Power Station, dismantling asbestos linings, something which now would make you shudder. He worked in a bakery. He was to describe all this as the updated version of the Dickens blacking factory.

Eventually, in 1976, he went up to Manchester to read for an MSc in the Department of Liberal Studies in Science. One of the closest friends he made at this time wrote me a long letter after his death.

I can remember being introduced to him in our student house. He had got 'loads of books', according to one student, and we shook hands rather tentatively. Marek's eyes narrowed a little, and it was the first of many assessing looks that he gave to anything or anyone new to him.

It soon became clear how self-sufficient he was. He... cooked from scratch, and he had an enormous appetite. In a house filled with language and philosophy students, we didn't know much about the environment, nor did he feel the need to explain what he was doing. What did strike me, however, was the amount of hard work he put in, working late into the night and often on Saturdays...

There are certain things that I will never forget and will always be grateful for: it was Marek who was there for me when I had real trouble finishing a piece of work and getting upset about it. He was kind and attentive, happy to listen while I ranted and raved. He was the one who made the effort to intercept me on my way to re-sitting an exam which I thought I wouldn't pass, and who gave me plenty of encouragement. He was also an inspiration... The moment when he stated his belief in personal freedom, and insisted that we should live our lives as we want to, still sticks in the mind...

I shall always remember his love of football and his athleticism, his wolfish grin, his wit, his love of curry, ice cream, trifle, real ale, and his ability to switch on the cor-blimey accent when he felt like it. To have been a friend of his has been a real privilege, and I miss him.

'We didn't know much about the environment...' One might assume that Marek's MSc. would be a development of his undergraduate studies, related to environmental science. Much of it was. But for his thesis he chose to write about H.G. Wells: both science and literature attracted and absorbed him.

Prophecy without Politics: H.G. Wells and the Spirit of Science was submitted to the university in 1978. I don't know for how long Marek had been reading Wells, but he had certainly read the Polish science fiction writer Stanisław Lem, and Wells struck a deep chord in his own thinking about the future, and the possibilities of science. He developed an interest in artificial intelligence, corresponding for some time afterwards with a fellow post-graduate student, Jamie Fleck. Perhaps the shadow of the war which fell so deeply on his parents' lives and on his childhood drew him towards notions of utopia.

The thesis has two main chapters, the first on Wells's novels, the second on his political thinking. The two are drawn together. As rather often in academic writing, there is something of a chasm between the prose of the critic and that of the object of study. Marek, at this stage never one to use a short sentence where a long one (with detours) could go wandering down the page, was drawn to the dense, the convoluted, the circumlocution. In contrast, Wells, quoted in all his clarity and directness, leaps off the page.

This being said, the thesis is a prodigious piece of work, reflecting enormously intelligent reading and thinking. My inability, forty years later, to follow its thread, may well reflect more on my own limitations than the work itself. Marek himself, who was never shy of pointing out other people's failings – sometimes reducing them to helpless laughter, sometimes cutting them to the quick – would certainly say so. I can hear him say so now.

At all events, he received the MSc, was highly regarded in the department and was expected to go on to do a doctorate. According to the statement made in the preliminary pages of his thesis, it would have been in the sociology of scientific knowledge.

'Loads of books' in Manchester: this is perhaps the point at which to say more about Marek's reading, and his mind: original, sceptical, rich, wide-ranging. I move along the bookshelves in my house in Highbury, bought with great help from his bequest to me.

When I moved here I brought all his books from our house in Stoke Newington, and put them up in a separate tall alcove, in the expectation that one day he might come back, and want to read them again. I suppose this is what Joan Didion would call magical thinking.

And I gaze now at the spines: all those worn old Pelicans, many of which date from Wye: *Nuclear Power, Derelict Britain, Polluting Britain...* There are books on political economics, climate and weather, agriculture, with the seminal authors of the environmental movement: Rachel Carson, James Lovelock. There are spine-cracked Penguin editions of two books he read over and over: John Stewart Collis, *The Vision of Glory* and *The Worm Forgives the Plough*, the author's account of working with the Land Army during the war. First published in 1946, it is now a Vintage Classic. And there's a hardback of *The Environmental Revolution*, by Max Nicholson. It was Nicholson who founded the company where Marek finally got his first proper job, where he stayed for the rest of his life.

And then there are the Poles: Adam Sienkiewicz, *Pan Tadeusz*, considered to be the last great epic poem in European literature; the Nobel Laureate Czeslaw Milosz, *The Captive Mind*, his examination of Stalinism, and his unforgettable memoirs, *Native Realm* and *The Issa Valley*. Twentieth-century Polish history is very much there, with more than one book about Katyn, the forest where in 1940 over four thousand members of the Polish intelligentsia held at Kozielsk Camp were murdered by the Russians. Hanna's father, Dr Szamota, was imprisoned in another camp, Starobielsk: eventually he was confirmed as one of those buried in mass graves at Karkhov, west of Starobielsk, in Ukraine.

There is Holocaust literature: Primo Levi; Eli Wiesel; Tadeusz Borowski's *This Way to the Gas Chambers, Ladies and Gentlemen*. And there are seminal reflective books about loss, exile and nostalgia, most notably Eva Hoffman's *Lost in Translation*. I think almost all her subsequent work is on those shelves, together with *The War After*, by Anne Karpf, which looks importantly at the effect of the Holocaust on the children of survivors.

Here and there are the essays of Isaiah Berlin and the Alan Clark *Diaries*; Russian novels; modern Polish poetry; the translations of Ovid's *Metamorphoses*, read in the last months of his life.

Little books which somehow aren't there, but which made him and our young son laugh a great deal, are Garfield cartoons. This lazy, goofy, overweight and malevolent ginger cat was good to turn to at difficult points in our family life. There were quite a few of those.

Marek and I met in the summer of 1976. He was about to go up to Manchester; I was about to enter the third year of the degree I was finally undertaking as a mature student. We both had temping jobs at Marshall Cavendish, a hugely successful publisher of part works – on gardening, cookery, crafts – with offices in Soho. Robert Paulley (he of Wye College) was Production Manager for the Encyclopedia division: our jobs came thanks to him.

I was cutting up one part-work to turn it into another; Marek, down in the basement, was sorting vast quantities of film in what Robert recalls as 'a steel-reinforced room which had once stored mink furs'. But he was also packing books with a couple of friends, 'which always seemed to involve a lot of football with an empty beer can'.

It was a long, scorchingly hot summer. A large roof terrace was the place for lunch: eating salad sandwiches, flicking cherry stones. Marek's stones went the distance. We got to know one another, we fell deeply in love. But for reasons outside the scope of this essay this was not the moment to do anything about it: in the autumn he went up to Manchester, and I returned to the life I was living then. For two years, intermittently, we wrote to one another; occasionally I went up to see him.

It rains a lot in Manchester. By the time he began his PhD, without a grant, Marek had very little money, and his life was not much fun. By the spring of 1978, a year after completing my degree, I was working for a very different publisher, Wildwood House, in Covent Garden. Small, radical, independent, it was founded at about the same time as Virago. Marek came down to London to see his family, and me. Through the back streets of Covent Garden we walked and talked. That summer he abandoned his PhD, unable to see how he could possibly fund it, and at last we got together.

Our first home was at 9 Highbury Crescent – Number Nine, as those of us who had lived there in the early seventies always referred to it. We lived in a vast, cold, ground-floor room overlooking the garden, sharing the flat with two others.

At first we were very happy. But Marek was someone of enormous intellectual energy, who had been pouring it into his studies. Suddenly without them, and without a job, he entered something of a crisis. He began a voracious reading of Graham Greene, which helped, but I often came home from work to find him sunk in gloom.

It was a colleague at Wildwood House who saved the day. This was Elaine Elkington, a lovely person who spoke of having once had 'a tea and buns sort of job'. Most of us have had one of those at some point. She was married to John Elkington, a clever, kind and ambitious young man, now a world authority on sustainability and corporate responsibility. In 1977, with Max Nicholson, founder of the World Wildlife Fund, and the economist David Layton, John had founded Environmental Data Services (ENDS).

ENDS was a subsidiary of Income Data Services (IDS), founded by David Layton in 1966. Both companies published journals intended above all to inform professionals in their specialist fields: IDS was dedicated to all aspects of employment practice – pay, human resources policy, law. ENDS published news, analysis and reference right across the environmental spectrum. It now, of course, emphasises carbon-cutting and sustainability.

The sixties and early seventies had seen the green movement really getting under way. *Silent Spring*, Rachel Carson's ground-breaking investigation into the effects of pesticides, was published in 1962: a wake-up call. Friends of the Earth was founded in San Francisco in 1969, the same year as several major environmental disasters: the pollution of the Rhine by an insecticide which killed twenty million fish; the collapse of the Icelandic herring stock due to over-fishing and deteriorating waters; Hurricane Camille, which swept across the US Gulf Coast leaving devastation.

To read through a timeline of the following years is like watching a pendulum swinging wildly across the world, between catastrophes and the attempt to contain and legislate against them. Greenpeace was founded in Vancouver in 1971; in 1972, the year that the UN Environment Programme came into being, DDT was banned by the USA. In 1974, it was realised that chlorofluorocarbons, widely used in the manufacture of aerosol sprays and refrigerators, were damaging the ozone layer. The Control Act was made law in 1974. A year later, the accidental release of the chemical compound Dioxin in the Italian town of Seveso, killed animals and traumatised the population. 1979 saw the worst nuclear power accident in US history: the partial meltdown of a reactor in the Three Mile Island plant.

The founding of ENDS, dedicated to following, uncovering and analysing environmental news stories for a readership of those at the heart of industry, who urgently needed to get themselves informed, had been very timely.

In early 1979, John Elkington, presiding over ENDS as its first editor, was in need of a staff journalist. Over our Wildwood tea and buns, Elaine and I had talked a lot about Marek; she mentioned him to John, who interviewed and appointed him.

For the first six months, John wondered if he had made a terrible mistake.

It was the environmental lawyer Richard Macrory, now Emeritus Professor of Environmental Law at University College, London, who, as one of his best friends, recorded those early days in an obituary for the *Independent*.

'Mayer read and read, and talked endlessly to people involved in environmental policy but, to the despair of his editor, wrote almost nothing. But then, as Elkington recalls, after this lengthy gestation period he suddenly went critical, like a nuclear reactor, and poured forth a regular stream of insightful and authoritative copy, something that he continued to do for the rest of his life.'

Everything that he had absorbed at Wye College, and developed in his MSc studies at Manchester, together with his deep feelings for truth and principle, came into play once Marek got to grips with ENDS. He was twenty-seven then, very fit, very strong, and now very focussed. But in that year, 1979, he did take time off: in the summer, we went to Poland.

He had been once before, at nineteen, to visit his mother's cousin and her family in Warsaw. He was the only person in his family to have done so: his parents and grandparents refused even to recognise Communist Poland, let alone visit it. Perhaps it was the time he'd spent in Polish Scouts which sharpened Marek's curiosity; perhaps, feeling so out of English life in his first year at Wye, he wanted to make a connection with his roots. At all events, he had had this brief, affectionate visit, but had not seen very much of the country. Our holiday now felt momentous: preparing for an engagement with places which had meant so much to his parents; affirming his own background and identity; sharing all this with me.

Before we left, we went to visit his grandparents. They were tiny, courteous, charming people, deeply involved with their grandchildren, but living quietly in their mansion flat. On that visit, his grandfather gave Marek an empty jam jar: it was to be filled with Polish soil.

We left in mid-August, taking the ferry to the Hook of Holland, then travelling by overnight train to Warsaw. This involved crossing the border from West to East Germany, from West to East Berlin: we were woken in our bunks four times with shouts for passports. In the morning we woke to a country of sunflowers, hayricks, silver birches, cornfields, storks. We saw women gathering hay into stooks by hand, as agricultural workers had done for centuries: modernity had passed Poland by. Marek translated the names of stations: Stumps; This is Rome; Hawks Nest; In the Manner of a Wolf. He also, as we journeyed, translated the Soviet slogans, painted in huge red capitals on white station walls: LET US STRENGTHEN SOCIALIST JUSTICE!

Poland in 1979 was living through Communism's final years. The Solidarity Campaign was yet to gather strength and momentum; the Velvet Revolution of 1989 in Prague, and the fall of the Berlin Wall, were all in an unimagined future. We stayed in Warsaw, whose Old Town had been entirely rebuilt, reconstructing the medieval buildings which had been destroyed in 1944. The whole city had, indeed, been razed to the ground.

We hired a car which broke down, and another which did the same, stranding us on a country road, miles from anywhere; eventually Avis provided one which stayed the course. We drove to industrial towns belching black smoke; through country villages adorned with sunflowers, white geese, blue-painted houses, where children rode home at the end of the day on wagons piled up with hay, and men lay on roadside verges in a drunken stupor.

We went to Krakow, one of the loveliest cities in Europe, whose shops were simply empty. We put up our tent on a campsite where Marek's jeans, like the coffee we put in a thermos, were stolen. And what we experienced was a country of real impoverishment: food shortages, black-market currency, towns where the street lights went on and off at random, villages where agricultural labourers struggled to bring in a harvest: the communal equipment, powered by a communal electricity plant, constantly failed.

'Everywhere they show us on the television how much we have,' one despairing farmer told Marek. He had been waiting for five hours for the electricity to come on again, so he could use the combine. 'Where is it all?'

It was a country where few people smiled, a place of beauty and desolation.

In a flower-strewn meadow in the south, Marek filled a jar of Polish soil for his grandfather. In Warsaw, we stayed as B&B guests in a house whose elegant owner was a survivor of Dachau. Now, dressed in different satin dressing gowns throughout our visit, he prepared extensive breakfasts: bread, sausage, curd cheese, tomatoes, hard-boiled eggs, apples and preserves. All this was bought on the black market, which is how we were paying him for our stay.

We went to the museum commemorating the 1944 Uprising and gazed at photographs of everything his mother had talked of, over and over again down the years: the barricades, the bomb-shattered streets, the makeshift funerals, a street full of corpses. 'No place for tears,' said Marek, as we talked it all over, sitting on steps nearby. 'There was no place for tears then.'

Next day we visited the cemetery which commemorates the dead of that desperate battle. It took a long time to find the right headstone, walking at the end of an autumnal afternoon along paths between dozens of others. We were looking for Marek's uncle, after whom he had been named, just nineteen when he was killed. Candles flickered on the graves, bunches of red and white flowers were laid beneath the stones. At last we found it: Marek Prawdicz-Szamota, that name among row upon row of others. There were thousands engraved on those tall granite stones.

Marek lit a candle; it burned with all the others as we walked away.

In 1981 Marek succeeded John Elkington as editor of ENDS. He had an excellent colleague: Georgina McAughtry, who had been there since the beginning and was to show herself over the years to be a brilliant businesswoman. It was Georgina who, as the company grew gradually in staff numbers and reputation, took over its management, production, marketing and expansion. As principled as Marek, she also became a true friend.

But it was Marek who wrote the copy which eventually made the journal a byword. There was no byline, which perhaps was just as well, since in the early years almost every word of it came from him.

And he became a very powerful writer: the over-elaborate prose of his MSc days was gradually refined and streamlined; everything was underpinned by meticulous research and searching interviews. 'I came to regard him as the most penetrating and thought-provoking journalist who ever interviewed me,' said one man after his death. This was Andrew Warren, Director of the Association for the Conservation of Energy.

Marek was covering everything, large and small, as ENDS, with many more writers now, has continued to do. Major features on major international disasters and events – Bhopal, in 1984; Chernobyl in 1986; the world's worst oil spill in Kuwait during the Iraq War of 1991; the Earth Summit at Rio in 1992 – were published alongside accounts of damage done in this country: river pollution, irresponsible landfill, hazardous waste spills, the campaign to remove lead from petrol; together with reports of small business enterprises which put environmental responsibility at the top of their agenda.

Reporting on court cases and on legislation became a regular feature: Richard Macrory published 'In Court' every month, detailing prosecutions and convictions. Marek was also following legislation closely, attending House of Commons Select Committees and getting to know many MPs. His contact list became enormous, his editorials were robust. He pursued and worried the wrongdoer – the lawbreaker, the spiller of chemicals, the concealer of damage – like a terrier with a rat. With a different temperament he could have been a formidable barrister. Writing suited his need for solitude.

All this involved a working life which might at the least be described as eccentric. Computers were only just beginning to come into the workplace in the late seventies, and there was certainly no digital printing. Most publishers were still at the hard-copy-turned-into-camera-ready-copy stage, and in the early days of ENDS we were talking scissors and cow gum.

This was where Danuta, Marek's youngest sister, came in. Invaluably, she had trained as an illustrator, knew about graphic design. Now, putting the journal to press each month meant turning up with her dog at about 10 p.m., settling down at a large desk and cutting and pasting the sheets that Marek gave her until dawn.

Essentially, he became nocturnal: the long quiet hours of the night were when he got most of his writing done, after a day on the phone, or visiting companies, or attending Select Committees. Recovering, he slept for Poland.

In 1982 we moved from that huge cold room in Highbury to our first flat: pretty but small, on the borders of Highbury and Stoke Newington. In 1983 our son was born.

'I never knew,' Marek said, when James was a few months old, meaning he had never known what joy a baby could bring. There was a lot of laughter between them when James was small. But his hours grew longer and longer. 'When I've finished the issue' became a running joke – or a running sore: no sooner was it finished than the next began, and I think perhaps he did become physically addicted to this workaholic cycle. Our move in 1989 to a house in Stoke Newington – more space, eventually his own study – did little to change things.

As the years went on, it all took a huge toll: he was under immense pressure, trying to balance an over-demanding working life with life at home; his health and his temper suffered. We survived as a family, but it wasn't easy for any of us. This is the truth.

It is also true to say that in the midst of all this Marek could be the kindest, most tender-hearted and most generous person: to his family and to his friends. And although I have painted a picture of solitary, night-owl years he was not, of course, working in isolation, but as part of a group of deeply committed and hugely influential Greens.

Tom Burke, Nigel Haigh, Richard Macrory, Tom Radice, Tessa Tennant (who, like Marek, died far too young), Fiona Reynolds and Robin Grove-White all were, and continue to be, important in different fields, linked by environmental issues: the law; academic research, analysis and teaching; policy-making; green investment. Some are now the recipients of CBEs; all are at the very top of their respective trees, but if that smacks too much of the establishment let it be said now that it would be hard to find a group of funnier, more individual, interesting and engaging people. At work and outside it, Marek was close to them all.

And then there was Andrew Lees.

In Marek's early days at ENDS, Andrew was a radical campaigner on projects in Wales and then Norfolk, his home county. In 1985 he came to London to work for Friends of the Earth; in 1990, by which time he and Marek had become close friends, he was appointed National Campaigns Director. Perhaps, as with Marek, passion describes Andrew's attitude to his work more accurately than commitment. He wasn't a shouter, but he really did believe in making a difference and getting out there, and directed several major international campaigns, not least exposing the covert shipping of European toxic waste to a little Nigerian port.

At the end of 1994 he flew out to Madagascar, where Rio Tinto Zinc were planning to mine for titanium oxide – whitener for toothpaste is one of its uses. The mine would provide employment in one of the poorest countries in the world, but it would also destroy mangrove swamps, lagoons and forest, home to rare plants and animals like the lemurs; it would uproot coastal villagers and destroy their ancestral burial grounds.

Andrew had gone out to make a documentary. He did not return. A week of huge anxiety went by, covered extensively by the British press; his partner, Christine Orengo, flew out with a friend to join the search. His body was found on 7 January in a forest clearing: he had died of heat exhaustion.

In the wake of his death, Christine's sister Yvonne, Marek, Mary Taylor of Friends of the Earth, and one of Andrew's brothers, all founded the Andrew Lees Trust. Its aim was to develop environmental projects to help an impoverished community manage and protect their health, food supply and land. Under Yvonne Orengo's directorship – she went out to Madagascar and stayed for many years – the Trust planted a tree nursery, trained local women to make clay ovens, supplied wind-up radios and sponsored students, as well as eventually entering into a dialogue with Rio Tinto Zinc to hold them accountable as the mine developed. For her services to the Trust Yvonne was honoured in 2012 with an MBE.

Marek, deeply saddened by Andrew's death, became one of the Trustees, involved from the beginning and able to be generous: ENDS was now growing financially. With Andrew he had shared a left-field view of the world, and many late-night conversations. Essentially, they were soulmates.

★

Marek continued to cover the major issues of the day. In 1995 these included the founding of the Environment Agency, whose sometimes less than ideal work he reported on in unrelenting detail. In 1997 came the drafting of the Kyoto Protocol: the international agreement to commit to reduce carbon emissions and other greenhouse gases. Again, he would follow its progress closely. And in that year he became Editorial Director of ENDS.

The following year, two other important things happened. The first was that to his astonishment he was awarded a medal. It was bestowed by the Society of Chemical Industry, a learned society founded in 1881 'to further the application of chemistry and related sciences for public benefit'. Now offering an international forum for dialogue between science and industry, the Society gave Marek its Environmental Medal 'for outstanding and sustained contributions to the analysis and industrial dissemination of environmental policy and legislation'. He was the last person to seek recognition for his work, but this really did please him, and the blue-ribboned medal, bestowed at a special ceremony, is a handsome thing.

The other major event of 1998 was our purchase of a rundown cottage on the Welsh borders. It was about an hour's drive from the Herefordshire farm where the three of us had spent many good holidays; finding this lovely old place felt like putting down roots in a county we had come to love.

The cottage dated back in part to the sixteenth century; it had a stream, and a little land, and was set between pasture and woodland. We had it restored by a local builder, and happy times began, with friends and family coming to stay and Marek discovering the delights of vegetable gardening. I have an enduring memory of him out in the orchard, digging and sowing, with cricket on the radio and a robin on the top.

I have another memory of him on that farm, sitting outside on a wooden chair reading *To the Lighthouse*, with a hen perched on his walking boots. Flash, the family sheepdog, came with us on our walks in the valley; Marek, a tremendous walker, loved dogs, and James (now Will) has inherited his easy and affectionate way with them. On the farm, at the cottage, running down the long lane which passed it, walking up in the Radnor Hills, Marek was often at his happiest and most relaxed.

Over the years we did have some very good holidays, on the farm, at the cottage and in Europe, sometimes with friends, sometimes just the three of us. In the summer of 2003 we went on a big family holiday to Turkey: we three, two sisters, Turkish brother-in-law and nephew. We were staying in a little fishing village, and Marek ran a great deal there, out every morning, up in the hills overlooking the bay. We celebrated his fifty-second birthday; a photograph shows him wearing on his head the fruit strainer I'd bought for his cottage jam-making. We swam, we climbed, we had a long day sailing and a lot of laughs.

It was only towards the end that Marek began to ask himself on those long morning runs if he was beginning to slow down a bit, perhaps not as fit as he was.

One morning in September, not long after our return, he found a lump in his neck. In a very short time, he was given a diagnosis: kidney cancer. He could live for perhaps two years; it was possible it would be two weeks.

As with all else, he made it his business to understand every aspect of what was going on. He became an expert in what turned out to be a very rare, genetic form of the disease. I do not find the image of 'battling' with cancer useful, but he did fight it, with every ounce of his considerable strength. He continued to work at ENDS, and almost all through his treatment continued to keep mad, indefatigable hours.

One of his last editorials, in February 2005, was headed 'Crunch time on climate change'. In it, he celebrated the final coming into force of the Kyoto Protocol – from which the USA had notoriously withdrawn – as 'a vital milestone in the effort to tackle the threat of climate change'. He went on:

> The enormity of that threat is becoming ever more apparent. A major scientific conference in Exeter has confirmed that the world is perilously close to several serious, and potentially irreversible, tipping points…the melting of the polar ice caps, significant rise in sea level, abrupt shut down of the Gulf Stream, loss of the Amazon rainforest, widespread drought and loss of ecosystems… The unavoidable conclusion is that the most polluting industries, such as aviation and coal production, must deliver radical improvements in technology…

What would Marek have made of Greta Thunberg? Of Extinction Rebellion, demanding, almost fifteen years later, that the world and its leaders wake up once and for all to this threat?

The truth is that I do not know. He would not have been glueing himself to railings. I very much doubt if he would have been out on the streets, though he would have enjoyed the policeman skateboarding dreamily through the protestors on Westminster Bridge. But I think he would have been with Greta and all XR in spirit. He would have been up in that office at three in the morning: following the protests, writing editorials on the urgency of the need to act, analysing and writing about the response of government. He would certainly have had something to say about that.

In the last weeks of Marek's life several things sustained him. The flowers his mother brought to the house, fresh cut, dripping with rain, tied with string. The sudden arrival of a gorgeous basket of fruit from Michael Heseltine who, as Marek's illness progressed, added ENDS to his stable of publications at Haymarket Press. More of this below.

What else? Long nocturnal email conversations with his sister Barbara, another night-owl. Visits and letters from his closest friends. James and I in our different ways. Cricket. Cricket really helped: a television monitor hung above his bed in the Marsden Hospital, and he followed the Test Match all day – indeed, as the long twenty-three months of his illness approached its end, the only time a look of horror crossed his face in the Marsden was when he thought he'd missed a catch. On went his specs in a flash.

His wit never left him. Two days before the end, the pretty young nurse who'd been looking after him said she was going on holiday. Oh really? Where? Tunisia. And with whom? Three friends: another nurse and two geography students. There was a fractional pause, then one of his elegant eyebrows went up. 'I'm sure the Tunisians will be glad to see your theodolites.'

Thanks to modern medicine, his death two nights later could not have been more peaceful.

The obituaries, written by some of the environmentalists whose friendship he had most cherished, spoke of how ENDS had become a by-word for authoritative analysis; of Marek's extraordinary memory for detail, knowing that the devil lies therein.

'His persistence, penetration and refusal to be fobbed off with spin or platitudes, coupled with objectivity, good writing and a pleasing lack of arrogance, served as a beacon to a generation of environmental journalists,' wrote Tom Radice in *The Times*. In the *Guardian* Nigel Haigh said that 'ENDS became essential reading for anyone professionally involved in the environment, both in Britain and, because of its coverage of the EU, outside it, too.'

'He probably did more for environmental protection than Greenpeace and Friends of the Earth put together,' one man wrote to me. This was John Stevens, once Head of the Department of the Environment Press Office.

Michael Heseltine held a party in a grand room at the House

of Lords, to mark his purchase of ENDS. Marek, he told every-one, was the only editor of any of the magazines he had bought for Haymarket Press who had said that the money was not important. What mattered was that the Press honoured the high standards he and his colleagues had set.

In November 2006 the Environment Agency published a list of the one hundred people it considered to be the top green campaigners of all time. It was headed by Rachel Carson. Marek was sixtieth. I can see that eyebrow rise.

In the year after his death we did many things in his memory. There was a big memorial party at the Polish Hearth Club, where three years earlier we had celebrated his fiftieth birthday. Mamta Patel and her husband Geraint, two good colleagues from ENDS, organised a memorial walk over the Sussex Downs. The whole family scattered his ashes in the places he had wanted them to be scattered: first of all, up in the Radnor Hills; then beneath a quince tree, his favourite, which we planted at the cottage, and where we set a stone.

And then we all went to Poland, where his mother was reunited with members of her family she had not seen since the war. Together, we scattered ashes in the racing Vistula in Warsaw, and at the river's source in a mountain stream.

In the cemetery commemorating the Warsaw Uprising of 1944, Hanna scattered more at the foot of the headstone commemorating the death of her brother, killed with so many, many others. It was over sixty years since she had left that ruined city, twenty-seven since Marek and I had lit a candle there.

The next summer James flew out to Madagascar, met Yvonne Orengo at the Andrew Lees Trust, and scattered the last of those ashes beneath a permanent memorial stone.

Finally, we raised funds for the Herefordshire Wildlife Trust, to have a neglected wetland site restored, and dedicated to him. Many generous friends contributed.

To reach Parky Meadow you walk down a stony lane outside the village of Wigmore, and turn down a long old cart track. You come to two great fields, bordered by stream and willows, filled with every kind of grass. Barn Owls hunt here; sometimes there are cattle grazing in the distance; not much else goes on. It's very quiet. A notice at the gate describes the place, and in small type at the bottom announces:

> *This site is dedicated to Marek Mayer (1952-2005),*
> *outstanding environmental journalist.*

A great many people attended the ceremony in October 2006 at which the Director of the Trust unveiled this modest notice-board. I'm not sure if anyone really goes to Parky Meadow now. But then, as my old friend Patrick Cullen remarked, knowing of Marek's love of solitude: he wouldn't have wanted them there. It's true. For this quiet, hidden place to exist, to be safe and maintained for wild plants and creatures: that would be enough.

The Diarist

ROY STRONG

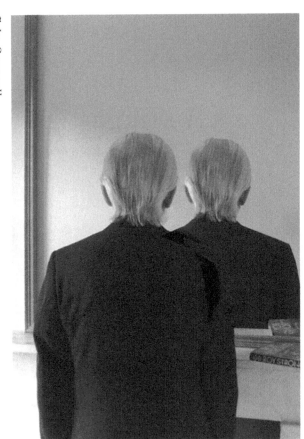

John Swannell

A young man from nowhere who went somewhere.

We are (pre-Covid) in Hereford Cathedral: the Sunday morning service of Eucharist. As choir and congregation join in singing the first hymn, a procession makes its way down the nave towards the choir and altar: the Cross-bearer and candle-bearers; the choristers in their blue cassocks and white ruffs, the lay clerks and Director of Music; the clergy and attendants, the Dean of the Cathedral. One of those in this procession is an altar server, Roy Strong, clothed, like the clergy, in fine vestments. With his snowy head bowed just a little, his distinctive ears, and his hands clasped reverently before him, a dignified prelate meets a beautifully brushed Arctic hare.

The sceptical observer, recalling the flamboyant figure of Roy Strong's London past, might be inclined to think: he just loves dressing up, that's what all this is about. The sceptical observer would be quite wrong. Since his conversion to Anglo-Catholicism in 1955, at the age of twenty, a deep faith has sustained him for the whole of his adult life.

He does, of course, adore dressing up. The image opposite, Roy Strong after Magritte is taken from *Sir Portrait*, a collection of portraits by the distinguished photographer John Swannell, which features its subject in thirty guises: a Renaissance prince, Chekhov, Tennyson, Isambard Kingdom Brunel, Henry VIII… In 2015, marking Strong's eightieth birthday, these photographs were shown at the National Portrait Gallery, where his life as a brilliant young man had begun.

It has been a long life, full of contrasts, even extremes: the worldly, which made him famous, and the spiritual, which has offered hope and comfort in dark times. He has had a house and celebrated garden in Herefordshire for over forty years, but he made his name in London. Above all, there is the extraordinary journey he made from a lonely, bitterly unhappy childhood and youth to a place at the centre of everything in the art and museum world, and, through this, to the centre of London society.

He was to write about it all – the rich, the brilliant, the eccentric and the intolerable; the glittering first nights and exhibitions, the dinner parties and the country house weekends – in his unputdownable Diaries. And yet he remained an outsider: a highly observant individual looking in at a world which most people had been born into, and took for granted. This, as Roy has said himself, is the Diaries' strength.

'The reader at Weidenfeld & Nicolson thought they were absolutely marvellous,' he tells me. 'No one had ever written anything like this before.'

It is 2019, and we are talking in the comfortable conservatory of The Laskett, the country house a few miles outside Hereford which he bought with his wife, Julia Trevelyan Oman, in 1973. It's a warm spring afternoon, the sun shining on a large round table heaped with biographies and the page proofs of his new book, *The Elizabethan Image*. Tabitha, the current cat – there have always been cats – is asleep beneath a potted palm.

We are not so very far from the Radnorshire village of Clyro, home of another great diarist, the Victorian country curate Francis Kilvert. Between 1870-1879 Kilvert wrote about every aspect of his life: his parishioners, his family, the beauty of the natural world, his love of God. He wrote about the young women he fell in love with, and the little girls to whom he was perhaps too greatly attracted. But he was doing so simply for himself; when he died his wife burned many of the volumes, and the rediscovery in the late 1930s of those that remained is one of the more satisfactory stories in the literary world.

Roy Strong's own diaries began in 1967, at someone else's suggestion. We talk about them a great deal this afternoon, but we also talk about his troubled family background and his long, contented, unexpected marriage. And he gives me a copy of his memoir, *Self-Portrait as a Young Man*, published in 2013 and dedicated to Antonia Fraser, 'who had always wondered where I came from'. The opening quotation in my essay comes from this compelling autobiography: I draw on both the book and our conversation in what follows.

There is a photograph of the young Roy Strong taken in about 1953, standing outside the suburban family home in Winchmore Hill, north London. Solemn, bespectacled, in suit and tie, he resembles no one so much as another celebrated diarist, one Adrian Mole. And indeed, in the crammed folio of his early art work is a copy of a Velasquez portrait inscribed *RC Strong 19 June Age 12½*. At this stage in his life – on the cusp of school and university – and for years afterwards, he was cripplingly shy. There were good reasons.

Strong, born in 1935, was the third son of a bullying, self-centred, uneducated father and a cowed, weeping, over-possessive mother. The marriage was utterly miserable. But 'divorce then was the ultimate disgrace and carried with it a huge social stigma.'

The household was run on the lines of 'Whatever you do, don't tell your father', and of this man, a hat salesman, he writes, 'I have never, but never, felt anger, rage or resentment so deeply, so bitterly, as I did in my early teens.' Both in this book and in our conversation he describes presenting a good school report only to have it slammed back at him, unread. 'You don't forget things like that,' he says, and some of the pain he felt then clearly remains with him to this day.

The fact that the report was so good can be ascribed to three things. The 1944 Education Act took him to Edmonton County

Grammar School, where he received an excellent education from dedicated teachers. His abilities were developed both through that teaching and his own unremitting hard work. And while his father filled him with such rage and unhappiness, he owes a great deal to his devoted, anxious mother. She believed in education, and she did everything to ensure that her bright, hard-working son received it, scrimping and saving the money from any number of low-paid jobs to help him.

'She loved children and being a mother to them. The downside was that she would have preferred it if none of us had ever grown up.'

We meet his two brothers now and then in the Diaries, where amidst all the talk of parties and glamour they strike notes of sorrow and fury. Derek, the oldest, Strong describes as saintly – 'I have known few other people who have had such a strong sense of responsibility and caring.' Brian, the one in the middle, was the brutal black sheep: violent even as a child, he grew up to lead a life of drugs, crime and deception. Both were evacuated during the war, leaving Roy as the only child, into whom his mother poured all her love and ambition. Even after their return, this made him 'Mother's boy' until manhood, something he bitterly resented. He is also aware that such a situation can lie behind the life of a gay man: more of this below.

Yet despite the suffering he endured, he once began a lecture on happiness at Birmingham University, with: 'Can I now give thanks for unhappiness? Because it gave me my life's work. It led me to find refuge in distant worlds of the mind and the imagination.'

A deep love of history began at a very early age. 'I was swallowed up by the past,' he says. He had an inspirational teacher, Joan Henderson, with whom he maintained a lifelong friendship. And it was history, specifically of the first Elizabethan age, of court and costume, which opened a door on to everything he hadn't known he longed for: the distant worlds of drama, theatre, beauty, glory.

He was also born at the right time to experience the post-war, post-austerity renaissance of ballet and theatre – he spent hours at home with his Pollocks toy theatre, which he still owns – and the reopening of museums and galleries. In 1946 his mother took him to an exhibition of French tapestries at the V&A, which thrilled him.

'By the time I was fourteen my idea of bliss was to travel to South Kensington with my friend James Platt, both of us with a packet of sandwiches. He went to the Science Museum and I went to explore the V&A, and in particular the Costume Court. I took a sketchbook with me...'

James Platt, who sat at the next desk at Edmonton, was Roy Strong's only school friend, and one he could never take home. He could never take anyone home. On Sunday afternoons they used to meet for a walk: once round Grovelands Park and back again. That was it. After O-levels, James, like many of the boys in that year, left school to go to work. Roy, with a clutch of form prizes, had exam results so good that the school encouraged him to stay on. He went into the sixth form and flourished.

'I was treated as an intelligent human being and what creativity I had was put to good use... What I learnt early on was an ability to work ferociously hard on my own.' Coached in Latin after school by another dedicated teacher, Doris Staples, he passed well enough for university entrance and, with three good A-levels, was in 1953 admitted to Queen Mary College, University of London, to read History.

He was still living at home, still sharing a bedroom with Brian, colonising the dining room with his books and papers, and at QMC became aware of the yawning gap in background between himself and the other undergraduates. 'I entered a world of upper classes, aristocrats,' he tells me. Some of the young women were waiting to be presented at court: he was cut dead by one when he told her that his father had no club. I ask how he had coped with that. 'I had to learn an awful lot very fast. I had to be a very good actor.' And he subsumed himself in work.

'I had gone up...with one end in view,' he writes in his memoir, 'to write a book on the portraits of Queen Elizabeth the First. An undergraduate course had to be endured in order for that aim to be achieved.' At the end of his first year, he wrote a long letter to Miss Staples, she of the Latin coaching. She kept it, and returned it years later, when certain things had been accomplished.

I do hope to go on to the Warburg – that is if the grant continues or I can get a scholarship.

I realise that one degree is not really of much use – interesting jobs are so difficult to get. All I want to be is something like the Director of the National Portrait Gallery or the Head of a Department in the Victoria and Albert Museum!

The rest, as they say, is history. He graduated with a First, and was indeed given a scholarship to go to the Warburg Institute, where in 1953 he embarked on a PhD on Elizabethan court pageantry under the supervision of Frances Yates, another woman who was to become hugely influential intellectual mentor. 'The boundaries of knowledge widened dramatically. I was taught to think horizontally.'

One might think that at this point, with his wings stretching, and the beginnings of an interest in his own clothes, as well as in the costumes of the sixteenth century, he might have begun at last to feel comfortable in his own skin. But this was not to happen for another few years. In the meantime, he writes:

> I was not only cripplingly shy [except in seminars, where he seems to have shone] but aware that I was sexually ambiguous... At twenty I was totally bottled up and inhibited. There was a homosexual side to myself, that much I knew; but whenever, later, I got glimpses into that world I knew equally that I did not wish to enter it. There was another side to me: emotionally and intellectually I

was also hugely attracted to women and I knew that, if I found the right person, I would like the stability of an old-fashioned Christian marriage.

It was while he was at the Warburg that through a friend he was introduced to the Anglican chaplain of London University, Father Gardiner. He invited Roy to accompany a small group going one weekend to the shrine at Walsingham Abbey. 'There was no religion at all in my background,' he says. But at Walsingham he had his first profound spiritual experience: 'Just the piety of the people there, and a hugely powerful atmosphere that the place has...' His voice begins to drop. 'That is where I – well, I suppose I had a kind of conversion. I went back there twice, and then I asked to be instructed, and I was confirmed.'

At different points in his life, his faith has been of the greatest importance. In his old age, Hereford Cathedral has offered him a kind of family. But when I ask him about his relationship with God now, he laughs, and doesn't really answer. 'I never go through any particular angst about it.' It's a very Anglican cast of mind.

At the end of his time at the Warburg, he still had not really discovered where he might be heading. He had a doctorate; he was scholarly, lonely, shy and impractical. He had begun to publish papers, and in the New Year of 1959 sent one on Nicholas Hilliard to David Piper, a senior curator at the National Portrait Gallery, later to become its Director (1964-67). In July, a post as assistant keeper was advertised: they wanted someone to catalogue their sixteenth-century collection.

He can remember little about his interview except that after answering questions in the high-flown manner of the Warburg he was asked by one of the Board: 'What would you do if the window-cord broke?' History does not relate what he replied, but he got the job.

He took up his post of assistant keeper in the autumn of 1959, joining what he has described as a great institution which had gone to sleep. The Sixties were on the horizon, and though Roy Strong was then what we (and he) would now call a young fogey, rather than an angry young man, he was to play a huge part in the revolution in British life and manners. To do so involved a metamorphosis.

'It somehow came back to me that I was considered a humourless bore,' he writes in *Self-Portrait.* 'It came as quite a shock, but it was one to which I responded. I therefore deliberately set out to transform myself, if not into a delight at least into an amusing companion at table.'

By the time this transformation began, Roy Strong had been at the National Portrait Gallery for some two years, spending much of his time in the basement, sorting through thousands of old saleroom catalogues. Still horribly shy, he was in a state of utter loneliness. And he had entered an institution largely ossified in its attitudes and practice. No one who had been dead for less than a decade could be brought before the Trustees. Not a single photograph graced the walls. If a journalist rang the rule was to put the phone down.

However, there were gleams of light. Every Monday he attended the auctions at Sotheby's and Christie's; there were visits to see the portraits in grand country houses; after a while he was put on to identifying those brought in by members of the public: 'a marvellous way to learn...and to acquire finesse in terms of courtesy'. He was involved in a minor way with exhibitions, though this was at a time when private views were often dismally unattended. Above all, he began to distinguish himself as a scholar.

In 1963 he came into the limelight by identifying a lost Holbein cartoon, concealed beneath the artist's painting of Henry VIII bestowing the charter on the Company of Barber Surgeons. It had taken him weeks of painstaking work, peering through a microscope, to make this discovery. The article he then wrote for *The Burlington Magazine* was published to coincide with a major Holbein exhibition into which he threw himself heart and soul.

He wrote to his Dutch friend Jan van Dorsten – letters to this fellow-scholar appear not infrequently in the Diaries – of 'an unending battle over curtains, lighting, wallpaper, captions... Forays for invitation cards, for posters, for gorgeous *mise-en-scene* of yards of rich damask and rich wallpapers...' He was to write in the Diaries that he approached every exhibition as if preparing for a first night, and here it all began. The result was a triumph: a glamorous private view attended by the great and the good, and huge coverage in the press. It was a turning point both for the Gallery and for him.

In 1964 Roy finally moved out of the constricting suburban house in Winchmore Hill, which he later described as less a home than a detention centre. With Michael Borrie, who was to become Head of Manuscripts at the British Library, and a lifelong friend, he moved into a flat in Lancaster Gate. Carefree bachelor days began, and with them the purchase of interesting clothes for the evenings: a double-breasted Blades suit, a Regency frock coat. He was out and about in a big way; he was cooking with Elizabeth David and entertaining. The shy young man had at last begun to feel at ease.

At the Gallery he was in the ascendant, and in 1967, eight years after he had gazed at those serried ranks of catalogues, he applied for the post of Director. In the strategy document he prepared for the Trustees, outlining his vision of the next ten years, he was uncompromising. It is quoted in *Self-portrait as a Young Man*.

> The National Portrait Gallery, as is well known, houses the nation's collection of famous British men and women of the past. It was founded in 1856 for this purpose, but also embodies a reflection of Victorian attitudes to portraiture, i.e. moral didacticism. The latter attitude can

no longer be sustained...We have passed the age when to
be instructive was to be dreary...

He was interviewed on 16 March, 1967, and on the 17th
inscribed in his appointments diary, 'THE DAY I HEARD'.The
news had to kept under wraps for a week, until it was officially
announced in the Court Circular of *The Times*. But on 25th
March he wrote to Jan van Dorsten: 'GOT IT.' He was thirty-
two, the youngest person ever to hold the post. And it was in this
year that he began to keep a very different diary.

He was living in interesting times, Lady Carlisle told him at a
dinner party in the autumn of 1967, soon after he had become
Director. He would meet interesting people – he should record
it all. So he began, at first just jotting things down on loose sheets
or whatever notebooks came to hand. It was when he read Cecil
Beaton's diaries, just coming out at that time, that he settled on
quite how to do it, and began to take it seriously.

Beaton penetratingly describes individuals at length: Diana
Cooper becoming a bore in old age; Noel Coward suffering
from poor circulation and taking too much to his bed; his own
difficult relationship with a lonely, demanding mother. And of
course there is Garbo, and their long on-off romance. He
spends pages on a single event: a picnic on holiday in Italy; the
royal family attending a play; the state opening of Parliament.
He is writing what Roy Strong came to realise were elegant set
pieces, or miniature retrospective essays. They became his
inspiration.

30 November 1968
Christabel, Lady Aberconway
I was bidden to lunch by Brinsley Ford to that treasure
house, 14 Wyndham Place. Joanna Ford was ill, so it
turned out to be a [accent] trois with Christabel, Lady
Aberconway. And what enchantment that proved to be.

For one thing she knew how to make an entry to effect, even though she's short in stature, arriving with one hand engulfed in a vast fur muff and the other resting on the gold and onyx handle of her walking stick...

This account, Roy tells me, is the one where everything gets going. It covers three pages, and all these years later, almost word for word, he re-describes that entry into the room, that gorgeous walking stick.

'She took a fancy to me,' he says. 'She was Samuel Courtauld's mistress, a completely mesmerising woman, adored cats, too. After lunch she took us back to her own house in North Audley Street and showed us round. "A bathroom for Venuses...a staircase for lovers..." He laughs. Well, I mean, you would remember all that!'

And he adds, 'I'm aware that Volume I records a complete world that's gone. I set out to record the passing social scene – it was an amazing period.'

Cecil Beaton, then in his sixties, was still very much part of that scene. Introduced by the ballet critic Richard (Dicky) Buckle he was to feature hugely in Roy Strong's life: the exhibition of his portraits in 1968 was both the first smash hit of his directorship and the crown of Beaton's career. Opening on 31 October, with a private view attended by the Queen Mother, it turned the Gallery into the stage set for a three-act play.

29 October
To Jan van Dorsten

And now one is on the eve of the great Beaton show and the whole of London agog for it... No one will ever be able to do a photographic exhibition again in the same way... Act I: A drawing room pre-war with a great frieze of beauties, the Queen Mother seen in the distance through a Venetian window flitting across sunlit lawns... Thirties popular music playing. Interlude: The war, a corridor of sailors, bomber pilots, etc., hung like banners; a bombed-out room... St Paul's arising from smoking ruins. Act II The Coronation. Act III A studio today, a huge studio stove, vast Beaton hat, postcard stand ten feet high with twenty photos of Marilyn Monroe slowly revolving... It will cause a furore!

Sixteen thousand visitors passed through in a fortnight. *The Sunday Mirror* billed Roy as 'the man who is giving history a facelift'. It is indeed extraordinary to think of the Gallery's embargo on the photographic portrait at last being swept away. Enter the honouring of Beaton, David Bailey everywhere, photography itself to become the medium of the age. In June, at the annual meeting of the Trustees, Roy recorded in his diary, 'I got them to agree to purchase portraits of the LIVING, an astounding change...'

In October he wrote to van Dorsten: 'I have suddenly found myself shot into the limelight as a kind of messiah of the London museums. Very dangerous, this pop idol stuff.' But he was riding high. 'I do seem to get involved with smart people these days,' he added, having the night before the private view gone to a *Vogue* party where, he recorded in the Diary, 'the *beau monde* floated by like the waves of the sea.' Among the dozens of guests were Mick Jagger, Lee Radizwill, 'stunning in Courreges black and white', Noel Coward, looking 'very decayed', and David Hockney, 'with a beautiful blond Jewish boy... It was so terrific, so glamorous. And I loved every minute of it.'

A cast of thousands appears in the Diaries, the chief players identified in a list at the back of each volume. In the first, *Splendours & Miseries 1967-1987*, it runs into some hundred and fifty pages. 'Barley Alison (1920-1989) Publisher, spy and first mistress of Roy Jenkins (q.v.)' is one entry.

'The year as a whole was one long whizz,' he writes of 1968. This was the year in which he decided to ditch the sober grey suits which he – and everyone else – had always worn at the

Gallery, and wear his gorgeous evening clothes to work. In came the fedora hat, the cravat, the frock coat, the entirely individual and eccentric look. By now, inspired by those the Beatles wore for the LP sleeve of *Sergeant Pepper*, he had grown the signature moustache which he wears to this day, now accompanied by a snowy goatee beard. And from then on, he says, 'Everything took off like a rocket.'

The following year he was invited to George Weidenfeld's fiftieth birthday party, which demanded 'exotic dress'. He recorded this in the Diary: 'I went as Aubrey Beardsley's idea of the Regency in black and velvet silver spangles swagged in purple sashes and carrying a huge fur muff.'

Amidst all this glamour and exhibitionism, however, he remained deadly serious about his ambitions.

27 March 1970
To Jan van Dorsten

I have turned down everything that is showered on me in the last two months, and it is a great decision...I had no idea that being successful was so difficult to handle. However, 'No' has been firmly said to all projects, and a curtain has come down on any requests for personal coverage... I have no desire to go down in history as the young man who went around in a funny hat and wrote a few books in the early Seventies. I intend to have a long, immensely hard-working and distinguished career.

The following year was to see a huge change in his life. He had by then bought a little house in Brighton, but his working week was of course in London, and amongst the huge circle he had by now acquired he was enjoying the company of a celebrated theatre designer, Julia Trevelyan Oman. She was older by five years; like many of his friends she was from the totally different background of the upper classes, but she was also deeply involved in a world which as a boy he had longed for: the mystery and romance of the theatre. They grew close; they shared a great deal, not least that both were, deep down, very shy people. Both had been told by their families that they would never marry.

21 July 1971
I propose to Julia Trevelyan Oman

Egocentric as I am, I go through such agonies of shyness over close personal relationships. I never thought I'd ever make it. At my hurried morning prayers I can remember promising that I would do it, but never thinking that I would actually make it. We went to a terrible film premiere of *Lear*, awful and boring, and had dinner after. Then we couldn't get a taxi so we walked back through St James's Park. Suddenly we stopped by the lake and the moon shone through the trees on Buckingham Palace. Very French, we both said, and then I proposed. Julia began to cry and then we hugged and kissed each other and then tottered through the darkness to a seat... We are both so utterly shy and unprepared for this. It was a moment of the deepest happiness...

He was thirty-five, she was forty-one. The first time they met, she had watched him walking away and thought: He needs looking after. He had at last found someone with whom he could lay to rest the misery of his parents' marriage, and create a new, lastingly happy home life, and when we talk he is adamant about what that meant.

'There would never be a row about money. There'd never be a row about anything, ever. And neither of us wanted children – I really couldn't bear to have done to children what was done to me.'

In an email sent after our interview, he writes: 'I have always had a drive as a homemaker and I've always enjoyed the company of women more than men. I knew that if I married I wanted to marry someone who was a person in her own right, who had her own existence... Also I wanted to marry someone with a bond of mutual interests, as the greater part of marriage is conversation and domestic life and community of interests...in a sense it was a marriage which could have been arranged in the Victorian period... Also, as a Christian I regarded marriage as a sacrament which could not be betrayed.' And he adds, disarmingly: 'We in fact weren't really sixties people but [got] caught up in it.'

In the Diaries he always refers to their wedding as an elope-ment, which is perhaps a typical Strong way of glamourising what was simply a quiet, very private service away from the press of London. They were married on 10 September at Wilmcote church, near Stratford-upon-Avon. Father Gerard Irvine, a very good friend, officiated; David Hutt, another, was best man. All this, together with – of course – details of what he and Julia wore, is recorded in a long letter to Jan van Dorsten.

And it was to van Dorsten that he wrote in 1979 about 'all the loving kindness that we have had and have every day together, all the eating, the cooking, the washing-up, the planting and weeding, the shopping, the working, the everything – it is the most precious thing ever to be given.'

Within two years of their marriage, years in which they were both working at full-tilt in London, they bought The Laskett, an early nineteeth-century vicarage outside Hereford. Though they enter-tained a great deal there, it became, with their creation of a garden, a blessed retreat. In that same year, 1973, Strong was appointed the Director of the V&A.

He had reached the summit of his ambition, running a great museum which he had loved since boyhood. But the years he was there do reflect the splendours and miseries of the title of this first volume of the Diaries: he was to become a contentious figure, arriving in the midst of the miners' strike and later becoming embroiled in a bitter dispute between the Heath government, who demanded he make cuts, and the unions who resisted them. He eventually succeeded in wresting the Museum away from the Department of Education and Science, but the Board of Trustees who then took charge were to prove as difficult to work with, and he did make enemies. The Diaries, of course, reflect and record all this.

If the NPG was a great institution gone to sleep, the V&A was a 'closed, hermetic world'. None of the Keepers of each of the great departments spoke to one another, nor wanted to. Peter Thornton, Keeper of Woodwork, told him 'You have to earn our respect.' There was an outcry when Strong claimed a taxi fare. 'No Director had ever done such a thing before. The salary was £8500 and I was the first Director in the Museum's history not to have a private income.'

9 February 1974
To Jan van Dorsten

The first three weeks at the V&A were HELL. The dreary Civil Service-ness of it all, the terrible forms, files, signing, the filth, the smell of Jeyes Fluid, the dirty loos, all the things I can't stand, but I will change it... There are some very good young people and the point is to draw out their talent, let them have their heads, and we ought to raise the roof in a year or two. I want to get the twentieth-century into that place... I want provocative exhibitions...happenings in the quadrangle...huge catalogues...

Within that first year all this began to happen. He mounted a landmark exhibition, The Destruction of the Country House, which has never been forgotten. 'At one blow,' Roy writes in his Introduction to that year in Volume I of the Diaries, 'it removed the country house out of the political arena and into the cultural one, in which it has remained ever since as one of [this country's] achievements in the arts.'

In terms of exhibitions he was off to a flying start, and during his tenure, which lasted until 1987, he created and oversaw many others which were both popular and influential: Change & Decay: The future of our churches; The Garden: A celebration of a thousand years of British Gardening; The Way We Live Now. He was also instrumental in major acquisitions. In 1982 he was knighted. But behind the scenes things were often extremely difficult.

20 September 1975
Eighteen months on at the V&A

It has been a very tough eighteen months. I succeeded on a wave of optimism: the Pope [John Pope-Hennessy] had gone, with his remote autocratic ways and ruthlessness to the staff. But...the whole set-up was archaic from the moment I arrived. It has taken me almost a year to create an efficient, loyal team around me. [And] of all the battles those with the unions have been the most unbelievable... Their greatest objective is to achieve a union closed shop...no recruitment from outside except at the very lowest levels...no changes, no new broom, no new ideas. The Director, in short, is there to follow the policy laid down by the unions. It has been total confrontation all the way and, if lost, the Director would be reduced to being merely a cipher of the unions.

The press turned against him. Liz Forgan, who was to rise to great heights in the BBC, came for an interview which began: 'Your staff don't like you, do they?' One journalist shouted down the phone, 'We made you, Roy Strong, and now we're going to destroy you.' He was forced to make staff cuts and to close the Museum for one day a week: announcing this to the entire staff he was on the brink of tears. 'I walked away alone, broken and defeated. My world seemed in ruins.'

It took two years to get the Museum out of the DES, but even in 1985, as he later wrote: 'This was a year where I seemed to move from disaster to disaster. Having striven to remove the V&A from Government I now found myself at the mercy of an intractable and capricious Board of Trustees.' There were huge public protests at the idea of 'voluntary donations' in lieu of admissions charges which no one wanted but at one point had seemed essential to keep the ship afloat. Terence Conran was trying to get him out. He felt at a dead end.

Various possibilities came into view. Beatrix Miller, the editor of *Vogue* and for decades one of his closest friends, mooted the possibility of his taking over. There was much talk of his joining the board of the new arts complex on the South Bank; nothing came of it.

But by now he was deep into creating the garden at The Laskett. He was publishing successfully and importantly: *The English Renaissance Miniature*, the first comprehensive survey of the portrait miniature, England's unique contribution to Renaissance art, came out in 1983, fulfilling an early ambition. In 1987 he published *Gloriana: The Portraits of Elizabeth I* and *A Small Garden Designer's Handbook*: in that year, he resigned from the V&A. 'From the moment [it] was made public it was as if some terrible weight had been lifted from me.'

It was ten years before Roy Strong published the first volume of the Diaries: this, as he says now, was the etiquette of the time. 'For most people, notably political diarists, that has gone to the wall,' he writes in an email. But he wanted to publish while people still remembered who everyone was. When he did, they caused a sensation. Serial rights had been sold to the *Daily Mail*, for a whopping sum which, he says, enabled him to stay at The Laskett. They ran front-page headlines he could hardly bear to look at – 'Princess Margaret topless, that sort of thing,' he says. 'And the Museum staff all rushed out thinking it was all about them. But I'd always thought I wouldn't waste my writing skills on that lot.'

Their overall reception was very mixed, Terence Conran taking the opportunity to pronounce his directorship of the V&A a catastrophe, Sheridan Morley declaring, 'This is a major diary on a level with Harold Nicolson and Chips Channon.'

Strong himself makes a modest, cool-eyed assessment. '… although they're no masterpiece, they record a life and period. My instincts tell me that they will grow as a point of reference.'

He writes thus in the second volume, *Scenes and Apparitions: The Roy Strong Diaries 1998-2003*, which he published in 2016. By then, he had long since retired to Herefordshire. This being said, it was anything but a retirement.

'I resigned with precisely £12,000 a year,' he says, as we continue our conversation in The Laskett conservatory. He is speaking not without some bitterness, even after all this time. 'After directing two great institutions, I was effectively *dumped*. So – you just had to get on with it.'

For some time he was very involved with the Canary Wharf project: there was talk of moving the NPG out there. But what he mostly got on with was reinventing himself once more: this time as a best-selling author.

He had already published scholarly works on the Elizabethan age and portraiture; he had begun to write successful garden books. Now he began a huge project: a complete history of Britain for the general reader. *The Story of Britain* came out with much fanfare in 1998. It's a book which has really lasted: hardback and paperback are still in print. This was quickly followed by *The Spirit of Britain: A Narrative History of the Arts* (1999) and *The Artist and the Garden* (2000).

Publication, of this and much more, took him back to London, and all round the country on book tours. To say that he had begun a new, and very demanding life is an understatement: he was also involved in radio and television projects, for a long time had a column in the *Financial Times*, and all the while was entertaining at The Laskett – Antonia Fraser and Harold Pinter are divertingly described – and continuing to develop the garden. In short, he never stopped.

All of this is absorbingly recounted in *Scenes and Apparitions*. But despite the vast amount of work he was doing, this volume of the Diaries is generally characterised by a thoughtful and reflective tone, and there is often a wise judgement of people and events.

The news of the death of Princess Diana came early on a Sunday morning: 31st August, 1997. Like most people in this country, no matter what their views on the monarchy, Strong heard it with shock and disbelief.

Within the day, he was rung by *The Times* and asked to write a piece for Monday morning. He wrote of Diana as an icon: 'another message to the Palace that won't be listened to'. By mid-week, with the whole of the Mall a mass of flowers, 'there was little or no reaction from those up in Balmoral…[and] it was clear that something serious needed to be said.' On the Wednesday morning he went on the *Today* programme.

'By then I had marshalled my views: firstly that the reaction was so extreme that it revealed an emotional vacuum which no one could fill. Secondly, never had the gap between the monarchy and the people been wider… Not even was the flag at Buckingham Palace at half-mast. The lack of response was appalling…'

Since Cecil Beaton first introduced him to the Queen Mother in 1968, Strong had been both friend and close observer of the royal family; he was a knight of the realm. But none of this prevented his honest and accurate assessment of this event, and honesty and accuracy are hallmarks of his diary writing as a whole. He divides opinion, but he is who he is, unflinchingly. He is conservative: he wants to honour what was good about the past.

'My earliest awareness of anything to do with things cultural was of an England under threat,' he writes in *Self-Portrait as a*

Young Man. 'That has coloured my entire creative life…' He does rail in the second volume of the Diaries against the spin of the Blair years and what he sees as a dumbed-down denial of the past. 'New Labour may be refreshing, but they're not the Second Coming… It is so easy to destroy things but so very difficult ever to put them back.'

But he has not turned into an old fogey, and what the diaries show, as well as the ability to capture people in a sentence (John Betjeman 'a cross between Margaret Rutherford and Billy Bunter'), is an acute perception of the complexity of the individual life.

'Jennifer Jenkins [wife of Roy] was in a long black dress and wearing enormous emerald chandelier earrings. I felt her to be a sad woman with intellectual and emotional possibilities unfulfilled. It would need someone other than her husband to achieve this.'

Princess Margaret, he writes in 1975, 'is, as we all know, tiresome, spoilt, idle and irritating… She has no direction, no overriding interest.' But he also records her loneliness as her marriage to Snowdon deteriorates. 'God, what a sod *he* was,' he says in our interview, talking about people he'd deliberately excluded from the first volume for fear of litigation. 'I thought he'd be dead by the time Volume II came out, but he wasn't. I just didn't want to get into all that.'

He is always moving on the decline of cats and people: Beaton in Volume I 'a tragic, furrowed bundle' after his stroke, wrapped up to see him off with a weak little wave at the gate of his country house. He gives a fine posthumous portrait of the historian A.L. Rowse, whose *Elizabethan England* inspired him as a boy; who damned Roy's early books but later became a kind of friend.

Appraising his own life, in his late sixties, he writes in 2002 of a deep contentment, far from the madding crowd. He describes 'that unchanging day' of order and simplicity, beginning at 9 am in his Writing Room and encompassing work, jogging, meals, gardening, ending with the news at 10.00 and bed.

'I like to keep abreast of current news and gossip, but I don't want to be part of it. I don't want the London scene... I want tranquillity. I'm no longer after anything, and everything is over to a new generation.'

This was written a year before Julia fell suddenly very ill. Her diagnosis of terminal pancreatic cancer shocked them both, but the care he gave her, and her own courage, are what make up the last part of this second volume. It is, he tells me, the only time he has written about really intimate things. 'And then I did write every day, because it kind of steadied me.'

His grief at losing the great companion of his middle age, with whom he had talked endlessly, worked, entertained, and done the washing-up, is everywhere in these last long entries. Yet in the account of her death he does reveal a cast of mind in both of them which many of us might hope for in such circumstances: 'Everything was faced up to and said.'

Scenes & Apparitions concludes with her Service of Thanksgiving, held on 22 January 2004 in St Paul's, the actors' church, in Covent Garden.

The third volume of the Diaries, *Types & Shadows, 2004-2015* was published in November 2020, not without a struggle. He had begun using a laptop, and the result was short, bitty pieces, which both his editor and his agent, Felicity Bryan, told him were simply no good. It was the photographer John Swannell's cry 'But you're Mr Pepys!' which gave him the impetus to start again, and this volume is dedicated to him.

Roy's grief at Julia's death runs all the way through – 'I think of her every day' – but the writing (in a return to longhand) reflects above all else the determination to draw strength from her memory and to make his old age 'a wind-up, not a wind-down'. Making exercise a priority as the years go by, he appoints a personal trainer and learns to ride a tricycle.

These Diaries span eleven years, in which a very great deal

goes on. He weeps for Julia, but from her London workroom and the studio in The Laskett he clears out completely 'the world of Miss Havisham in which [she] liked to dwell'. This means hiring seventy skips: clearly, she was more than a bit of a hoarder.

Craving 'light, air and clarity', he has the house and garden redesigned, publishes *The Remaking of a Garden: The Laskett Transformed* and eventually opens it to the public – 'publicity, merchandise, the lot'. In 2011 there were almost three thousand visitors. There are more books, and plenty of appearances at literary festivals to promote them: *Self-Portrait as a Young Man* creates something of a storm in its revelations about his background; *A Little History of the English Country Church* (2007) becomes a much-loved bestseller.

Increasingly involved in the life of Hereford Cathedral – to which he has made very generous gifts – he would not want to miss 'the uplift of London', where he keeps a toe-hold for visits to the ballet, theatre, opera. He also travels widely: to Europe on restorative holidays with friends; to Burma (where he is relieved to see the LBT: the Last Bloody Temple) and to India, which exhilarates and distresses him. 'Calcutta is the city as car crash, bewilderingly beautiful, and outside is squalor, rubbish, chaos.' In a four-lecture tour of Rajasthan, everyone in his group falls ill.

Over three years he sits (sometimes uncomfortably but always entertainingly) in thirty guises for John Swannell's magnificent *Sir Portrait*, the subject of that 2015 exhibition at the National Portrait Gallery. This is where his astonishing career began, but he is now very glad to have left. Of the celebration dinner held to mark its 150th anniversary, he is scathing. 'All those living whose portrait is still there should have been invited. As it was, the evening was given by the rich for the rich.'

His television appearances on Channel 4 are frivolous – *The Diets that Time Forgot*, in 2008, and serious – a co-presenter of

The Genius of British Art in 2010. He does collapse from time to time, but essentially he is indefatigable, in a round of memorial services, birthday parties, special events to mark the Queen's Diamond Jubilee, dinners to mark the opening of exhibitions, and private dinners in homes which are sometimes elegant and sometimes on the edge of decay: old age can be perilous. Of Beatrix Miller, once editor of *Vogue*, whose phone calls helped to keep him going in Julia's long illness, he writes in 2004: 'I have no idea what she does all day beyond shuffling around in this shadowed limbo.'

In the autumn of 2014, 'I looked at my 1967-1987 Diaries and realised they had a wicked flare, which has gone now.' I don't think this is true. Shrewd, funny, sometimes lethal, he has lost none of his razor-sharp ability to skewer a prominent figure ('Nick Serota of the glinting, predatory eyes') but is often tender and compassionate. Entries recording the decline and death of dear old friends – Beatrix Miller, Michael Borrie – are very moving. And he is sharply observant of his times.

'This is a flashy, trashy age,' he writes in 2004. 'Where are the Isaiah Berlins, the Kenneth Clarks?' In 2011 he notes 'a gulf between rich and poor on a scale unknown since Edwardian England', and wonders, 'If university fees had existed in 1953, would I ever have gone?'

Above all, in *Types & Shadows* he is honest: about other people, and about himself. When an *Evening Standard* journalist tells him that the subtext of any interview with him is of a gay man in 'a lavender marriage', he writes simply: 'I did fall in love with Julia, and to me our marriage was sacred and in every sense fulfilling. I can write with truth that I have never been to bed with a man, but, yes, I have with a woman. But sex was never the driving force of that marriage, although it was certainly part of it.'

It was his abiding love for Julia which kept him going through the sorry saga of his attempted bequest of The Laskett to the National Trust, something she had longed for. 'I so want this to happen,' he writes in 2010, as negotiations begin. It is the start of a ride of yes-and-no which went on for a disgracefully long time, concluding in 2014 with a final No.

'I wasted four years of my old age on this,' Roy writes then. 'It is hard not to feel quite bitter about it.' But the Diaries do not end in bitterness: in 2015 the gift of The Laskett was gratefully accepted by The Royal Gardeners' Benevolent Fund, known as Perennial. It is they who will run the open house and garden – not when Roy dies, as the plan had been, but when he leaves the place, as, unexpectedly, he has done.

'Lord knows if I'll make eighty,' he had written in 2005, the year of his seventieth birthday, 'but I'm all for it if I can.' In August 2015 he did indeed make eighty, with a splash. He gave a splendid, twinkling interview to Lucy Worsley for BBC Four; he gave parties at The Laskett, and fizz and birthday cake to the entire congregation of Hereford Cathedral. Above all, there came a letter which made him burst into tears: for services to the cultural life of the country, the Queen was appointing him Companion of Honour. He threw another party at The Laskett, held in torrential rain, and the Diaries conclude with an account of the investiture at Buckingham Palace by Prince William, 'a sweet prince, thoughtful, a little shy'.

Five years have passed since then, in which Roy Strong, only a little less out and about, has continued to publish extensively. Here are the Diaries, and there, on the table in the conservatory where we talked in 2019, were the lavish colour proofs of *The Elizabethan Age: English Portraiture, 1558-1603*, greeted by the *TLS* on publication as 'this gorgeous, ardent book', surpassing all his earlier work. He was deep in *The Stuart Image*. 'I'm writing my fiftieth book, you know,' he told me. I asked if he thought of himself as primarily an historian or a diarist.

'They come together,' he said without hesitation. He's a writer – a visual, observant writer – above all. As for whether he thinks of himself as a diarist in the great tradition, 'That's for someone else to say. But I mean, if you look at the Peter Hall diaries – just dictated into a microphone. Mine are very considered pieces of writing.'

When I asked what was important to him now, with all he had achieved, he said slowly, 'Friendship. Companionship. Peace in the house. Creating an environment in the home. And a sustaining faith, I suppose. Not bad.'

He was living the life he wanted. But then something happened: in January 2020 he had a bad fall which put him into hospital and seclusion for some weeks. He could have lost his spirit, succumbing to the retreat from life which, throughout the Diaries, he has observed can happen to the old and frail. However, the dedication given to exercise over the past few years paid off: he was not frail, he recovered, and despite many slings and arrows Roy Strong has never been one to lose spirit. But he did realise that he no longer wanted to live in the isolating depths of the countryside. The next time I saw him, at a film festival in the Hereford arts centre, he had news.

'I'm leaving The Laskett! I've bought a Georgian house in Ledbury! It's given me a whole new lease of life.'

The pandemic struck. We all went into lockdown. But the purchase of the Georgian house proceeded, and as we cautiously emerged into socially-distanced meet-ups, my partner and I were invited to tea. Greeted by Roy's new, part-time house-keeper, we saw the kitchen full of boxes, the table heaped with glass and china. 'I've had enough of Victorian clutter,' Roy announced. Before we left, he took us round the ground floor, whose walls are filled with fine pictures: portraits, landscapes, miniatures, many (many) photographs of himself in costume. 'That's going, that's going, that I've sold. This is coming with me.' He would be gone by the autumn, without a backward glance. 'It's over.'

★

Ever since he worked his way through grammar school and out of the misery of his youth and childhood, Roy Strong has reinvented his life. The bitterly unhappy boy became a scholar. The shy, lonely young man, quite out of his depth with the upper-class students at Queen Mary College, turned himself into one of the most flamboyant figures of London society, an ambitious and imaginative man who brought the National Portrait Gallery out of its slumber and into a triumphant modern age.

At the V&A he created exhibitions which changed the whole face of museum culture. When his life there fell apart, he, the half-gay man who became a loving, full-time husband, began a new career as a writer and lecturer, much of whose work has reached readers in every social class. And he, whose father's rose bushes all stood in an untouchable row, became an extravagantly romantic gardener.

Through it all, since the 1960s, he has observed and chronicled society in volumes of diaries which, it is a certainty, will endure as important and wholly individual records of a vanishing world. And now, on his way to ninety, the last new life begins.

The Novelist

CHARLES PALLISER

The idea that I write in order to find things out perhaps needs some explaining, since the conventional view of the writer is of someone who has something he or she already knows and wants to communicate. Instead, as I suspect many writers do, I see the novel as a tool for making discoveries and one of the strongest motives that drives me to write is curiosity.

A wet night in November 1995: I'm giving a reading in Hackney. Afterwards, a tall man in a winter coat comes up and quietly introduces himself. 'Charles. Charles Palliser.' So modest is his demeanour, and so old the coat, that it never occurs to me that this is the author of a masterpiece.

> It must have been late autumn that year, and probably it was towards dusk for the sake of being less conspicuous. And yet a meeting between two professional people representing the chief branches of the law should surely not need to be concealed. Let us imagine, then, how Law might have waited upon Equity. Approaching a particular house in a street near Lincoln's-Inn-Fields, Law, embodied in the person of a small, pale-faced gentleman of about forty years of age with a large head, mounts the steps and rings the bell...

This is the opening of *The Quincunx*, a novel published in 1989 which received critical acclaim around the world, has sold a million copies and been translated into a dozen languages. These facts astonished its author, a university lecturer in his early forties. It had taken him twelve years to write, and a long time to find a publisher: when Canongate brought out an edition of no more than 1000 copies, he bought fifty, thinking it was going to sink without trace and wanting to be able to say, 'Look, I once published this novel.' But its success enabled him to leave the University of Strathclyde in Glasgow, where he had been teaching literature for some fifteen years, buy a house in London and settle to the life of a full-time writer. With all that that implies.

This is the opening of the second chapter:

> Our house, the garden, the village and the country for a mile or two thereabouts – this was my world, for it was all I had known, until that last summer, when a new one opened before me at Hougham...
>
> The first moment that separates itself from what had come before is late on an afternoon of cloudless sunshine when the shadows were beginning to lengthen. Tired after my play, I was swinging on the gate into the lane that ran along the side of the garden... I knew I wasn't supposed to do this, of course, and my mother had already reproved me as she sat on a garden seat at her work a few paces away... Backwards and forwards I swung, lulled by the rhythm of the squeaking hinge, with the sun warm on my face and the soft breeze carrying to me the scent of flowers and the smell of freshly cut grass...
>
> Suddenly a harsh voice that seemed to be right at my ear said: 'Stop that at once, you wicked creature. You know that ain't allowed.'

Within a few pages of *The Quincunx*, everything is set up: London, with a Dickensian dusk and an implied Dickensian disdain for the machinations of finance and the law; a quiet village where a dreamy small boy, watched over by his mother, is suddenly the victim of an act of violence. In these two opposing worlds of the novel, with a cast of countless characters, innocence and cruelty will collide, in a narrative as compelling, a plot as intricate, as anything by Wilkie Collins. There will be many acts of violence. And here in this opening are the novel's two main voices (others emerge): the one dry, ironic, omniscient, from time to time openly addressing the reader; the other a narrator with whom we identify entirely as the world of his childhood is snatched away and he enters a maze of fear and danger.

Both voices belong to the classic Victorian novel – Dickens uses them in *Bleak House*, and that vulnerable little boy at once calls Pip and David Copperfield to mind. Yet in writing *The Quincunx*, brilliant pastiche though it is, Charles Palliser intended not to mimic but subvert the conventions of Victorian fiction. In particular, as he writes in an Afterword to the Penguin edition of 1992, he wanted to break what he describes as 'the implied contract between writer and reader on which the nineteenth-century novel is based... This contract assumes that everything to do with both plot and character is eventually explained in full by a narrator or author who is completely trust-worthy... I wanted to turn that upside down...'

This is why, although many of its readers – including me – have been happy to take the novel at face value, it has also attracted those who suspect that it is more than it seems, and could be read quite differently. In the Afterword Palliser addresses all this, discussing his intentions, and its genesis and development, with one or two startling revelations.

'I write very slowly,' he said in our interview, 'and I often put things aside and come back to them, and I think that reflects my belief that the most creative part of a writer is the unconscious, and you've got to let it take its time. The passing of time will solve a lot of the problems.'

That small boy swinging on a garden gate in about 1818 is John Mellamphy, living in modest seclusion with his beloved mother Mary and their servants in the little village of Melthorpe, somewhere in the north of England. Who is his father? Who, in London, is managing his mother's financial affairs? Why is he so strictly forbidden to walk far from their quiet house?

When, one summer's day, he ventures further, he encounters a mysteriously unhappy little girl, living in the great Hall of Mompesson Park. This is Henrietta, whose story will become most fatefully entwined with his own. Meanwhile, Mary Mellamphy – 'once the adored child of a wealthy gentleman', as we learn much later – is tricked into investing in a bogus property company, and loses almost all her savings.

It gradually transpires that she is in hiding, that Mellamphy is not her real name, that through a disputed will John is heir (under certain conditions) to a great estate, and that a great many people want him dead. An attempt is made to abduct him: the pair flee to London. There, as Mary struggles to earn a living as a seamstress, they begin their descent into poverty, terror and despair.

No one they encounter – and as they cling to one another they encounter extraordinary people – can be trusted, no one is who they seem. There is blackmail and betrayal; there are names and false names, recognitions, reversals. In all this, as they move from one dreadful lodging to another, hastening through the streets, the grand houses and filthy slums of Victorian London are unforgettably evoked. This is a novel whose author had read all Dickens and much of Henry Mayhew by the age of twelve; he knows everything about the city and its malignant river.

And on the past events which so haunt the narrative, he offers different perspectives: old letters; long recountings by unsuspected people; the journal kept hidden by Mary and found by John after her death. In this, however, crucial pages are missing.

He also offers an intriguing structure. *The Quincunx* consists of five parts, each named after a family. In his quest for the missing will, for the truth about his father, and, after his mother's death, for revenge, John will meet, and find enemies, in all of them. Each has a coat of arms; each bears a quincunx, the quatre-foil symbol with a centre, as on the fifth side of a dice. It's a design which John has known all his life, 'from the crests on my mother's plates and from the Mompesson and Huffam tombs in the church at Melthorpe'. Each part consists of five long books, with one petal of the symbol on the opening page gradually acquiring the others as the book progresses; each book has five chapters.

'We must remember that a pattern – whether of past or future – is always arbitrary,' cautions a nameless voice towards the very end of the novel, '...there could always be a different one or a further elaboration of the same one.' This is perhaps one of Palliser's hints at a way in which the events of *The Quincunx*, despite all its unmaskings and explanations, could be read and interpreted differently. None the less, this is the pattern which he gave to its immense complexities, and in the Afterword he explains how he came to do so. If ever there were evidence needed of how the unconscious does its work, it is surely here.

By Christmas 1986 the Edinburgh publishers of Canongate were keen to publish, but would not commit until they had seen the final version. As it stood, the typescript was a 'sprawling randomness' of some 750,000 words. In seeking to rein it in, and give the conspiracy against John a proper shape, Palliser tried to fit it into a pattern, perhaps a mathematical structure. It failed to subdivide convincingly into the numbers three, four or six.

Then he tried the number five.

'At that moment,' he writes, 'the word "quincunx" and a striking image of the thing itself surfaced from somewhere in the recesses of my memory.' With this, he knew he had the perfect title.

Furthermore, he realised that this structure had been there all along, waiting for him to perceive it: here were five families, who would give their names to each of five parts in which their affairs were already prominent. Finally, he realised that the fact that five is an odd number meant that he had a structure with a centre. 'It was therefore not long before I had the idea of making this an empty centre and the pivot on which the book revolves in terms of both form and content: the missing sections of Mary's journal.'

Others have made of this empty centre a philosophical under-pinning of the novel: its events stand between the certainties of pre-Darwinian Victorian England and the void of a world then drained of meaning. Palliser himself aligns it with his central character: 'The linchpin of the whole novel is therefore a gap, a dizzying void of exactly the kind that John constantly fears to find beneath his feet.' And on the death of his mother John does indeed come to a bleak, almost nihilistic philosophical position, unable to believe in a God who could have allowed this to happen. As he walks through Soho, he is filled with a profound distaste for humanity as a whole:

'As I walked along I saw all those I encountered as pigs, brutal animals, self-interested creatures of mere appetite. I did not wish to belong to such a race.'

It is not until much later, when he himself is facing almost certain death, that some of his own humanity returns: he is flooded with remorse at the memory of occasions of unkindness to his mother, determined to live a better life if he survives. Which, of course, he does. But it is Palliser's feeling that he is too damaged – 'embittered and money-obsessed' is how he described it to me – to be given a happy ending.

This refusal to close the novel – as Dickens almost always does – with the satisfactions of marriage, prosperity and a bright future is one of the ways in which Charles Palliser was seeking to write 'an ironic reconstruction of the Victorian novel', as he puts it in the Afterword.

But above all, inspired by his childhood reading of Mayhew's *London Labour and the London Poor,* he wanted to give voices and validity to those poor in a way in which the conventional Victorian novel does not. There are, of course, exceptions – like Mrs Gaskell – but largely the impoverished and dispossessed are villains or figures of fun. Palliser wanted to bring them fully to life as individual human beings, as well as truly to show the conditions under which they struggled – or failed – to survive.

There is another family in *The Quincunx*. These are the Cockney Digweeds, who first make an appearance when seeking shelter from a storm in Melthorpe. Taken in by trusting Mary, they are later to play a huge part in John's life in London. And through one of them, as he was writing, Palliser had already been made strikingly aware of the power of the unconscious.

He had reached a point where John finds himself imprisoned in the madhouse where he finds his father, who shortly afterwards meets a dreadful death. ('A Victorian melodramatic absurdity,' as he said with a laugh in our interview.) How is he to escape? Palliser racked his brains. Until he knew this, the story could not proceed, and he went to bed filled with anxiety. Next morning, as he lay dozing, he heard a Cockney voice speaking in urgent tones. What was it saying?

It came again, and at last he made out 'Hide in the coffin!' It was the voice of Mrs Digweed, who was working in the asylum, and he realised what she was telling him: that John should hide in his father's coffin, soon to be borne out of the place. 'And I thought, my God, that is extraordinary,' he says now. 'And I had the answer – it came to me while I was asleep.'

Although he has never had quite such an experience again, he acknowledges in the Afterword that some of the genesis of *The Quincunx* is mysterious. Images appeared early on – a face appearing, impossibly, at a high window; another, very disturbing face, pitted and staring; a little girl on the other side of a huge wrought-iron gate, with a big house behind her. All these found their place in the drama; two were major players.

Where does the power of this novel reside? Perhaps the answer to that depends on your cast of mind. If, like its author, you are endlessly fascinated by all things cryptic – plots, puzzles, secrets and complicated solutions – you will relish its intricate construction. If you are naturally sceptical, and well versed in postmodern metafictional novels – it was reading Umberto Eco's *The Name of the Rose* which showed Palliser that he needed to raise his game – you will look further, perhaps read it again, for an alternative account of what is already a dazzling concatenation of events. Whatever kind of reader you are, you will be gripped by the story, and relish the prose.

Palliser himself is explicit about the power of his narrative hook: a child in danger, fleeing from all he has known, surrounded by enemies, telling his story from some unknown point in the future. We are, throughout, on the edge of our seats in wanting to know what happens next, something of which the author is keenly aware, and who is plotting accordingly.

But I suggest that although the drama itself is so compelling it is the individual characters through whom it is mediated who so engage and lead us on, and above all John himself, with his love and anxiety for his mother and his attraction to the pitiful Henrietta. Her sadness and vulnerability, and her lonely seclusion in the gloom of Mompesson Hall, all strike a note which is sounded nowhere else in the novel. Amidst the clamour of London, and the heaping up of terrible events, her situation is immensely sympathetic.

John, furthermore, is himself loveable and appealing: we are beside him and rooting for him at every turn. Palliser – apart from the desire to subvert the conventional happy ending – may feel that a relentless pursuit of his inheritance has made him less of a moral person, and that he is unworthy of marriage and happiness, but I would take issue with this. John may in the subtext prove to be an unreliable narrator, we may need to re-evaluate everything that has happened, but read at face value he has been through a progress of the soul, and far from craving money has now a distaste for it. And there is a real poignancy to his feelings about Mompesson Hall at the end – a place which may, or may not, ever be his.

I could see through a window in the empty, shut up mansion the branches of the great elms of the park waving gently in the wind against the pale blue sky and at that moment a great longing welled up in me to feel this place my own.

It is the power of place, and his childhood experience of being transposed from one part of the world to another, which Charles Palliser identifies as one of the things which made him a writer. We have been friends for twenty-five years. For many of those years we have together run monthly author events at the bookshop in Stoke Newington, north London, where we both, at different times, used to live. Now we live a quarter-hour's walk from one another in Highbury.

If there is an object in Charles's own house which is not a book, I have yet to see it. Not true: I have from time to time seen tea cups. We take tea – a slice of cake for me, nothing for him; milk for me, lemon for him – in one half of the long ground-floor room divided by wooden shutters. Teetering piles of paperbacks surround us; on the other side of the shutters is his study, where no doubt there are hundreds more. I have never been in there; I don't know if anyone has. The shutters to the street are also closed: it's a dark, womb-like space, where he is unendingly at work.

I am forgetting the piano, which I have seen once. A modern grand, it stands in a top-floor room (think piles of books in the hall, and on the flights of stairs) where perhaps a thousand CDs line the walls. Charles has taught himself the piano, not something which people of advancing years do easily, and is as modest and self-deprecating about this achievement as about all else. Though he talks of 'fumbling assaults', I know he is good, from what he says he is playing – Bach, Handel, Telemann, Purcell. 'The thing is that it's you making these sounds – that's where the pleasure lies.'

We talk in my house – plenty of books, but a few more bookshelves – on a summer afternoon. Children play outside in the street. One of the things we talk about is Charles's own childhood.

This, as he might understatedly express it, was not always easy, but although he is a thoughtful and eloquent talker he is not one to lay out his private life in public. Let us just say that he was born in Massachusetts of an American father and Irish mother, whose wartime marriage was not a success. They had three sons – Charles is the middle one – and separated when the children were very young. Because of this, there was a great deal of moving about.

'I suppose all one's early experiences shape you. All I can say is that I was woken at quite an early age to the differentness of different places. By the time I was eight I'd experienced three completely different cultures.' One was upper-middle-class English society in the elegance of Bath, where his (essentially Victorian) grandmother and (difficult) aunt shared a house. At different times, mother and sons lived uneasily with them.

'Bath was full of the most amazing cityscapes – you'd just go round a corner and see something extraordinary.'

When he was four or five they moved to a remote mountain village in Switzerland. 'It was such a spectacular change. I became very aware of the place – I remember standing gazing at the mountains, watching the sun rising or setting, and then of course the snow: it was an amazing experience. Apparently I was speaking fluent French, which I don't remember at all.'

His time in America could not have been more different: living on a run-down post-war public-housing estate in 'this awful decaying industrial city in Massachusetts. Though there was also the astonishing grandeur of the Connecticut River which ran through the middle of it.

'I think that being made aware at a very early age of the differentness of several places, dialects, languages, and social forms means that you don't take things for granted. You become aware that there are different options for how individuals live or societies function and your curiosity is aroused.'

What was common to all these experiences was poverty and anxiety: about money, and about family relationships. It was a fractured family, full of contrasts and powerful characters. A child of essentially gentle, philosophical temperament, Charles experienced dramatic and disturbing events. As for money: his mother – 'the sweetest person in the world' – had suffered a major accident during the war and was living on child allowance and a tiny pension, unable to work. No one, for whatever reason, was helping to support her or her children.

'You see how powerless we are without money!' John exclaims to Henrietta in *The Quincunx*. 'Is poverty so terrible?" she has asked him. 'Yes.'

Family relationships were difficult or fraught. 'I suppose the only proper loving relationship in the family was between me and my mother.' But here, too, there were distressing times: on several occasions, when she returned to America to seek a divorce, she and the little boys were separated. Charles slows right down in talking about this.

'I suppose that's always the worst thing – being separated from the person you love and feel secure with, and I suppose I always had that fear that it would keep happening. And it's part of life, but it shouldn't be part of a child's life...' But once again, he plays things down, talking about a university friend who suffered a great family loss. 'So I'm not going to claim that I had really terrible experiences.'

One other thing he recalls as having had a powerful effect on his psyche: it constitutes his first memory. This was at the age of three, when he witnessed a girl drown in the river Avon. 'I can still see her white form as she struggled in the water, and for many years that gave me nightmares even though I didn't know until much later that she'd died. I suppose that was a primal experience of some kind.' It's an experience which, trans-figured into a disturbing dream, makes an appearance in his second novel.

Life began to settle down when his mother took him and his younger brother (the older by now living with his father in America) to live in Cornwall, a place of which she had happy holiday memories as a child. Again, their arrival in this very different environment made a great impact.

'I remember that as the train approached Looe, suddenly the whole landscape opened out and I saw the river and the lake and the bridge and beyond it the painted houses of East and West Looe climbing the steep sides of the valley and further on the sea pounding against the cliffs. I was seven or eight and I remember thinking, This is an astonishing place.'

For a short time he attended 'a funny little school' in Looe, and it was here, for the first time, that he realised how much he enjoyed writing. 'We were asked to write stories, and I decided This is great fun, I want to do this. I want to become a writer.' It was when he was twelve, he writes in the Afterword to *The Quincunx*, and had devoured Dickens, that he realised not just that he wanted this, but that it was a certainty.

Devouring Dickens was a pleasurable activity he shared with his mother, and when they all moved to settle down in Truro life took on a calmer, happier tone, despite the fact that he and his brother attended 'a terrible, terrible school'. This was the run-down Cathedral School, to which they were sent out of pure snobbery by the great-aunt who was paying the fees. 'We were both bullied, my brother and I, and the teaching was absolutely awful, but because we were both academic we survived.'

At home, he was reading voraciously, not only Dickens but most of the children's classics: Stevenson, H.G. Wells, Sherlock Holmes, Arthur Ransome, Philippa Pearce. With a troubled background, was he seeking and loving getting lost in reading?

'I think that was a large part of it. I don't want to exaggerate the difficulties I faced because my mother and I had an extremely close, loving, talkative relationship, and we read and discussed books together. But yes, for anyone who becomes a writer books are an alternative reality. A better reality. Or a worse reality, because that's important, too: you live through other people's appalling experiences and then you come back to the real world and feel very grateful to have warm clothes and three meals a day.'

A-levels arrived. 'And I just thought, I must do well because it's all down to me and so I worked very, very hard, and set my sights on Oxford or Cambridge.' He got in to Exeter College, Oxford, 'and that was a turning point. I thought then that things could be all right for the three of us. As they turned out to be.'

He graduated with a First in English and subsequently moved to Wolfson College, Oxford, and gained a B. Litt. in Modern English Literature.

He then lectured for a year at Huddersfield Polytechnic and in 1974 took up his post at Strathclyde. 'Earning a living by teaching literature was paradise for me.' By then, he was already writing seriously.

There are two major elements in Charles Palliser's novels. One is his love of the cryptic. Driven by curiosity, as he writes in the Afterword to *The Quincunx*, he delights in devising plots whose solutions demand a great deal both of him and of the reader. He himself doesn't know how a novel is going to end, although he works out almost everything before he begins to write – an extremely detailed, intricate synopsis, in effect. When this is done, 'I write the thing, and only then fill in the last movement.' I ask where all this interest in clues and complication comes from, and he laughs and says he wonders if it goes back to the fact that one of the interests he shared with his sweet and gentle mother was murder.

'We loved cases where there was mystery about the identity or motive of the murderer because that made it an issue of psychology. We would read and discuss a book about a particular case and I think it was the fascination of not knowing for sure what the truth was that gripped me. That, I suppose, became the guiding principle of the way I write: You don't disclose everything so that the reader has to collaborate in the novel. And the mystery can work at different levels: the literal level of what has happened and the meta-level of how and why the story is being told.'

Is unreliable narration at the heart of his work? He prefers the term 'compromised narration', an idea which he has made his own. 'I do think that almost any voice you're reading in a novel should be compromised; that is to say, the reader ought to have to put it through some kind of reinterpretation, even if it's very minimal.'

The other notable thing about his fiction is how truly violent and shocking much of it is. Somehow in *The Quincunx* – perhaps because we have the safety of knowing that a first-person narrator must survive in order to tell his story – the effect is not as chilling as in other books. But in *Betrayals* (1994), his third novel, and *Rustication* (2013), the most recent, there are scenes which almost unbearable to read. I think of the torture and dismemberment of a young African in *Betrayals*. And the language of the poison-pen letters in *Rustication* is unimaginable in *The Quincunx*, which, subversion of the genre or no, does preserve some of the decorum of the nineteenth-century novel. In *Rustication*:

> *You think you can fuck any girl you like and just walk away because of who you are... I am going to kill you but before I do that I am going to hurt you so badly you will scream for mercy. You are so proud of your cock. See if it will get you an heir when it's stuffed down your lying throat!* [sic italics]

Charles is a courteous, kind and generous person who endured and came through distressing, even terrifying events as a child. What lies behind this aspect of his work?

'When I was a child I had the belief that if I imagined in great detail something which I was terrified might happen, it wouldn't happen,' he says. 'Because it would be too improbable for it to occur exactly as I had foreseen it. So it was a kind of superstitious magic, in a way. I thought of things like being separated from my mother, which did keep happening, and I'd imagine in detail some horrible way it might come about and then I'd think: now that I've invented it, that can't happen. But, of course, it did. And I think my writing is a bit like that. If I think of really awful things, and describe them, I'm keeping them at a distance, I'm somehow protecting myself from them.'

I think about this for quite a while after our interview is over. And I think – as Charles himself must have done – about the core relationship in *The Quincunx*: a loving mother and child in such poverty and danger. I recall, too, something else Charles says when I ask what it's like to spend time writing about very dark, violent things.

'It feels odd to say it, but I feel I am distancing myself from it while I'm writing it. It's as if I'm saying, This is the monster, and I've got the upper hand now.'

How do you follow a book like *The Quincunx*? By the time it was published, Charles had almost completed his second novel, *The Sensationist* (1991) and decided to publish it 'to make clear to myself and to others that I was not going to produce big historical epics for the rest of my life'. He thought at the time that the two novels could not have been more different; subsequently he began to see similarities.

We spend quite a long time talking about this slender novel. Spare and elliptical, presented in sixteen short chapters, the dialogue without quotation marks, it refuses to orientate the reader but has a haunting power.

In dark wet autumn weather, a young man arrives in an unnamed, unstable city. There are mountains: it feels mittel-European. Gradually we realise – heather, a loch – that we are in Scotland, but the place is made all the more uneasy for its Kafkaesque anonymity. The man, eventually named as David, has come to take up a job of which we learn nothing, save that he is working on 'the concept'.

'We're in the business of foreseeing the unforeseeable,' a colleague tells him, an idea which is returned to over and over again in the novel. Bit by bit his place in the company is eroded. He works alone in the silent building at weekends. He applies for a promotion and doesn't get it. The company collapses.

'A lot of money was involved. Of course, it wasn't down only to him. Nobody could have predicted how the systems would behave under those conditions. But then, he supposed, you could say he was paid to predict that...'

He is isolated; he has failed to predict. These two themes are played out obsessively in the foreground of the novel, in which David drifts in and out of beds and parties in a city of warehouses and tenements, elegant parks and squares, having sex with any number of anonymous young women. There's a lot of drink, drugs, groups and hazy stuff. One of these women, a painter met at a gallery, becomes a more serious lover.

Lucy is highly strung, intense, unpredictable; she has a little girl. As their relationship intensifies, repeatedly falls apart and is rekindled; as David falls in and out of love with her, and sleeps with other women, he reflects endlessly on the part he might have played in the climax of events.

'How could I have known? Was I responsible for what happened?'

'What I did was harmless enough. No worse than many. Nobody ought to have got hurt...'

'How could I have predicted it? Was it my job to foresee the unforeseeable? And yet I can't help blaming myself.'

Dark notes are sounded from the beginning. The first night of his arrival he dreams of an old school friend, someone he has barely thought of for years, whom he now sees 'drowning in front of him, crying out speechlessly, his white legs descending an invisible stairway'. He has other nightmares, of the city collapsing, of rot and decay. He is woken 'by cries of pain or rage in the street'. A mouse threshes wildly, caught in a trap. Despite all this, the real horror of the ending is something the reader can predict only in the last few pages.

The Sensationist began with a dream, though not the one David has on the night of his arrival, of a schoolfriend drowning. Charles acknowledges that this 'might be a kind of echo' of the girl he saw struggling in a river when he was such a young child, but talks more of the dream he had about the shock of moving to Glasgow – another great move in his life, recalling those contrasted city and landscapes of his early boyhood.

'It was a vision of being out of place, and scared, and wondering what am I doing here, how can I make sense of this? That's how I felt about finding myself in Glasgow, for a long time.'

As in *The Quincunx*, a young man is on his own in an alien city; both novels offer at times a profound disgust with humanity; both end with a sorrowful exchange between a man and woman who once were close, but who have no chance of a future.

The novel is suffused with anomie; David's voice and perception are bleak. But it also has a melancholy beauty, deriving from the taut, declarative prose.

> They had reached the edge of the water whose surface was metallic grey. There was no wind and the water rippled like the veins on the back of an ancient hand.

> Beyond he could see the glitter of other waters... The
> clarity of the light gave the landscape the vividness of a
> dream.

'Every sentence was agony,' Charles recalls, 'because I was
trying to pare it down and make it striking, visually striking. And
trying to evoke a consciousness that was very different from
mine.'

The Sensationist was published to considerable acclaim. 'Here
are passion and despair in all their tragic glory... Here is a novelist who should never stop,' said the *Independent*. The *Scotsman*
thought it 'a dazzling performance which leaves one wondering
whose voice he will employ next, or whether this is perhaps his
own.'

This was a remark which found an unfortunate echo in a
number of readers who, says Charles, 'simply loathed' the book.
Perhaps many were disappointed not to be continuing their
immersion in a Victorian novel. *City Limits* seems to have been
the only publication to realise that *The Sensationist* confronts the
reader with 'the inescapable vacuity of contemporary Britain'.
But far from seeing the novel as a Swiftian morality tale, many
did indeed mistake the central character for its author.

'How can you sleep under the same roof as That Man?'
someone asked a female lodger living in his London house.

One might say that such a reaction is a tribute to the power of
the voice which Palliser has created. In his next novel he tried
any number of voices.

Betrayals (1994) consists of a series of interlinked macabre and
vengeful stories, each told by the most unreliable of narrators.
Often very funny, it uses frame after frame like a Russian doll,
requiring every detective skill the reader might possess. Literary
sophistication – or post-modern tricksiness – doesn't begin to
describe it. Clever clogs might be one description, and the book

itself now and then refers to things being too clever by half. Playing with genre, referencing everything from Jack the Ripper to Jeffrey Archer, via freemasonry, academic life and the self-destructive scorpion, it has been compared to Nabokov and John Barth. Its American publishers called it 'an astonishing virtuoso by a modern master'; many critics in this country admired it. How had Charles done it all?

'I do remember it was very, very hard work. I don't know if I bit off more than I could chew but it was probably more than most readers were prepared to chew. I was intrigued by the idea of a novel where the same stories and motifs are broken up in order to be reassembled and reappear in a different context so that the solution to one mystery will be in a completely different story, set in a different country, and perhaps even in a totally different time... The central idea is that revenge is self-destructive. I use the image of the scorpion that stings itself to death. It's my belief that malignancy is always its own punishment. That evil is the consequence of unhappiness.'

Much of the novel is parody or pastiche: it is in one, Kiplingesque story that, as I said earlier, an African boy is tortured and dismembered. In our discussion, Charles reveals that he had thought of this as a parody of literary theory's dismemberment of the text – 'killing the thing they're trying to deal with', something which he felt had got out of control by the time he left Strathclyde.

'I suppose the book is about revenge, and the only way to escape from someone who has done you wrong is to more or less forgive them... I'm not saying that I've always forgiven people who've done me wrong, but – ' he begins to laugh, 'I can at least see that that's what you ought to do.'

Not every critic loved *Betrayals*. In a long piece in the *London Review of Books* Jonathan Coe, a huge admirer of *The Quincunx*, looked at Palliser's work to date and found this third novel both overcomplicated and philosophically unsound. He pointed out that *The Quincunx* was written out of love and admiration for the Victorian novel, even as it sought to challenge its conventions, and that many readers, sharing these feelings, would probably feel excluded by *Betrayals*, and be only too happy for the author to give them *Quincunx 2*.

'I think one of the problems for me is that my books are so different that I don't really fit into any genre,' says Charles now. 'Was *The Quincunx* a literary novel or a pastiche that just tried to tell a good story? I think you do pay a price if you don't put yourself in a pigeonhole.'

It was five years before he published another novel. In many readers' eyes *The Unburied* (1999) was a return to that which they felt he did best: an atmospheric Victorian Gothic murder mystery.

Set in a country cathedral town in the winter of 1881, the novel features Edward Courtine, a lonely Oxford historian; the old college friend who once betrayed him; a miserly banker who is bludgeoned to death and, once more, a contested will and a question of large inheritance. Layered into the drama are Courtine's research into a questionable incident in the life of King Alfred; the town ghost, a man murdered in the Civil War; and the possibility of another, more recent murder within the gloomy cathedral.

There is much to be solved, in an atmosphere of mist, lamplight, bitter cold, distant choral voices and night-time assignations. The infinitely complex plot rests on documents and keys, but also contains more human moments in Courtine's recovery from a broken heart. It is his quiet voice which leads the reader on – with a thrilling court scene in which he is far from quiet – and the novel as a whole is reflective as much as it is dramatic.

'People think of my three novels, *The Quincunx*, *The Unburied* and *Rustication* as belonging in some way to the category of the imitation Victorian novel,' says Charles, 'but I think of them as being incredibly different. For a start, they're set in such different periods – it's like saying that a novel set in 1920 is like one set in 1964. Because it's our own era, we can see how different those periods are.'

This is a remark which perhaps asks quite a lot of the general reader of the Victorian age, and even the literary critic.

'But also,' he adds, 'the structure and tone of voice are totally different in each of them.' Having said this, he does identify parallels between his second and his most recent novel. 'In a way you might say that *Rustication* has more in common with *The Sensationist* then the other "Victorian" novels: an intense vision from the limited point of view of a young male, who is obsessed by drugs and sex, and so on – but they're set in such different periods that readers wouldn't think of connecting them.'

Rustication was launched with a big drinks party at Daunt's Marylebone Bookshop in the autumn of 2013. The atmosphere was buoyant: this was Charles Palliser's first novel for fifteen years, published by Norton on both sides of the Atlantic, and it drew attention.

> It is December 1863, dark, dank and ominous, and to a decayed and apparently haunted house in the Kentish marshlands journeys Richard Shenstone, lately sent down from Cambridge for smoking opium and being involved, in some as yet unexplained way, in the suicide of a similarly intoxicated friend.

This is D.J. Taylor, writing in the *Spectator* of Palliser's darkest novel yet. In the story of a young man in disgrace, told through his feverish diary entries, obscene poison-pen letters, animal mutilation and a brutal murder combine to create terror in the local community of village and country town. As an incomer, Richard will find himself chief suspect.

Like almost all the other reviews, Taylor's opened with *The Quincunx*, and if Charles feels that general readers ignore the different periods in which his nineteenth-century novels are set then he is up against astute critics who make no such distinction either. But Taylor, writing of an author who had virtually inaugurated the genre of 'neo-Victorian literature', was mostly admiring, like most other critics. In this novel the author had created through his masterly handling of suspense 'an exercise in pure form', a remark which must have pleased Charles, who talked in our interview of how much he thinks about structure and technique. 'That's one of the great pleasures of writing a novel: the quest to find out how to match the content with the technique.'

The *Independent* wrote of 'the nasty underbelly of Victorian society' being revealed – as of course it was in both *The Quincunx* and *The Unburied*. The novel was 'Dickens without sentimentality or euphemism'. But it also talked perceptively of 'another great Victorian terror, that of social rejection', and the novel is indeed charged by the slights, cuts and outright disdain by the local gentry which torment Richard's impoverished widowed mother and ambitious older sister. Richard himself transgresses all of this by having sex with their little servant Betsy, in a relationship which by the end has become something of a real love affair. A largely unhinged young man, forced to confront shocking revelations about his family's past, as well as his own failings, he is, Charles feels, redeemed by almost the only character in the novel who has some goodness in her. Not one of his reviews discussed redemption.

At the beginning of this essay I referred to Charles settling to the life of a full-time writer. The life of a full-time writer is tough. So are a lot of jobs, but writing, with its swathes of solitude, and endless room for doubt, perhaps makes particular demands. The days when writers could hope to be taken on by a publisher in early days and nurtured, perhaps for years, until they fulfilled their promise, have largely gone, although there are, of course, laudable exceptions: Headline's long and fruitful relationship with Andrea Levy was one.

In the thirty years since *The Quincunx* was published there have been many literary flashes in the pan, and seismic shifts in publishing. Astonishing advances are still paid, but to far fewer authors, and even those who once commanded six figures can find themselves after some years living on tea and toast. Many once-acclaimed writers can no longer find a publisher, and this – I have it on good authority – includes not a few who were once on the Booker shortlist. You are only as good not so much as your last book, but your last sales figures. From time spent on both sides of literary life, I have a theory. No publisher or agent really understands an author, and vice versa: our lives are just so different.

The Society of Authors, where Charles has in recent years been active, exists to try to interpret the one to the other. And teaching has offered salvation: the proliferation of creative writing courses up and down the country has benefitted a great many writers, as well as gifted students. The other good news is that the small independent publishers – Serpent's Tail, And Other Stories, Galley Beggar Press, Blue Moose and many others, not to mention the publishers of this very book, have often been the ones to take on the unknown author, publish the debut novel, and see both win a major prize. There is also, of course, the growth of crowd-funding, Unbound an honourable leader here, and the whole world of online and self-publishing.

In the midst of all this, where is Charles Palliser? It was a small independent publisher, Canongate of Edinburgh – now hugely respected – who bravely took on his first novel, and saw its fabulous success. Has it overshadowed all his other work? If the answer to this is yes, it has not deflected him from writing what he wants to write. And what is that? Talking to him I am aware of several important things in his life and work.

One is that he is constantly thinking about the relationship between writer and reader. The curiosity of which he wrote in *The Quincunx* Afterword relates not only to his own drive to explore different ways of telling a story, but to the desire to tantalise the reader's curiosity. 'I like devising a strong narrative,' he says, 'putting my characters into a difficult situation which they've got to negotiate their way out of by a series of surprising and audacious, unpredictable moves.' Through these moves and discoveries, he likes to keep the reader guessing ahead, anticipating – 'to be intrigued but not baffled'.

I note that *The Sensationist* is the only one of his five novels not to be told in the first person, and even here the third-person perspective is so limited that you are right inside the mind of the main character. All his narrators are male, whether a lonely middle-aged don, a man on his own in an alien city, a scheming serial killer, drug-addicted student or the desperate young son of a naive and trusting mother. And almost all call into question the nature of the story they tell: they are unreliable, or compromised: they demand that the reader burrow through layers of plot and meaning.

As for meaning, it seems that the morality of the individual is essentially what interests Charles in all his work. He talks of revenge being its own punishment; of the corruption that the obsessive quest for money brings; of the importance of forgiveness; of redemption through love.

This last feels an extraordinary phrase to associate with a writer whose subject matter is often so dark, but, like most serious writers, he is holding dark matter up to the light, exposing it for what it is.

Finally, I'm aware of his childhood: of the power of place, and the ways in which the different places he experienced awakened his visual imagination. 'I have the sense when I'm writing that I've got to give the reader the pictures, the material to have the pictures in their own head.' And I think of all that early uprooting, and fear and loss, and how his work reflects not only a ferocious intellect, but the fear, loss and danger which he writes about in order – among other things –– to keep it at bay.

Where is he now, six years on from the publication of his last novel? Living quietly, but very much out and about; playing the piano; at work on many things. A writer who is often engaged with more than one project at any one time, he has had plays performed in the past on stage and radio, and is working on another one now. There are two or three novels on the go, at different stages, in different computer files, in the quiet, solitary, shuttered space of his study.

'I'm writing what I want to write, and loving it. The important thing is to enjoy what you're doing, and I am. If I suddenly found that I no longer wanted to write, I can't imagine what I'd do with my time.'

The Translator

ANTONY WOOD

Hazel Wood

It's a creation – like an explorer, or a geologist, searching for the ore inside the rock, getting through the outer layers to get to the original writer's secret. You have to recreate, *not reproduce. Translation is a new beginning.*

His study is right at the top of a four-storey late-Victorian house: quite a climb, especially in your eighties. The desk in the gabled window overlooks a tree-lined street; upon it this summer afternoon in 2019, amidst much else, are the proofs of website revisions for Angel Classics, the tiny publishing company Antony Wood founded in 1982 'to push back the frontiers of world literature'. It was a move which raised eyebrows, he recalls. 'In those days, publishing translations was thought of as a nut's game.'

A lot has changed since then: high-profile prizes, many more translations published by much larger companies, much more reviewing and attention in general. Antony was a pioneer, and Angel Classics, 'dedicated to casting foreign fiction and poetry into live, convincing, lasting English form', lives on, with thirty titles still in print. They range from work by leading German and Russian authors to lesser-known classics from less familiar languages: Modern Greek (the early Modernist K. Theotokis) and Danish (two selections of adult novellas and short stories by Hans Christian Andersen).

Antony shows me a vast old ledger, bound in green, in which for years he has meticulously kept Angel Classics' accounts. And here, in a crammed bookcase, are rows of Angel Books: Pushkin, *Mozart & Salieri, The Little Tragedies* and *The Tales of Belkin*; Dostoevsky, *The Village of Stepanchikovo*; Ivan Bunin, *Long Ago*; Heinrich Heine, *Deutschland: A Winter's Tale.* There are trans-lations of Goethe, Theodor Fontaine, Theodor Storm, Schnitzler, Tagore.

For decades, from up in this gabled attic, Antony has run two careers: as publisher and as translator. And here on his computer this very afternoon is an email from Penguin acknowledging receipt of the typescript of *Alexander Pushkin: Selected Poetry*. The crown of his achievement as translator of Pushkin, the volume represents the work of almost half a century. It contains the most lucid and engaging Introduction, and eighty-two lyric and ten narrative poems, including *The Bronze Horseman, The Gypsies, Count Nulin* and *The Tale of the Golden Cockerel.* We do not know it now, but in 2020 this book will win a major prize.

I look round this crowded place before we settle down to talk. Pleasingly old spines run along the bookshelves, with a row of stoutly-bound dictionaries including a multi-volume one 'of the language of Pushkin'. The poet's works in many original editions and translations run along two shelves. Vladimir Nabokov's edition of *Eugene Onegin,* in four volumes, famous for its treasure-trove of notes, occupies a higher one.

Other shelves are crammed end to end: Russian essays on Pushkin; editions of Turgenev, Gogol, Chekhov, Solzhenitsyn and a mix of Tennyson, Yeats, T.S. Eliot, Virgil, Horace, Goethe. There are rows of reference books, of dictionaries – Russian, German, French and English. There are also heaps of files piled on top of an old concealed sink. Waste-paper baskets and filing cabinets overflow; there's a lot of stuff on the floor. A very great deal is going on in here.

Some of Angel books are also on my shelves at home: gifts on publication down the years. But although Antony, his wife and I have been friends for so long, in and out of each other's houses, I haven't been up here since 1988.

In that year, Antony asked me to proof-read a new edition of poems by Osip Mandelstam (1891-1938) the great Russian poet, contemporary of Akhmatova, Pasternak and Marina Tsveteyava, who perished in a Stalinist transit camp. He may have asked me to do this out of the kindness of his heart. Living with my partner and our little boy in a small flat round the corner, I didn't have much money, nor much space, and, thanks to more kindness from him and his wife Hazel, was writing my first novel in the basement of this house, surrounded by bicycles and spiders. Maps of wartime Warsaw were taped to the wall; for two playgroup hours each morning, I inhabited a different world.

A great deal has happened to both our families since then, but nothing has ever taken Antony (for the purpose of this essay I shall now call him AW) from the work which for many years has nurtured, inspired and sustained him: his own translations of Alexander Pushkin. They are creations of great beauty, power and vitality.

> Time to be off! Loud blows the horn;
> The whippers-in in hunting dress
> Have mounted promptly with the dawn,
> The close-leashed borzois prance and press.
> The master of the house appears,
> And pausing in the porch awhile
> He looks about; his visage bears
> A proud, proprietorial smile.
> He wears a fastened Cossack coat
> With sash in which a blade is stowed,
> A rum-flask hangs below his throat,
> A horn upon a bronzen chain.
> His blear-eyed wife, in cap and shawl,
> Looks from her window, vexed, it's plain,
> By all the din and caterwaul...
> They bring the master of the house
> His mount; he grabs the withers, gets
> Foot firmly in the stirrup, shouts
> Not to wait up – and off he sets.

This is the opening of *Count Nulin*, a narrative poem published by Pushkin in 1825. You need know nothing about the subject (a parody of Shakespeare's *The Rape of Lucrece*), nor the poet himself, to be at once engaged by the energy, rhythm and straightforward humanity of these lines in AW's translation. Here he stands, the master of the house, in his Cossack coat, with his beaming smile and grumpy wife (soon to be discovered reading a romantic novel instead of feeding the geese), the horses and dogs of the hunt pressing all around. Up he swings into the saddle, and away he goes. It has a terrific immediacy.

There are two leading points to be made about Pushkin. One is how little known he is in this country. Everyone has heard of *Eugene Onegin*, but although there have been celebrated translations few people could quote from it, or tell you much about the author beyond the fact that he died much too young, in a duel.

In contrast, it is impossible to overestimate the regard with which he is held in Russia. He is to Russian readers and writers as Chaucer and Shakespeare are in England, and more: he has penetrated every layer of society.

> In Russian culture, Pushkin is all-important, omnipresent, taken for granted – and often barely noticeable, like the air we breathe. A Russian's first encounter with Pushkin is likely to be as a child: "Who is going to close the door after you – Pushkin?!" He is a sort of domestic god... [He] wrote in every genre and style, was Russia's paramount poet, publisher, pornographer, rebel, pragmatist, lover, duellist, jokester, victim, Christ-figure; he even had the foresight of securing an ethnically correct – African – descent... Russians are puzzled to discover that Pushkin is not a household word in the West...

This is the translator Alexander Zholkovsky, in his essay 'Pushkin under our Skin', published in *Alexander Pushkin: A celebration of Russia's best-loved writer*, a lively collection of essays edited in 1999 by A.D. Briggs for the bicentenary of Pushkin's birth. Here, distinguished translators, including AW, discuss their often passionate relationship with the poet.

Reading Zholkovsky's words I am reminded of the summer of 2008, when I travelled by train through the Baltic States with my friend Ruth Pavey. Our first country was Lithuania, where Ruth assigned to herself the role of stork-spotter, counting over fifty in the gentle farming countryside through which we passed. From Vilnius, the capital, we set forth by taxi one sunny morning to visit the Literary Museum of Alexander Pushkin, located outside the city in an old manor house which once belonged to the poet's son.

Our driver, a man of some size in his fifties, with a thick white moustache, was kindly and conversational in halting English. He told us his name was Tadeusz. When we arrived at the gates, he got out and accompanied us into the empty lodge, from where a woodland path led down to the house itself. It was very hot. All at once Tadeusz spread wide his arms and in that echoing little building, sweat staining his blue cotton shirt, he burst into declamation: verses from *Eugene Onegin*. He had learned it at school; clearly, it meant everything to him.

Alexander Pushkin (1799-1837) was born into the Golden Age of Russian literature, and became its supreme artist. *Eugene Onegin* (1833) is his masterpiece: a novel in verse – sonnet-like stanzas, indeed, a startlingly original form – which moves from the glittering balls and ballets of St Petersburg to the great lonely stretches of the countryside, where estates are farmed by peasants and run by men with libraries.

In its long tragic story of love unrequited, and love too late discovered, evocatively set against the passing of the seasons, Pushkin notices every detail of Russian life: the way a young man flicks back his hair as he ascends a marble staircase; the hiss of the evening samovar on a gleaming table; the little feet of a girl at a dance; the sound of a shepherd's horn in a misty valley; the way a heavy goose struggles to gain purchase on the ice.

Above all, the novel conjures huge emotions experienced by

vividly realised individuals who live and breathe as we all do: it gives weight to human feeling. This was something new, just as that which Pushkin gave to the Russian language was new – indeed, as AW explains to me, transformative.

Much of his greatest work was accomplished in the six years of his exile: banished for writing verse attacking autocracy. The solitary years between 1820 and 1826 were spent in various places including Odessa and his father's family estate in Mihailovskoe, in north-west Russia. In these years he began *Eugene Onegin*, wrote the historical drama *Boris Godunov* and completed several narrative poems, including *The Gypsies* and *Count Nulin*. In all this work what he was doing to the Russian language was revolutionary.

Russian before Pushkin was 'harsh, military, ecclesiastic, impersonal': this is how AW described it our conversations for this book, up in his attic study. 'Poets were writing about weather, stone, waterfalls, battles, God.'

At the end of the eighteenth century, as he explains in the Introduction to his Penguin selection, 'the Russian language still lacked words with subjective and emotional meanings, such as "touching", "influence", "nuance", "interesting".' A new layer of words modelled on French was now being ushered into the Russian literary language: *intéressant – interesny*; *touchant – trogatelny*.

'It was Pushkin, born in the last year of that century, who most of all brought the new style into currency. In so doing, he gave Russian voice to human feelings and preoccupations. And in verse, he gave the natural rhythms of the Russian language perfect metrical form. In the words of Kyril FitzLyon, Pushkin "took a lumbering carthorse of a language and turned it into a Pegasus." The Russians have never got over this miracle.'

His life was difficult: 'raffish, unsalaried, harried and constricted by authorities... writing continuously through it all,' AW writes to me after our conversations. It was also tragically brief. In 1826 Tsar Nicholas summoned him from exile for an interview, at the end of which he pronounced him the most intelligent man in all Russia, granted him political freedom and announced that from now on he himself would become the poet's personal censor.

By 1831, when he married the beautiful Natalya Goncharova, Pushkin had completed *Onegin*, and composed *The Little Tragedies*, *Tales of Belkin* and the mock-classical verse tale *The Little House in Kolomna*. He and Natalya settled in St Petersburg; four children were to follow. An autumn in 1833 in Boldino, an obscure, run-down family estate, produced the magnificent *The Bronze Horseman* and much other verse, but on return to St Petersburg in 1833 unhappy years began: Pushkin continued to work but was plagued by debts and by anxiety about his wife's fidelity. On 27 January 1837 he was provoked into a duel, and shot in the stomach. He died two days later, at the age of thirty-seven.

It has been said that Pushkin was married to literature, that he almost walked into poetry, as if it had an existence of its own.

> His completed work, [writes Antony Wood, in the Penguin Introduction], includes over 800 lyric poems, a dozen long narrative poems (*poemy*), six folk or fairy tales (*skazki*) in verse, six verse plays, a novel in verse, a novel in prose, six short prose tales and a history of the Pugachev Rebellion.... [He] is central not only to Russian culture, but to Russian identity. He gave the Russians their own language, a classical literature, and an inspirational demonstration of human claims against state power. His extensive and varied oeuvre fertilised the soil for Russian literature throughout the rest of the nineteenth century and the next.

How did Antony himself discover him? The answer is through doing National Service. 'Pushkin saw more military action than I did,' he writes in his engaging essay 'The Carthorse, The

Posthorse and Pegasus: My Relationship with Pushkin' (1999). In 1956, before Cambridge (where he read Modern Languages, French and German, and English) AW went through the Joint Services School for Linguists, which trained Russian speakers to be called upon to interrogate prisoners in the event of war. 'But the only prisoner I found turned out to be myself,' he tells us. 'I became a prisoner of Pushkin.' He found himself in the middle of Bodmin Moor – 'a fair imitation of the Siberian steppe'. The first Russian poem he ever read was taught on this course: Lermontov's 'The Sail', a lovely thing which, some years later, he translated during what was supposed to be a sailing lesson. It is a miracle of compression: less than half the original's syllable-count.

> Lone sail against blue sea-mist:
>   what is it seeking?
>   what forsaking?
>
> Wind, waves, and bending mast:
>   not happiness...
>   not happiness.
>
> In beams of gold, on azure
>   the rebel flees
>   for stormy seas.

After Cambridge, trying out different kinds of editing jobs, AW spent a year as Editorial Secretary for *The Slavonic and East European Review*, University of London. He regards this as his academic training. It was here that he picked up a Russian school edition of *Eugene Onegin*, reading it in his bedsitter after work.

'I opened *Eugene Onegin* and was immediately captivated, although I found it difficult, largely because of vocabulary. I got on faster with it when I read and discussed it with an eighteen-year-old Russian ballerina, to whom I had been introduced to improve my Russian conversation...'

What excited him was 'the way that ordinary words are threaded through the metre, with the speech rhythm dominant, not the metre itself... Pushkin takes everyday language and lifts it to the skies. The second thing that stirred me in *Onegin* was the overwhelming sense of energy and physical concreteness...'

His next editorial job was in the uneventful 'general books department' of the popular magazine house George Newnes. 'In the same bedsitter where I found myself under the spell of Onegin and his world, I first read *The Bronze Horseman* [the dramatic narrative poem on the catastrophic flooding of St Petersburg in 1824] and it was the sonorous lofty prologue that first impelled me to try to translate Pushkin... After this first effort I embarked on *Onegin*.'

And from now on, translating Pushkin became a passion. He wanted to share it, 'with friends, family, anyone I met'. He discovered that quarto sheets could be neatly folded inside his school edition of *Onegin*, and took them out to scribble a first version of the latest passage wherever he happened to be – 'on the tube, in lunchtime pub or café, lingering in the office after work, in the loo (at home or in other people's houses)...'

By now he had moved into a two-room flat with his girlfriend Hazel, soon to be his wife, who remembers calling him in those days 'a translating machine, translating as it moved, text in hand, from one room to another'.

'Translating Pushkin became an almost secret, almost illicit pastime for me... But if my publishing career was to take off, I had to stop fiddling about with translations in my spare time... I should be researching projects, cultivating agents and experts, lunching prospective authors. So, moving to a more exciting book publisher than George Newnes, I did these necessary things, my career as a commissioning editor took off at last, and for a number of years I went about with a normal look in my eyes, having left Pushkin.'

But Pushkin did not leave him. He had been inspired; he had, essentially, fallen in love. And then, in 1982, he left John Murray and founded Angel Classics. In spite of the demands this new venture made, he finally had time in which to return to his own translations.

To render prose in another language is one thing. Constance Garnett's beloved translations of Tolstoy, Dostoyevsky and Chekhov, dating from the late nineteenth and early twentieth century, have enabled generations to feel as if they have read this great literature in the Russian of the original. Tolstoy himself praised Garnett.

But poetry makes particular demands, raises particular questions. Do you – can you – keep to the original metre? How can you – should you – find equivalents for rhyme? How do you move from a literal to a literary translation?

A good translation, AW believes, is one which makes you think the author wrote it.

'It gives a *flavour* of the original,' he says. 'It gives a character-ful form of the original. You have to *hear* – in Pushkin the sound is almost more important than the sense. Those sonorous vowels, that buzz: zh, dsh. What Nabokov called "the hum, buzz and click of vowels and consonants".'

Yet Pushkin has been described as untranslatable. What especial challenges does he present? How does AW work to render his nineteenth-century verse in the English language and idiom of the twentieth and twenty-first? Above all, what does he want the English reader to take from Pushkin?

'Poetry,' he says simply. 'Magical effect. Flavour, nuance, the architecture of the poem. If you translate him literally, it sounds flat. He used ordinary words, but the patchwork he made of them was unique.'

And as an example of how he works, he directs me to the short lyric poem 'My beauty, sing to me no more' (1828), which is filled with yearning for a past too achingly sad to revisit. Below (taken from AW's Appendix to his Penguin selection) are the first two verses, in both literal and literary translation.

Literal translation

> Do not sing, beauty, to me
> The songs of sad Georgia:
> They remind me
> Of another life and a far-off shore.
>
> Alas! They remind me,
> Your cruel melodies,
> Of the steppe, and night – and beneath the moon
> The features of a distant, poor girl.

Literary translation

> My beauty, sing to me no more
> Sad Georgian songs
> They bring to me
> Another life, a distant shore.
>
> Alas! Your cruel melodies
> Bring back to me
> The steppe, at night –
> Far off, beneath the moon, a face.

In the literal translation we have no real sense of what the Russian metre might have sounded like – only a reader of Russian could know that. In the literary translation, where AW is seeking to represent Pushkin's melodic melancholy, the first line has a rhythmic sonority and flow which are immediately beguiling. Read it aloud and at once you understand what the translator has achieved.

He has given this line an iambic cadence immediately recognisable to the English ear, even though it is in tetrameter: the translation keeps Pushkin's four beats, or stresses, as opposed to the five beats of the pentameter familiar from any English sonnet. It's as if Shakespeare's 'Shall I compare thee to a summer's day?' has been amended to 'Shall I compare thee to the sky?' AW's translated line is no less lyrical for having two syllables fewer.

Now comes the interesting bit. Instead of sailing on in the same metre as the original, AW has lopped off half a line's length in Englishing (ie 'giving English form to', a literary term more nuanced than 'translating') the middle lines of the first stanza, before returning to the full four stresses in the fourth and last line. AW is a great lopper-off of syllables. Why has he done this here?

'Pushkin's poem, in four stanzas of iambic tetrameters,' he explains, 'is a poem of rhythmic opposition and contrast, with the phrase *napominayut mne* ("they remind me") having a dominant effect. In translation the over-plentiful English syllables naturally dropped away, giving rise to a new metric pattern of longer and shorter lines. In tightening the middle two lines of each stanza, I give variety and rhythmic emphasis to the whole and bring out more strongly Pushkin's key words "bring" or "bring back to me" which occur three times in the whole poem. I follow the dynamic rather than the formal structure of the poem.'

And the greatest challenge of translating Pushkin is, he says, the challenge of translating Russian itself: the Russian language is polysyllabic, where English is full of monosyllables. (I have it on good authority that Isaiah Berlin pronounced 'epistemological' as a single syllable.) There is often, as AW puts it, 'a syllabic shortfall' from Russian to English: a Russian word contains five or six syllables, yet only one of them will be stressed. Here, for example, is a line from *Eugene Onegin*: '*Ostanovilasysa ona*' – 'She stopped'. Metre therefore needs constant thought.

Here, taken again from the Penguin Appendix, are the first six (of fourteen) lines of Pushkin's *Elegy* of 1830 in literal translation.

The madcap years' faded merriment
Weighs on me like a drunken haze.
But, like wine – the sadness of past days
In my soul, the older it stays, the stronger it gets.
My path is bleak. Toil and grief [accus.] promise me
The future's turbulent sea [nom.].

In turning them into a literary translation, AW originally short-ened Pushkin's pentameter to tetrameter, 'to avoid drag in English'. But the effect is pretty spartan.

The madcap years now gone to waste
Hang on me like a drunken haze.
But in me, sadness from the past
Strengthens, like wine, with lengthening days.
My way is bleak. Adversity
Haunts the future's heavy sea.

'I came to realise,' he writes to me, 'this was surely too controlled and impersonal, unexploratory, too pat. So I went back to Pushkin's pentameter.' The result is less terse, the longer line has more room to linger and hesitate, is more truly elegiac.

The madcap years have long since gone to waste;
They hang upon me like a drunken haze,
And deep inside me, sadness from the past
Grows in strength, like wine, with lengthening days.
The course that I must take will offer me
Troubles and toil, and a tormented sea.

Perhaps this is the place to note how continually AW revises. Over the years I have quite often woken to the sound of an A4 envelope falling on to the doormat, and found there a recent translation, hand-delivered, with a little introductory note. It is a certainty that within days this will be followed by another:

pencilled emendations to the original, with a few words of expla-
nation. And quite possibly a third, as an email attachment: *See
lines 4 and 6. What think you?*

I am tempted to say that this is the life of the translator: obsessive, unable to let go, starting up in the night with a sudden
thought, but in truth, although AW is almost emblematic in his
desire to 'get what seems to be right', it is simply the life of a
writer, where every comma counts.

Below are three recent AW versions of the opening stanza of
'Bound for your distant homeland' (1830), a love poem written
in memory of Amalia Riznich, an Italian woman who once
beguiled the author.

> Bound for your distant homeland
> You left an alien shore,
> That hour I wept before you
> Till I could weep no more.
> How I strove to keep you,
> In pleading hands grown cold;
> The torment of our parting
> I tried my best to hold.

In giving me his selection of work to read before our interview,
AW asked which I preferred, the one above, or this below:

> Bound for your distant homeland
> You left an alien shore,
> That hour I wept before you
>   To weep no more.
> I did my best to hold you
> In pleading hands grown chill,
> The torment of our parting –
>   To hold it still.

I much preferred the second, whose abruptly-appearing but
weighty short lines made me think of Hardy. It seemed that AW

was pleased with this response, but he then had a discussion with Hazel. A used A4 envelope (they are always used ones) arrived through the letterbox some days later.

> Bound for your distant homeland
> You left an alien shore,
> That hour I wept before you
> And I could weep no more.
> I did my best to hold you
> In pleading hands grown chill,
> The torment of our parting,
> I strove to hold it still.

I was sorry to see the disappearance of those Hardeyesque short lines, and said so. AW's dry response was to say he was considering my views very carefully, but I sensed that this third version would be the one he would now stay with, and I was right. Hardy was all very well, he wrote, 'but in this poem Pushkin doesn't change his rhythm in this way, so better to keep his smooth-running syllables, but make an effort to give them real weight in English. That way they don't come over as make-weight just to keep up with the polysyllabic original – which I think they do in my first version.'

AW has been translating Pushkin for some fifty years. How, I ask him, does his mind work when he is deep in this endeavour?

'I'd rather turn it around,' he writes in an email. 'When I'm on holiday, I think about Pushkin. Walking across the fields, I think about Pushkin. I can date holidays by what I was translating at the time. We were in Italy in 1991, at the moment when Communism was in the process of falling, Yeltsin was in power, there was a counter-revolution by the Communists and the Russian Parliament was set on fire. I stood outside the house we were staying in, looking out over a beautiful Tuscan landscape, reciting a new translation of a – non-political – Pushkin lyric to see how sounded.

'But to answer your question properly – when I work, I'm addressing immediate aspects of translation: thinking of rhymes, considering meaning, finding a word or a phrase, the balance of a line. Rhymes come quite early in the process and often determine how the rest of a line goes. When I began to translate seriously, I used to work from isolated word to word, rhyme to rhyme, but then I began to think in terms of whole phrases and even in whole lines at once. And often in Pushkin the commoner and more everyday the word or phrase, the better it suits. But in narrative poems – Romantic or satirical or elevated and so on – or in verse fairy tales and ballads, it tends to be more a matter of stylisation.'

And at one point in our interview he gets up and peers down at the books running along the floor beneath one of the shelves. 'The crap translator goes for the exterior: form, metre and rhyme, but misses the secret.'

'Which is?'

He begins to pull out volumes. 'You have to *recreate*, not reproduce. I'm not trying to get the exact word, but find the *feeling* which the writer might have had. Ah, here we are.' He unbends, plonks two or three books on the table, and riffles through them. 'Here. Have a look at these.' I gaze at yellowing pages.

> I thought my heart had lost the power
>   Of suffering love's gentle pain:
> I said: 'The past, the fleeting hour
>   Comes not again, comes not again.
>   'They've gone, the raptures and the longing,
>   The flattering dreams that shone so bright...'
> But as I spoke, they came back thronging,
>   Called up by Beauty's sovran might.

He points to two more versions of this poem. 'See what I mean?' And after much digging around in a filing cabinet, he pulls out his own.

The ready power of suffering
The heart, I thought, had lost;
Those days are long since over,
I said: the past is past!
Gone are the joys and heartaches,
The make-believe and dream...
But now I feel them stirring,
For beauty rules supreme.

Yes, it's a different creature. And then I ask why, although *Eugene Onegin* so inspired him when he was young, he did not attempt to scale that mountain. 'Just too much of a task. Too much going on.' And the translation in 2008 by his old friend Stanley Mitchell (I shall return to him) could not be bettered. We begin, then, to talk about the poems he has worked on, over and over, all down the years, and settle on four more to discuss.

On the principle that an opening should whet the appetite, it is openings I select, followed in some cases by later stanzas.

AUTUMN: A FRAGMENT
(1833)
I

It is October, and the lingering leaves
Are disappearing from the naked branches;
The road is glazed, the cold of autumn breathes;
The millstream still sounds loudly as it passes,
But now the pond is hard...

The poem was written, AW notes, on Pushkin's family estate of Boldino, in 'one of Pushkin's famously creative autumns'. I can remember him working on this translation in late summer while staying with us in Herefordshire many years ago. As so often, he was using the back of an envelope, followed by handwritten A4 pages, to be typed up (with emendations) on return to London.

II

> This is my season: Spring is quite the worst,
> I hate the thaw, it makes me ill – stench, mire,
> The unsettled blood ferments, I am depressed.
> The sternness of Midwinter I prefer;
> How I love its snows, when free and fast
> The sled speeds on beneath the evening star,
> When she beside you gives your hand a squeeze,
> Warm beneath fur, fresh, trembling and ablaze!

The poem is written in *ottava rima*, the eight-line stanza form in which Byron wrote *Don Juan*, which Pushkin (the 'Russian Byron', as he was dubbed earlier in his career) had read in French. AW keeps Pushkin's rhyme scheme ababababcc, but with effective half-rhymes.

'Neat rhyme to me is like a greetings card,' he says. 'All Pushkin rhymes, except when he uses blank verse, but if you can't find a decent rhyme in English, forget it – don't flog a dead horse. An indecent rhyme can do perfectly well.' The whole of this stanza is full of vitality, the last two lines filled with romantic excitement. And the pentameter is cleverly varied: the stately iambic 'The sled speeds on beneath the evening star' giving way to the insistent trochaic beat of 'Warm beneath fur, fresh, trembling and ablaze!'

'Winter Evening' was written in the last two years of Pushkin's exile on his parents' estate in Mikhaylovskoye.

WINTER EVENING

> Heavy storm clouds hide the sky,
> Whirling snowflakes wild;
> Howling like a savage beast,

Sobbing like a child,
Rustling on the withered roof
Sheaves of ancient straw,
Like some late, lost traveller,
Beating on the door.

I once told AW that I loved his verbs, which pleased him: 'Pushkin is very much a poet of verbs: people do things.' In 'Winter Evening' it's all verbs, whose power is matched with those strong, full, alternate rhymes. And the trochaic metre – the style of the Russian folk song or tale, as AW explains it – beats out the relentless onslaught of the snowstorm: '*How*ling like a savage beast...' There are only four stanzas, but by the last, though the storm is unabated, the mood has changed, as the poem's narrator calls for a tankard and drinks with his companion.

Sing to me of how the blue-tit
Dwelt beyond the sea;
How the maiden went for water
Early on the lea.

The snowflakes whirl wildly on, but the maiden and that little bird – the stuff of folk-song – lighten the heart.

'The Prophet' leapt off the page when I first read it. Pushkin was working from a new Russian Orthodox translation of the Old Testament – specifically the Book of Isaiah – when he wrote this mighty thing. He dated it 8 September 1826, the date of his meeting with Tsar Nicholas I and his release from exile.

THE PROPHET

I wandered in a lonely place;
My soul's great thirst tormented me –
And at a crossing of the ways
A six-winged seraph came to me.

[...]
And to my lips he bent, tore out
My tongue, an idle, sinful thing;
With bloody hand, in my numb mouth
He placed a serpent's sapient tongue.
And with his sword he clove my breast,
And took my trembling heart entire;
A coal alight with brilliant fire
Into my opened breast he thrust.
In that lone place I lay as dead,
And God's voice called to me, and said:
'Prophet, arise, behold and hearken:
Over the world, by sea and land,
Go, and fulfil my word unshaken,
Burn with my Word the heart of man.'

In translating the poem, AW went back to the Bible (Isaiah 6:1-10) discovering that Pushkin's verses were more violent than Isaiah's. 'The elevated level of diction was important in the translation. It has a biblical grandeur.' And was it thrilling to work on a poem of this power?

'Yes. I myself felt like a coal alight with brilliant fire.'

The Bronze Horseman: A Petersburg Tale (1833) is one of Pushkin's great narrative poems (*poemy*). It takes its title from the bronze equestrian statue of Peter the Great, commissioned by Catherine the Great and unveiled on 7 August 1782, the official centenary date of Peter's accession to the throne. Standing in a square close to the river Neva, the statue has become the emblem of St Petersburg, and in the poem is the core presence, merging into the persona of Peter himself. AW suggested in our conversation that he is almost God, and that the Prologue has echoes of Genesis. It was, we remember, this 'lofty, sonorous' prologue which first inspired him in his twenties to begin translating Pushkin.

There are three parts: the Prologue, which celebrates Peter's founding of the new capital city in 1703 – on what AW describes in the Notes to his Penguin selection as 'a desolate, unhuman-friendly spot on the Gulf of Finland' – and the dramatic two-part account of the catastrophic flood of 1824 which wreaked devastation upon it.

These events are mediated through the Everyman figure of a poor clerk, Yevgeny, who on his way home from work finds his 'age-worn little house', caught up by the furious river. After his frantic search, he is finally found drowned upon its threshold. The poem presents Peter as both the creator of a mighty city and, by building it in such a vulnerable position, the architect of its near-destruction. (Pushkin was immersed in Shakespeare when he worked on it, and its resonance with *The Tempest*, and Prospero's conjuring of the shipwrecking storm, have been noted.) Because of this it was heavily censored; only the Prologue was published in Pushkin's lifetime.

Stanley Mitchell, the acclaimed translator of *Eugene Onegin* (2008), was translating this tremendous poem for Penguin in 2011, but died before he could begin work on the narrative parts. His Prologue is published in *The Penguin Book of Russian Poetry* (2015), followed by AW's newly commissioned translation of the whole. Here is an extract from the Prologue's opening lines, introducing the reader to the 'bronze horseman', in both their versions.

Stanley Mitchell: Where desolate breakers rolled, stood he,
immersed in thought and prophecy;
and looked afar. A spacious river
flowed by before him; hurriedly
a poor boat strove in lone endeavour.
Upon the mossy, swampy shore
huts showed up blackly here and there,
the shelters of the wretched Finn;
and forest that no light came near.
[...]

A hundred years have passed since then;
a northern city, young, a wonder,
has, from the forest and the fen,
risen in majesty and splendour.

Antony Wood: Beside the watery waste He stood,
And gave himself to lofty thought.
Before his far-fixed gaze the river
Vastly stretched; a humble boat
Strove on it in lone endeavour.
Against each mossy, marshy bank
Here and there low huts showed black,
The shelters of the wretched Finn;
The ancient forest, dark and dank,
Perpetual stranger to the sun,
Sounded around[...]
[...]
A century passed. Out of the forest,
Out of the marshy waste, the fort
Grew to a city of the fairest,
Jewel and wonder of the north.

Both translations use rhyme, and half-rhyme, only intermittently; each has its power. AW and I sit side by side comparing them. We look at his half-line 'A century passed', much tighter than Mitchell's measured 'A hundred years have passed since then'. How does he account for his own choice?

'The effect should be stark and grand. Germanic military language. Peter's language was strong, and militaristic and Germanic.' AW's rendering of the paean of praise to the city which opens a new section could not be more different from Stanley Mitchell's. Here are Mitchell's first twelve lines:

I love you, miracle of Peter's,
your stern and graceful countenance,
the broad Nevà's imperial waters,
the granite blocks that line your banks,

> the railings in cast-iron muster,
> the melancholy of your nights,
> transparent twilight, moonless lustre,
> when, in my room, I use no lights
> to write and read, when massed facades
> and sleeping empty boulevards
> are clear to see, and all afire
> gleams the admiralty's spire.
> [...]

It's slow and thoughtful, almost dreamlike. Here is Antony Wood:

> I love you, Peter's grand creation,
> I love your stern and stately face,
> The Nevà in majestic motion,
> Its stretching shoreline's granite grace
> And railings of ornate cast-iron,
> I love your meditative night
> And moonless gleam so bright that I can
> Read and write without a light,
> The streets with not a soul in sight,
> The slumbering mass of every building,
> The brilliant Admiralty spire
> Clear to the eye[...]

Both poetic translators are using tetrameter, four stresses to the line, but in Wood you can really hear it beating out in affirmation, almost like a (Germanic) march.

A small thing: that playful imprecise rhyme of 'cast-iron' with 'that I can' (and enjambment) is reminiscent of Wood's light verse and clerihews, where he will quite often force a rhyme to hilarious effect.

Another small thing: Mitchell puts the stress in 'Neva' on the second syllable, Wood on the first, as in English. A footnote in *The Penguin Book of Russian Verse* (2015) where both translations appear, points this out, adding simply, 'It seemed best to accept this clash as a salutary reminder that translation inevitably entails inconsistencies.' On which note I leave comparison between these two creative artists and look a little at what AW does with the main body of the poem.

> Soon the weather grew still worse,
> The angry Neva roared and swelled
> And like a cauldron seethed and swirled;
> As if a captive beast let loose
> Fell on the city.
> [...]
> Seige! Assault! Malicious waves
> Swarm over windowsills like thieves.
> Sterns of loose careering boats
> Smash through panes.

It's marvellous stuff. AW boldly switches from Pushkin's iambic to trochaic lines, putting the stress on the first syllable of a key word in order to give the whole more force and power. As for the verbs which both he and Pushkin so relish, here is the image of the river's cruel destruction:

> A band of robbers
> Thus takes a village, slashes, clobbers,
> Smashes, wrecks and seizes; howls,
> Violence, terror, oaths and wails!

In his essay on his relationship with Pushkin (2020) AW writes eloquently of *Boris Gudonov*, Pushkin's great blank verse Shakespearian play about the sixteenth-century ruler of Russia, arguing that it shows 'reaches private passion in the inexorable river of history, the fizz and bristle of life contained within a precise, classical plan'.

On a smaller scale, the same might be said about this epic, tragic poem, in which a humble clerk loses his wife, his home, his life, in floods which might be simply nature unleashed in all its power but might also be the act of a merciless God. Either way, the ruler has done nothing to protect his people, and when Yevgeny dares to raise his fist against that towering statue:

> The awesome tsar,
> It seemed, had slowly turned his head,
> In sudden rage begun to glare...
> Headlong across the empty square
> He ran, behind him as he fled,
> Like rumbling thunder, hooves resounding
> Upon the shaken thoroughfare.
> And all night long, astride his bounding
> Steed, the Horseman, hand held high,
> Outstretched beneath the moonlit sky,
> Followed Yevgeny; and no matter
> Whither the poor madman bent
> His steps, with heavy echoing clatter
> After him the Horseman went.

AW's decades of working and re-working many of Pushkin's poems have triumphantly paid off: from sonorous Russian verse come English lines which ring out as powerfully as those resounding hooves.

Antony Wood's career has been threaded through with marks of recognition: distinguished radio and theatre productions of Pushkin in his translations; the Max Hayward Award, bestowed by Columbia University in 1987 for work in progress on Boris Gudonov; the Pushkin Medal, awarded by the Russian Government for dissemination of knowledge of Pushkin in Britain – I shall return to this.

But the crowning achievement came in September 2020, when his *Alexander Pushkin: Selected Poetry* won the $10,000 Read Russia Prize. Read Russia, founded in 2012 and based in New York, London and Moscow, is an organisation dedicated to the celebration of Russian literature and book culture. Their substantial citation for this award speaks of how the 'bold and intelligent versions delight at every page with their masterful technique and fine poetic sensibility, conveying the tender, lyrical qualities of Pushkin's verse, as well as their wit and humour, with a sustained excellence never previously attained in English...[The book] represents Antony Wood's crowning accomplishment of a lifetime dedicated to bringing Russian literature, and Pushkin's verse in particular, to a wider English-speaking audience.'

The presentation had perforce to be made online, but was no less exciting for that, and Antony was, of course, very happy. 'Tis mine, he had written to me in an email, after days of suspense.

Back to the Pushkin Medal. This honours not only translation but other ways in which knowledge of Pushkin is disseminated in Britain, and AW, the most convivial of people, has for many years delightfully organised events which bring together other translators, Russian visitors, Russians long-domiciled here, and British readers.

Pushkin House, an independent Russian cultural centre in the heart of Bloomsbury, has played a considerable role here. In the large room on its upper floor – bare floorboards; dusty but elegant square-paned windows; throne-like red and gold chairs for special people – AW has from time to time gathered an audience to hear Pushkin read in Russian and English. There are not a few fine old faces in this crowd, and occasionally a hat. You hear Russian spoken as you sit down with your glass of wine, observe embraces. There's generally quite a bit of bumbling and fumbling from AW round the microphone. Then everything quietens down and the evening begins.

The most recent of these events was a celebration of Pushkin's birth date, held in June 2018. For *Pushkin through English Poets*, AW had selected twenty-three poems (one for each

year of Pushkin's writing life) translated over the years by distinguished poets and writers: Vladimir Nabokov, Frances
Cornford, Elaine Feinstein, Christopher Reid, Seamus Heaney,
Carol Ann Duffy, Michael Frayn and more. He had assembled
six Russian readers: full-figured and fresh-faced; tall and
glamorous in heels, lipstick and jet-black hair; in clean school
shirt and trousers – this was the fourteen-year-old Vanya
Geoghegan.

The seven English readers included the poet Peter Daniels,
the actor Andrew Hawkins and Antony himself, earlier in a
backstage panic looking for his hearing-aids. He found them, he
stepped forward; there was the usual wild screech and whistle of
the mike as he tapped it. Then he bid us good evening with the
smile which is always on the edge of a laugh, and made his introductions. The readings began, first in English, then in Russian.

There is nothing to compare with the mixture of gravity and
exaltation with which those Russian poems were read –- the lilt,
the rise and fall, Nabokov's 'buzz and click of vowels and consonants'. The readers looked out over us all, their gaze fixed, it
seemed, on Pushkin and the past.

There have been other cultural exchanges. In December 1994
AW encouraged a ten-member Russian consort visiting England
to stay on for a little while in London. The consort was an
'ensemble of soloists', as they described themselves, founded in
1989 to revive neglected music of the sixteenth to eighteenth
centuries. Where were the singers going to stay, and rehearse,
and sing? AW and Hazel found room for two; others were
billeted in various assortments on his friends. We put up a tenor,
married but flirtatious. I still listen from time to time to his
thrilling voice in *The Lamentations of Jeremiah*.

These were charming people, bringing gifts of flowery tin trays,
CDs of their music, and Russian dolls. They were actually in a
state of shock: Russia under Yeltsin was invading Chechnya. The

news showed tanks, ruins after a bombing raid, people racing for cover. Here in London the choir gathered for an informal candlelit concert in one of Islington's grander houses and tried to forget all this for a while.

Over the years there have been other visitors. We once or twice had two elderly academics to stay in our house in Stoke Newington: the literary scholar Professor Leonid Asinshtein and his colleague Irena Yur'yeva, whom AW had met on a visit to Russia, came for a few days in London, working with another academic and visiting the National Gallery. The Professor was small, grey-bearded, authoritative; he did not take kindly to being given the low-status basement bedroom. Irena was a pale, gentle-mannered person in specs.

They did everything on a shoestring, making sandwiches before they left each morning, and although we sometimes cooked for them I shall not forget the suppers they made for themselves: cold boiled potatoes, thinly sliced, with hard-boiled eggs and lettuce. Leonid kept a single teabag in an inner jacket pocket which he gradually used up when he had access to hot water. It was a humbling experience. After they left, he rang from time to time from Moscow, enquiring after our health, telling us about his own, and his literary activities. They are people we should never have met but for Antony.

'Pushkin has added colour and panache to my life,' he wrote at the end of his essay of 1999, and perhaps this is the place to acknowledge everything he has himself added to the lives of his family and friends.

Christmas would not be Christmas without the adornment of a hand-written clerihew on every side-plate, nor his own birth-day without a lapidary how-it-feels ditty. He is funny and kind and clever, and extraordinarily generous with his time: in spite of everything he has on, he never refuses an invitation, nor a helping hand with the projects of others. Quite simply, he is always there. And although this is not quite the place to say so, the same is true of Hazel, literary journalist and co-editor of *Slightly Foxed: The real reader's quarterly*, and his wife of almost fifty years. They have been incomparable friends.

The Novelist & Activist

DARRAGH MARTIN

Being away from Ireland helps you look at it – Irish and irish: how can the self be bigger than the nation? I do think being away from Ireland helped me to write about it.

It is the summer of 2012. A young writer and academic has been granted a month's writing residency at the Blue Mountain Centre – 'supporting writers, artists and activists in Blue Mountain Lake, New York'. It's a place he'd describe as idyllic: a large, roomy lodge overlooking a lake filled with water lillies and set in a 1600-acre estate. Simple meals are provided; the atmosphere is calm and purposeful.

In the previous few months, a lot of this writer's life has been anything but. Since university, even since school, he has had an interest in politics and activism, most recently in the Occupy Wall Street campaign: a lot of meetings, marches and jail support. Soon, he will get involved in relief work in Brooklyn, in the wake of Hurricane Sandy.

He's secured these rare four weeks of peace in which to write and think by submitting a clever proposal: with a background in drama, and deep in a doctorate in Shakespeare studies, he will write a play which turns the little-performed *Timon of Athens* into a text for our times. In the wake of the global financial crash, *Tom of Athlone* will combine Shakespearian tragedy with a searing critique of modern capitalism.

Behind him are a good half-dozen plays he's written or co-written, directed and seen performed: hits on the fringes of Edinburgh, Adelaide, Melbourne, Georgetown and New York. He's been nominated for awards: people believe in him, and he believes in himself as a dramatist. He's also begun to see another direction: *The Keeper*, his first novel for children has just found an Irish publisher. But for now, for this precious four weeks, *Tom of Athlone* is the great new project.

He arrives. He settles into a pleasant, sunny room. When he's not writing he'll hike in the woods. Next morning, he opens his laptop, takes a breath, begins.

He sort of begins. Redrafts the outline. Starts to flesh out a scene. It doesn't quite work.

It's only Day One. It always takes a few days to get going – that moment when everything else falls away and you're lost in the thing is waiting somewhere towards Friday. A hike will shake things up.

Three weeks later he has one, terrible draft. The thing is inert, impossible. There are probably good reasons why *Timon of Athens* hasn't quite made the status of *Hamlet*. The whole *Tom of Athlone* idea was ill-judged, doomed, and no amount of reading about economics – those long, displacement-activity, wasted hours – is going to help him. He has nothing to show for three precious weeks but failure.

And then, in the last, despairing week of the residency, something happens. One morning, out walking round the lake, he has all at once the opening of a novel. He has the title, and the ending. Between them he has a central character he already knows through and through – he can hear her talking, right now. He has, incredibly, an entire cast of people taking shape in the shadows, and a terrific kick-off idea.

Back at the desk, in a sudden fever, he writes twenty-thousand words in four days. Granny Doyle, the lynchpin of the Irish Catholic family now pouring on to the page, and the lynchpin of the novel itself, would surely pronounce it a miracle.

Future Popes of Ireland, published in 2018, is Darragh Martin's debut novel. Set mostly in Dublin, where he grew up, and partly in New York, where he's studied and taught, it opens with the line which came to him like a gift, out by the Blue Mountain lake.

'It was September 1979 when Pope John Paul II brought sex to Ireland.'

The line – 'a gentle blasphemy', as one review describes it – demands unpacking. A Papal visit is never about sex, except to emphasise the values of celibacy and restraint, and indeed on this visit, the first of any Pope to Ireland, the message was about the hope for peace. But this is a novel set in Eire, and the Troubles of the North are largely offstage. Yet what drives much – by no means all – of the drama of *Future Popes of Ireland* is sex, and the suppression of its realities by the Catholic church.

Spanning the years 1979-2011, over three decades of modern Irish history, *Future Popes* is a clever, entertaining, warm-hearted book, shot through with pain and anger. Huge issues in Irish society – the law on abortion, the law on homosexuality, the climate of concealment and distress – are all within its sights, together with the roar of the Celtic Tiger and the rise of the Green Party, and all are mediated through an utterly engaging family saga. 'Think Zadie Smith, but much funnier,' said another review.

The opening scene is set in Dublin's Phoenix Park, where on 29th September 1979 Pope John Paul II celebrated Mass before more than a million people, a third of the population of Ireland.

> Granny Doyle understood his secret message immediately. An unholy trinity of evils knocked on Ireland's door (divorce! abortion! contraception!) so an army of bright young things with Miraculous Medals was required. Phoenix Park was already crammed with kids listening to the Pope's speech – chubby legs dangling around the legs of daddys; tired heads drooping against mammys – but Granny Doyle knew that none of these sticky-handed Seans or yawning Eamons would be up for the task. No, the ultimate position in the Vatican would have to come from a new generation; the Popemobile had scarcely shut its doors before the race was on to conceive the first Irish Pope.

Clutching a tiny bottle of holy water, Granny Doyle is amongst this vast press of people with her little family: her son Danny, his wife Catherine, their daughter Peg, aged four. The bottle is upheld and outstretched towards the distant figure of His Holiness as he waves his aspergillum over the joyful crowd, blessing and filling, miraculously, each one of such bottles. Granny Doyle puts back the pale blue lid and turns to her daughter-in-law, mother of just the one child.

'Sprinkle a bit of this on the bed tonight, there's a good girl.'

Catherine and Danny may or may not have obeyed this instruction, but their night is erotic and loving, and nine months later triplets arrive: three of the hundreds of babies born in the wake of that first papal visit to Ireland – including Darragh Martin – and many of them baptised John Paul. What singles out the Doyle family in this sudden spike in the birthrate is that Catherine dies in childbirth.

It is left to Granny Doyle to bring up motherless Peg and her three much younger siblings, Rosie, Damien and John Paul. Each child, crammed with the others into her three-bed house in Dunluce Crescent, will give her a different kind of trouble. Could one of them become the future pope she longs for?

A word about writers' block.

In the summer of 1973, another, very different writer took up a residency at another writers' colony: Yaddo, founded in 1900 by two billionaire idealists, and set on a great estate in Saratoga Springs, New York. This was Penelope Mortimer, a piercingly good novelist and short story writer, probably best known for *The Pumpkin Eater*. First published in 1962, the novel, about a married woman's breakdown, was made into a film starring Anne Bancroft, and is now a Penguin Modern Classic. By 1973 Penelope Mortimer was working – trying to work – on a novel called *Agatha*, expected by her publishers.

The temperature at Yaddo was in the nineties. She sat at her desk for twenty-one days. 'Thirty-five to go, and I'd written nothing...' she wrote ten years later in her memoir *About Time Too*, and went on:

> I've known torments of various sorts but none of them compares with the agony of not being able to write. What am I trying to say?... Move it about, dismember it, put it in italics, in quotes, puncture it with semi-colons, read it. It's still a cliché. Throw it out, start again. What am I trying to say? The sky is blue. The man is tall. The woman is fat. He said, she whispered, he shouted, she laughed, he mumbled, she protested, she stated. I have nothing to say.

Darragh Martin took himself out to the lake at Blue Mountain, in search of 'that lovely moment where a walk unlocks a different part of your brain'. In her own despair, Penelope Mortimer went to watch a dance class taken by the great ballet choreographer George Balanchine.

> Invertebrate dancers in ragged leg-warmers and thread-bare vests, arms like floating fronds...ran, leapt, to old pop tunes pounded out by an elderly woman on an upright piano. Balanchine, sloppy in sandals, snapped his fingers, sometimes their necks. There was a strong smell of sweat, floor polish, cigarette smoke.
>
> I don't know what happened to me during those few hours...but something broke, shifted, almost as if there had been an hormonal change. I went back to my room, pulled the paper out of the typewriter, threw it away and began *Long Distance*.
>
> Can it really have been so easy? It seemed to be. All the vague, inchoate masses of *Agatha* focused into one clear image: the room I was seeing at that moment, the woman who, at that moment, I actually was. This real place, with its people, relationships, anxieties, could expand to contain the past, even the future. The story would unravel minute by minute, each character and

incident bringing with it the shadow of its own history.
All I had to do was observe and report what happened.

With sudden but unswerving confidence, Mortimer was able to
'set facts tumbling about in time' as she moved fluidly from her
present to her darkly eventful past. *Long Distance* was published
the following year, acclaimed as containing 'some of the best
writing Mrs Mortimer has ever committed to the page'. She
herself considered it the most important achievement of her
career.

I give such space to her account of misery transformed partly
because it so mirrors what Darragh Martin experienced almost
forty years later, and partly to make a more general point. What
both these writers discovered was that the material which would
inspire them was already there, in the bloodstream, waiting to be
found. No writer can afford to ignore the power of the unconscious, however it may be unlocked: through a walk, a dream, a
dance class, any (Proustian) chance association of one thing
with another, where something – something you've always
known, perhaps – leaps all at once into life.

By the time Darragh Martin came to write his first novel he had
been away from Ireland for many years. 'Goldilocksing around
the world' is how he describes 2015, the year before he decided
to settle in London, but by then he had spent long, important
periods of time abroad, studying, writing, engaging in environmental activism.

He's a gay man of great humour, charm and drive. We met for
the first time in 2017 at Write to Life, the group within the
charity Freedom from Torture where he was working as the
administrator, and I as a volunteer writing mentor. He's tall and
quietly spoken; smiled shyly when introduced to us all as a
children's writer; had longish hair (this has changed – he has
quite a preppy haircut now) and was wearing iridescent green

nail polish. It was when he helped me in a struggle with an absurd on-line questionnaire that I realised how clever and funny he was. Within a few months, his debut adult novel had been bought by a major British publisher: in tough times, this was impressive. And when he ran a drama workshop for the first time, and had everyone completely engaged, it was clear that he was a person of substance.

He was born in 1980, the oldest of five children, growing up in the Rahenny/ Kilbarrack district of north Dublin. 'Being the eldest was fun,' he tells me in our long interview. 'I made booklets to help my younger siblings learn to read.' Two widowed grannies lived down the road, and the family visited one of them every Saturday: it was a large, close, Catholic family, for whom he retains great affection. He is godfather to his brother Brendan, fourteen years younger – 'in large families you sort of run out of godparents you can call on' – with three sisters in between.

Though he describes his school as 'pretty basic', Darragh was clearly a bright, enthusiastic student, soaking up the Irish language and Celtic myth along with the main curriculum. Much later, Celtic mythology would feed into his work as a writer, both for children and adults, but he was also very taken by animal stories – *The Animals of Farthing Wood* was one – and by what he describes as eco-non-fiction: new stories about environmental issues. These books were also to prove influential, both on his life as a considerable political and environmental activist, and on his work in drama and fiction. In 'transition year' – an extra-curricular year taken at fifteen or sixteen before studying for the Leaving Certificate – a course on global inequality made a great impact.

He became aware of Shell as a company with a troubling place in the world through the Ogoni scandal of 1995, in which an oil spill in Nigeria led to the devastation of Ogoni tribal land. A number of protesters, including the writer Ken Saro Wiwa, were executed. Darragh took part in a boycott of the local Shell petrol station, something he now describes as 'ridiculous, a failed rebellion'. None the less, his awareness of these terrible events was to feed into his first novel.

His writing life began at school. 'I was kind of precocious, entering writing competitions, writing stories: I really enjoyed that part of English from quite a young age, all those prompts – A day in the life of a stamp – I enjoyed that, and then when I was a teenager I got more into it, and into theatre.'

As a teenager he had got into something else: The Legion of Mary. Founded in Dublin in 1921, this is an international association of members of the Catholic Church who serve it on a voluntary basis. This is the sober description you find on Wikipedia. The organisation itself describes it as being 'under the powerful leadership of Mary Immaculate, Mediatrix of all Graces' which gives some insight into the world in which Darragh grew up. He joined when he was thirteen, 'one of the few people in Ireland who joined by my own volition, not forced by teachers or parents. I feel ambivalent about it. In some ways as a teenager it was a tremendously positive thing, because some of my friends now are from the Legion of Mary, and I really enjoyed the community service side of it.' He volunteered in a local nursing home: 'I loved all that – the nuns were amazing, and all the elderly men on the ward, all the talk.'

At this time in his life he was, like Damien in *Future Popes*, deeply religious, but his practice as a Catholic fed into his developing interest in theatre. 'I used to read the Rosary in church, and that gave me loads of confidence as a performer. We did a terrible, terrible play about the history of the Legion of Mary, but not having experience of anything else that was my experience of theatre – propaganda religious theatre – we didn't take it too seriously. Looking back, it was quite an intense space.'

It clearly was, but Darragh is someone who has managed to lose his faith, and loosen his ties with the Church, without the anguish which some Catholics suffer.

'It's been such a long time since I believed in God that the shadow is fairly small,' he says now. 'But I would say that while I'm personally at ease with the role of Catholicism in my life – I suppose I feel warmly towards aspects of it, and I suppose I was lucky - I remain very critical of the power of the Church in Irish history, and the Vatican's interventions in issues of personal morality – abortion, gay rights, and so on.'

With apparent ease, he lives and moves now between two worlds: the one secular, liberal-left, metropolitan, the other deeply traditional, in practice if not belief. I think he'd agree that he was formed by Catholic values. When we meet in my house to talk, he has just been home for his nephew's First Communion.

'And it is a bit of a scandal that children have to make their Communions – well, I would say maybe not scandalous, but it's not ideal having the education system so tied to the Catholic church. There's no separation between church and state. Certainly you wouldn't want the church not to be there, but I think it would be better if it was less embedded in the curriculum.'

A summer trip to Paris, made when he was seventeen, first opened his eyes to a wider world. In his first time away from home, he was staying with a friend, and working as a waiter to improve his French. He laughs. 'I remember my Granny saying: Don't go, it's full of iniquity.'

It was in his last year at school, just before final exams, that he wrote a story which raised questions he would spend a long time trying to answer.

'It was about this person saying, I am Irish, I am irish, and the capitals shifted – Irish or Ireland would be in lower case sometimes. I was thinking, How can the self be bigger than the nation?'

In 1999 Darragh went to study English and Drama at Trinity College, Dublin. He was reading widely, and had been working in a New Zealand bookshop, Unity Books, in Wellington, during the summer. Much of what he absorbed in these years, both on and off the course, he found inspirational: Virginia Woolf was important, but also Zadie Smith's first novel, *White Teeth* – 'this kind of rambunctious coming-of-age story, the idea of opposing siblings'. It was an idea which would eventually play into *Future Popes*.

In writing the novel he was also inspired by Salman Rushdie's central notion in *Midnight's Children* – of children all born at the same time, on that great stroke of midnight in 1947 when India finally gained independence. And its form intrigued him: 'that idea of being able to tell political stories through this very personal framework – that was really exciting for me.' The novels of Margaret Atwood and, later, Chimamanda Ngozi's *Half of a Yellow Sun*, which looks at the Biafran War through the eyes of several different characters, also made a great impact: 'that idea of telling political stories that are really accessible'.

At Trinity it was political realities which were beginning once again to involve him. He joined Amnesty International and took part in a campaign in support of a Chinese post-graduate student imprisoned in China. 'We had this grand idea of having this enormous envelope with a few hundred student signatures delivered to the Irish Home Office. They didn't want it.' In time, however, this student was released.

And then there was Roddy Doyle, whose novels are unputdownably personal but have, implicitly, a strong political edge. The film of *The Snapper*, the second novel in his Barrytown trilogy of working-class life, was made in Kilbarrack, near where Darragh and his family grew up.

'The parents and grandparents and the local radio stations were all talking about how Doyle's books were not a good representation of the area, but at university I thought, God, these are amazing, and that part of Dublin didn't feel represented in anything I'd read, so that was quite exciting – to see how everyday tragedies could have a space in a novel. That was a huge inspiration.'

It was while working in the Wellington bookshop that the idea of writing a novel had first begun to take shape, but at Trinity he was mostly engaged in writing and directing plays, often produced in three weeks on a shoestring budget – 'The first two I wrote were terrible.' Then, in his third year, he won a scholarship to study in Georgetown, USA.

'That was quite an important year for me as a writer. I took some really excellent classes in playwriting and directing. There was a lot more rehearsal time and money – the breathing time really helped.' And once again he became involved in activism, taking part here in demonstrations against the death penalty and the Iraq war.

His final-year dissertation at Trinity was about the ways in which Celtic myths are used in children's fiction to raise environmental issues, looking at how an appreciation of nature – often by having exciting adventures outside – was tied to campaigns against fox-hunting or for the preservation of native forest. Ancient Ireland had interested him since childhood; he'd developed 'an affinity with Celtic myth, Celtic stories, those kind of rituals'. He certainly wasn't inspired by the plays he saw in the theatres of Dublin. 'I wrote one play in college about Ireland, about Celtic myth. I wasn't interested in writing about Catholicism, and I found the Irish theatre world quite claustrophobic – I was really bored with all those kitchen-sink plays.'

He graduated in 2003, with First-Class Honours. By then, after good times in Paris, a summer in Canada and that year in Georgetown, Ireland had begun to feel pretty small.

Darragh left Ireland in 2004, and spent a year or more working his way round New Zealand and Australia – where he had friends from Georgetown – in bookshops and general temping jobs. His working life over the years is impressively varied, encompassing bookshops, 'a ridiculous gift shop', kitchen portering, bricklaying (that didn't last long) and briefly, at school, journalism: his Exam Diary for the *Irish Times* earned him a goodly sum. He's worked as a window dresser for Habitat, and in a charity; as a legal secretary and in a call centre, but the jobs he's enjoyed the most have been in theatre box offices.

And in 2004-2005, when he was travelling through New Zealand and Australia, he was writing primarily as a dramatist. The plays he wrote, performed on the fringes of Melbourne and Adelaide, as well as, later, in Edinburgh and New York ('so far off-off-Broadway it was practically in the Atlantic') show a playful, powerful, wide-ranging and surreal imagination.

An Air Balloon across Antartica (2004) is, as he describes it, about 'an explorer travelling across Antarctica in an air balloon, accompanied by the ghosts of several explorers, a hamster who wants to be a lemming, and an urn with her son's ashes'. Exploration also figures in both the epic drama *An Alphabet of Pluto* (2010) which dramatises adventures from the sixteenth century to astronauts on Pluto in 2204, and in *Why Pluto is a Planet* (2011) in which a gay teenager escapes to Pluto's underworld.

'The plays I wrote were set in space, Antarctica, anywhere but Ireland.' In truth, in his early twenties he'd had what he describes as a real aversion to thinking of himself as an Irish writer. It wasn't until his thirties, after a long absence, that he felt able to address issues which had been with him all his life.

Ireland is, of course, a country which has given the world some of its greatest literature. The huge figures of Joyce, Yeats, Beckett, O'Casey and Synge all stand behind any Irish writer, together with the moderns: William Trevor, John Banville, Brian Coffey, Edna O'Brien, Roddy Doyle, Colm Toibin, Anne Enright, Marion Keyes. And now there is a new wave, a renaissance, in which Darragh Martin belongs, together with Anna Burns, Sally Rooney, Eimar Macbride, Eoin McNamee and more.

Many of these writers have chosen to live outside Ireland, indeed you might say that exile is historically part of being an

Irish writer – for economic, social, political and artistic reasons. It's such a small country; it's been held for so long in the grip of the Catholic church.

Darragh knew, as a young man, that he wanted to leave, and he was also clear that he did not want to be part of the diaspora, recreating Ireland wherever he went. What he most wanted, after a year or more travelling and temping, was to use his brain again.

One evening in New Zealand he attended a lecture in which the Fulbright Scholarships were mentioned. In a life-changing decision, he applied, and was accepted to do an MA at Columbia University. He flew out in the autumn of 2006. There, in New York, his intellectual and artistic life were given real nourishment, and he re-immersed himself in the life of the academy, taking an MA within the Department of English and Comparative Literature which turned into a PhD.

The Master of the Rebels: Teenage Encounters with Shakespeare, 1944-2012 looked at the ways in which Shakespeare has been experienced in schools since World War II. He was asking how this experience had changed: what did it mean to be young, and exposed to Shakespeare? With the huge changes in youth culture in the twenty-first century, how have *Romeo & Juliet* and *Hamlet* shifted in their cultural meanings? How is Ophelia seen now? He included material on young adult novels inspired by Shakespeare, adaptations for children, and a chapter on children's literature and environmentalism. It sounds vibrant and important, but all he will say of it now is: 'Not my finest piece of work.'

Perhaps this is because much of his energy then was being directed towards playwriting. The PhD was funded: 'I was able to take amazing classes while being paid to do it.' He took classes with the radical playwright Charles Mee, Columbia's Professor of Theatre, alongside the MFA playwriting students while working on *The Last Brontosaurus*: a play about climate change which interwove a paleontologist with the Irish Famine. This was when he wrote *An Alphabet of Pluto*.

But he had also begun to teach, and teaching drew together major strands in his thinking. In a foundation course introducing students to the conventions of academic writing and research he developed special modules on Performance & Protest and Writing about the Environment. He devised a summer course on Literature & Climate Change, whose texts included novels by Barbara Kinsolver and Jeannette Winterson, as well as Ian McEwan's *Solar*. And between 2013 and 2015 he taught women held in Rikers Island, the large, infamously tough New York prison in the Bronx, directing a production of Macbeth interwoven with their own work. 'This was an amazing project.'

He was also writing fairy stories, contributing to collections of new Irish writing for children, as well as to academic books on teaching.

And then there were the mermaids. Google him, and you may well get 'Darragh Martin on how Catholicism was eclipsed by the Celtic Tiger and life as a drag mermaid.'

These lovely, mysterious creatures came to new, political life in the summer of 2014, on the People's Climate March through New York City. They had shiny emerald green fishy tails, sugar-pink tresses, starfish nipples. They made a lot of noise.

'I was helping with all these beautiful costumes. We announced that we were mer-people swimming through the ruins of humanity. It was a fun way to engage people in conversations about climate change and since then I've pulled out my tail and character (Crudella de Spill) for different protests or marches.'

In 2010, much of all this lay in the future. Darragh had been away from Ireland for a good six years. He had resisted writing about it, although with the collapse of the Irish economy in 2008 he had certainly thought about it. 'Immediately after the bust there was a time when things were pretty rough at home.' But in 2010 he wrote a play performed at Performance Space 122 for the first Irish Festival in New York.

This was *The Map of Lost Things*, a piece of puppet theatre in which he retold seven Celtic myths, returning to the stories and characters he'd loved since childhood. 'That was the first time I thought of myself within the Irish context, and I guess that *The Keeper* came from that. It's a story about an Irish kid in Dublin.'

There was something else: he'd turned thirty. 'And instead of keeping lots of things in the air, I wanted to do one thing well.' Settling into this first novel for children was important now: begun in Australia but completed here in New York it did quite profoundly reconnect him with Ireland, and for the established dramatist it also extended him as a writer: creating and sustaining a story in prose.

An engaging novel for nine- to twelve-year-olds, *The Keeper*, crammed as it is with all the elements of fantasy, has also the underlying values of classic children's literature, given here and there a gently modern gloss.

As it opens, Oisín, the twelve-year-old central character, is staying with his older brother Stephen and little sister Sorcha in their grandmother's house in Dublin. The middle child, he doesn't quite fit, either within the family, where Stephen mostly ignores or insults him, or at school. He's a reader, and that's not too fashionable now. When The Book of Magic leaps off one of Granny Keane's tottering piles of books and into his hands, he can't quite believe it. But a tiny inscription in green ink names him as The Book's Keeper, and from the moment he reads it, with a sense of wonder, ordinary life begins to dissolve.

The train home to their parents takes the children not to their station but to another, underwater world, the island of Tuatha Dé Danna – the people of the Celtic goddess Dana. Here, in a magical place complete with a dragon and an enchanted forest, a tremendous adventure unfolds. Sorcha is kidnapped by another figure from Celtic mythology, the evil Morrigan, a raven-goddess with dark and heartless powers. It is Oisín's quest, eventually with Stephen, but also with other inhabitants on the island, to find and rescue her.

Every trope and element of fantasy fiction is here: there are druids (one made out of smoke), alchemists, transformations, a magic sword, talismans. Not to mention seaweed stew, moonjuice, a tree house with duvets made of moss, and any number of weird lotions and potions. Not to mention the Great Irish Elk. It is imaginative, but also educative writing of a high order, introducing its young readers to the Celtic festival of Lughnasa (harvest), the season in which the drama takes place, and to a great deal of Celtic mythology. It's sprinkled with Gaelic, and includes a glossary. It's also quietly political, introducing themes of exile and home through the Nigerian Antimony, one of the children on the island.

The book is also underpinned by important and enduring values. Oisín (whose name means 'the gentle') is a lonely boy made to feel special, growing in confidence partly through the kindness of others and by his own courage. He and his brother end up as friends – for Sorcha is rescued, of course, the evil Morrigan turns out to be a lonely old woman, and the children at last return home. As for magic, it's like electricity, suddenly lighting a room: 'Everyday things were mysteries.' The Book of Magic itself is only what you make of it.

Near the end, when Stephen and Oisín fight for the last time, there's a nicely done pacifist message: 'As long as there were swords, and people willing to make them, there would always be ugliness and fighting in the world.'

Published in 2013, *The Keeper* was given a White Raven award by the Munich-based International Youth Library, and shortlisted for an Irish Book Award. It's a book which will last. Interestingly, the family structure figured in the novel – a strong, eccentric grandmother, absent parents, a trio of children, two boys and a girl – is mirrored in *The Future Popes of Ireland*.

'So I got back into Ireland through Celtic myth,' Darragh tells me. 'And then, in my thirties, I became much more interested in Ireland and questions I'd really steered away from – maybe it was through being away for so long. I do think it was being away from Ireland that made me able to write about it – I wouldn't have been ready to while I was living there in my twenties. And certainly the Peg story was about that: How can you understand a place you don't live in any more?'

It took him six years, and ten drafts of *Future Popes* to begin to answer this question.

'The Peg story.' This is where the novel all began, with those feverish twenty-thousand words written in the first person by the young woman who had left Ireland as a girl, in the wake of a scandal. Or a tragedy. Granny Doyle called it a disgrace, and quite a lot more. But that line of narrative disappeared as Darragh recast the novel in a polyphonic structure. It gives not just Peg's perspective but the Rosie story, the Damien story, the John Paul story: the lives of all these motherless (and then fatherless) children fiercely brought up by their widowed grandmother, cut, intercut and spliced in a flash back and forth through more than thirty years.

These triplets and their older sister are strong, deeply known characters, distinctively individual. We meet them first in Clougheally, the home by the sea in Erris, County Mayo, where Granny Doyle and her sister Mary grew up long ago.

Clougheally (an invented town) is something of a magical place, figuring (as Erris really does) in the Celtic myth of the Children of Lir, whose wicked stepmother, wife of King Lir, 'had them turned into swans and sentenced the poor creatures to nine hundred years of exile around the loneliest places in Ireland'. Local legend has it that three hundred of their years in exile were spent here, huddled on a boulder overlooking the Atlantic which still stands. The Children of Lir's boulder is the focal point of the beach where the children play, and comes to stand as a marker for each of them: terrified to leap off it and plunge into the waves below, each finds the courage to do so.

It is Peg, the clever little girl, a reading child, the child who could grow up to be anything, who seizes on the legend and, with the help of Aunty Mary (a beautifully drawn relationship) begins to write *The Chronicle of the Children of Lir* and dramatise it for the triplets to act out. It is John Paul and Granny Doyle who ruin this occasion, and it is they – so it seems – who stand behind Peg's eviction from Dunluce Crescent as a pregnant teenager. This is the great hinge in the novel, the before-and-after moment which will haunt and divide them all.

John Paul is 'a tornado of a boy', desperate to be OUTSIDE. A charmer, a chancer, a miracle worker, he is the character the least like Darragh Martin and the one who gave him the most trouble to develop, but is perhaps the most interesting.

'People have said they know people like him – he's quite an Irish character,' Darragh says. 'A very confident, braggy person with this idea that you must be in perpetual motion, who has a lot more going on under the surface.' He is, quite openly, Granny Doyle's favourite, 'the runt of the litter, the one who had struggled to stay alive', and even at eight he's a salesman, tranforming the shells of sea slugs on the beach at Clougheally into The Blessed Shells of Erris and selling them to a wondering church congregation.

He grows up to be a man whose dimpled smile can sell anything to anyone. Indeed, he eventually sells himself, turning into Pope John Paul III on YouTube, wearing a mitre, selling love hearts and his own phone-provider company in the boom years, attracting a huge following. He is the bragging new Ireland, carrying deep down a black hole of despair which at one point almost kills him. Its revelation is something of a masterstroke.

Damien is very different. He's a gentle, biddable little boy, placid even in his high chair, whose one aim in life is to be good. He's the devout one, the one who goes to church even when it's empty, 'his face shining as bright as the stained-glass windows'. 'God was like a radio channel that Damien could tune into...God understood that even if Damien was picked last in football or had a head that was made to throw milk cartons at, he was a good boy who would go far.'

Unfortunately, he's gay. This is something which comes as a devastating revelation to him when he glimpses, and then simply cannot forget, the scandalous sight of a young man's white buttocks squeezing themselves into a pair of tight jeans. They belong to Ruadhan Kennedy-Carthy, the sixth-form cad, as this type was once called, with whom Peg falls irresistibly in love, and has sex with, just the once.

At a time where to be gay in Ireland is not only criminalised but very dangerous – the murder of Declan Fynn in 1982 is referenced – Damien suffers secret torment as he grows up, and his tragi-comic attempt to come out to his grandmother is one of the highlights of the novel. But he does find love, albeit not for ever, and he also finds a purpose, working for the Green Party at a time when its rise towards power feels like a note of hope amidst corporate greed.

Rosie is also pretty green, but though she becomes an activist she's no party member. She's a dreamer, an idealistic New Ager. As a child in Clougheally she wants to grow up to be a swan; as a teenager she believes that crystals can repel mobile phone radiation; as a young woman she colours her hair bright blue, is tattooed in interesting places and lives with her lover in a tree-house, complete with named squirrel and a wooden dream-catcher.

This is in protest against a new dual carriageway in Wicklow, in 1997. By 2005 she's committed to preventing Shell from laying a new gas pipe in land leading down towards Clougheally. It is Rosie who is bold enough to seek out long-lost Peg in New York, where she fled in the wake of her banishment.

All these children grow up in a world of Catholic ritual and belief from which each one of them will, unequivocally, depart – although John Paul turns it all to his advantage.

'I mean, nobody in Ireland is *really* Catholic any more,' Rosie tells Peg as they talk for the first time in decades, out in New York.

But 'Ideology has long tentacles,' Peg thinks to herself. 'It seems premature to dismiss the effect of Catholicism on my – our? – generation. Catholicism is there, a pea at the bottom of a stack of mattresses, shaping our thoughts, even as we claim not to feel its presence.'

And the inventive, over-arching frame of the novel is drawn straight from Catholic liturgy. With sections titled after sacraments – Baptism, Beatification, Communion and Confirmation – and so on, it's as if the whole novel is held, ironically, within the embrace of the Church. Ireland in modern times is signalled by the sections Boom and Bust, returning elegiacally to Last Rites, as the stories are brought to a close.

Within this overall structure, each of the chapter titles is taken from an object. Darragh was inspired with this idea by Neil Macgregor's 2010 British Museum exhibition, A History of the World in 100 Objects.

It feels entirely fitting: Catholicism is full of objects, relics, artefacts, shrines – on many of which John Paul will capitalise. Holy Water Bottle is just the first of these titles. Others – there are just over the hundred – include Bloody Tea Towel and Catherine Doyle Memorial Card, from which we obliquely discover that poor Catherine has died giving birth to her triplets.

This a first taste of the novel's elliptical, show-don't-tell style: a great deal happens offstage, and we often learn what has happened to one character through the voice of another. There's a lot of cutting away: Darragh's years as a dramatist served him well in constructing short sharp scenes, and the whole is immaculately plotted.

He's also had a lot of fun with the chapter headings: The

Blessed Shells of Erris, the Miraculous Condom, Miraculous Fish Fingers and Scarlet Communion Dress all make an appearance; as the novel develops we zig-zag between Rucksack, Piggy Bank, Rosemary and Mint Hotel Shampoo and, memorably, Fallons French Regular and Irregular Verbs Book, which, with tremendous panache in the writing, draws Peg and her sixth-form lover together.

Statue of the Sacred Heart takes one of the several pieces of Catholic kitsch to be found in 7 Dunluce Crescent, where the children grow up. It's drawn from Darragh's own grandmother's house, where there was indeed a Statue of the Sacred Heart pulsating redly in the bedroom where he slept. Like Peg in the novel, he wanted to turn it off, but, as in the novel, this was unthinkable. Impossible, according to Granny Doyle.

'It was as if the statue knew,' Peg thought years later. 'The statue understood that 7 Dunluce Crescent was impossibly small for all the people and feelings it was suddenly asked to contain.'

The house, and the 'scrap of a street' with its rows of red-brick houses, are both unforgettably realised: the Sacred Heart in the bedroom, a holy water font in the hall, and in the kitchen 'more pictures of the Virgin Mary than Peg could count, as if she were a family member'. She finds the sitting room 'an eerie space with the telly turned off'. As Rosie grows up, she thinks of Dunluce Crescent as 'the furthest point in the world from anything relevant... It wasn't a structure where joy was possible.' And for John Paul 'The trick was to stay away...for as long as possible.'

But the house is where everything begins and ends. All of them long to leave, and all, despite themselves, are tugged back towards it, and the childhood they shared.

Socially and architecturally, its main feature is the glass front porch, wherein Granny Doyle's 'chorus of old ladies' gather to gossip and complain about the state of the world. News from the outer world is filtered through their coffee mornings, which act as a barometer of conservative Ireland's reaction to change.

> 1985. The porch of 7 Dunluce Crescent crackled with news of the Health and Family Planning Amendment Act [which made it possible to buy contraceptives without a doctor's prescription].
>
> 'An absolute disgrace it is,' Mrs McGinty said. 'We don't need Europeans poking their noses in. Charlie Haughey had it right before.'
>
> 'Do you think they'll be selling them in Brennan's?' Mrs Nugent asked, a certain thrill in her tone.

Meanwhile, Aunty Mary – Mary Nelligan – is making her own stand against the establishment: with a pounding heart she's on a train from Clougheally to Dublin with a pack of condoms in her bag, on the way to a protest by the Irish Women's Liberation Movement.

Mary, a quietly-spoken teacher, the antithesis of her sister Granny (Bridget) Doyle, is about to change her own world. Not only is she joining a demonstration for the first time in her life, but she's fallen in love – with another woman, the young radical feminist Stella, to be found in 1991 lobbying Mary Robinson for the decriminalisation of homosexuality. Mary has crept back to Clougheally by then: 'Past sixty now, she was best off leaving the revolutions to the young.'

All this is just to touch on the revolutions in Irish society towards which the action of *Future Popes* is heading. So much goes on in the novel that new readers will discover. But in 2008, as we know, the boom in the Irish economy had come crashing down, ruining John Paul and a great many other people. Then, in 2009, came the Ryan Report, or The Commision to Inquire into Child Abuse Report.

'That,' says Darragh, 'was a really big moment in breaking people's faith in Catholicism and the church, with all the uncovering of abuse. People were thinking: What are the alternatives? How can you have a sense of self, of morality, that's independent of these two forces, capitalism and Catholicism? And what's the role of activism in that space, what's the role of environmental activism? Perhaps the Celtic past gives you some of these values...

'That's why I wanted to think about who these characters are in the shadow of all this. For example, Rosie, she's not really in the shadow of Catholicism in the way that Peg and Damien are – she's kind of side-stepped that. And I think you see this in other writers – Sally Rooney is a really good example: Catholicism is there, in *Conversations with Friends*, but it's not the guiding frame.'

He adds, 'It's incredible to me – when I started, part of it was about anger at the state of things in Ireland, and since then the Eighth Amendment has been repealed, gay marriage has happened – these things felt so far away when I began the novel... Which is not to say that everything's great in Ireland now.'

We touch, tentatively on Brexit, in which the Irish border question looms so large.

'Brexit is alarming in the rise of the far right, the narrowing of identities and the anger that's involved...it sucks away all the energy from other conversations.' This is such a huge and urgent subject now that it threatens to take over the whole of our own conversation. We put it on one side, and turn to talk about his new novel.

'I keep saying that it's about the Higgs bosun, because that's the frame that holds it together – the search for this God-particle. But it's not really. It's set in London from the Sixties to the present – it has two strands, sort of like a helix – and it's about four housemates finding themselves in their early twenties in London.' He laughs. 'The working title is We Move in Extraordinary Circles.'

★

It's pouring with rain when we conclude our interview, and I run Darragh down to the tube. We've talked up to the last minute and he's in a hurry now to get to the National Portrait Gallery by five. I've asked him so many questions that I don't like to ask now: What's the hurry? What's going on?

That evening, I receive an email from an artist friend: 'On my way to the NPG for the BP Portrait Awards, but I'm not sure about it, I think there's a demonstration or something.'

Many years ago, this friend was the winner of one of these career-changing awards. It's not until next day that I learn about the 'BP or not BP' demonstration in which Darragh and a crowd of other activists chained themselves to the doors, forcing the great and the good attending the event to clamber awkwardly over the railings into another entrance.

For much of the following week, arts programmes were rekindling the debate which has been running on and off for a long time: should institutions like Tate and the NPG accept sponsorship from companies with disturbing associations? With a shocking record in environmental damage? Isn't the philanthropy of BP and others designed to distract our attention from oil spills and abuse of human rights?

Within days, Anthony Gormley and Rachel Whiteread had come out to support the BP or not BP movement. A few days later Mark Rylance resigned from the Royal Shakespeare Company over its BP sponsorship. Miriam Margoyles also protested; so did six thousand young supporters of the RSC. In response, the theatre severed its ties with the company. This is not going to go away.

Where does Darragh go from here? Involvement with climate activism is going to claim him for a good while yet. He is working on his new novel, working with Freedom from Torture – now with the Young Activists Group – and has been teaching on a local schools project, First Story, whose aim is to build confidence and raise aspirations. 'It's really trying to help young people feel their own lives are suitable material for writing.' All this makes for a pretty full working week. What lies behind his idealism?

'I'm not sure that I have a great answer to this,' he says in an email, 'but the stakes at this political moment feel incredibly high. I don't think we'll make progress on tackling the climate crisis or the hostile environment without grassroots action and political organizing.'

Perhaps the last word should go to *The Future Popes of Ireland*, where Rosie is out on a demonstration against the Shell pipeline.

> ...there was a lot one person could do with a square of cardboard. And she wasn't alone... Plenty of people had shouted at stone buildings before the world had changed. They were here now, ghosts filling the streets, looking on at the world, which would change one day; it had to.

The Multimodal Writer

JOSIE BARNARD

'New technologies have fundamentally changed what it means to be a writer, because you actually don't have control of your tools in the way that used to be the case. You have to be able to develop a creativity that will enable you to negotiate all this change.'

Josie Barnard is the author of two very fine novels, one set on the North Yorkshire Moors and the other in a Soho strip club. She is the daughter of an academic and a jazz musician. In just these two lines, you can see that contrast might be an important part of her make-up and her thinking, and indeed she is a writer who has worked in many different genres and media.

Between all, she sees profound connections: between her travel writing, her fiction, her radio and print journalism; between *The Book of Friendship* (2011) and her most recent book, *The Multimodal Writer* (2019). She is also at home with academic discourse, having a PhD by Public Works, from which this new book is drawn. As Senior Lecturer in Creative Writing with Journalism at Middlesex University, she was appointed in 2012 with a specific task: to enable students of creative writing to work with and think creatively about all aspects of the digital world.

'I absolutely love teaching,' she says. 'The opportunity to help people realise their creative dreams gives me enormous pleasure. And now I'm doing that when some of the challenges are new media technologies – I really do love helping people get to grips with what can feel like the enemy, to get them to the point when they are using technology to create something exciting and innovative.'

Under her tuition on the MA Writing for Creative and Professional Practice one student wrote a web novel accompanied by a Spotify playlist, another a traditional novel interspersed with a town's WhatsApp and Facebook conversations. Another expressed a love story entirely through graphs.

'You have to be able to help the student understand what stimulates them, and what they want to be able to achieve creatively. Once they've understood that, they have to be able to understand what technologies they can use to achieve it. Some of them are going to be interested in audio, some in game formats; one might be interested in making a podcast. What is right for the creative vision of each individual writer is going to be very different.'

On such a Master's programme students are asked not only to create, but to think and write critically about their work. Both in her teaching, and in *The Multimodal Writer*, Josie Barnard aims to give people a vocabulary to articulate what they're getting up to in a very fast-changing world. But above all, she wants to 'to remove the feeling of being bamboozled' by the digital world, to impart confidence to her students and readers of her academic writing.

'Then, when a new technology hits them, they already know their working practice – when they're at their most productive, what tools they're good at using. So they go: okay, this is the problem, I can assess what I need to do, knowing I've got a lot of resources, and if I apply this resource and add that new one in, then I can tackle it.'

There are still a very large number of people in this country for whom the 'digital turn' is something that's very much not for them. Statistics published in the Lloyds Bank UK Consumer Digital Index 2019 show that more than half of UK employees simply do not have the digital skills needed for work; almost five million of us cannot use a mouse or a touchscreen; and almost one in ten have no digital skills whatsoever.

Josie looked at all this for her 2019 programme for BBC Radio 4, *Digital Future: The New Underclass*, in which a wide range of people expressed their feelings of inadequacy, exclusion and frustration in the face of the new technologies which they either could not afford to buy or had never been taught to use.

'There's this idea of the "digital native": that anybody who grew up with technology is automatically able to deal with it easily,' she says. 'This is a complete myth. Yes, some can, but many young people, "millennials", find technology as difficult as anyone else. The assumption is that if a young person uses Facebook perpetually, or Twitter or Tumblr they can transfer all those skills to the workplace, and actually the transfer is very difficult.

'And the myth of the digital native undermines people's chances of becoming digitally enabled – they feel that they ought to know this stuff. There's a whole layer of people either too embarrassed to say they don't feel comfortable with all this change, or actively defensive.'

In the spring of 2020, after eight years at Middlesex University, Josie took up a new post: Associate Professor in Creative Writing at De Montfort University. At the same time, the Covid pandemic struck. When this happened, she says, 'All Higher Education was thrown in at the deep end.'

De Montfort could hardly have made a more valuable appointment. With Covid, conventional teaching – lectures in packed halls, group seminars and workshops, one-to-one tutorials; the whole business of face-to-face student interaction and encouragement – went out of the window. In the sudden move to online teaching, many students floundered: Josie's knowledge, skills, and above all her understanding of the challenge that digital technologies can present made her the ideal tutor now.

'The myth of the digital native meant many lecturers assumed young people would find the shift easy,' she tells me. 'But being at ease with social media as part of leisure time is one thing. Transferring those skills into a work or education context can be challenging and stressful. All sorts of details that nobody had anticipated made a difference. Students who'd relied on university printers, for example, couldn't print off drafts to edit in hard copy.'

Frustration with this kind of thing was compounded by being in lockdown. 'The sense of isolation many students felt has been widely chartered in the press,' Josie goes on. 'Students felt it at a time when they were submitting work for assessment, struggling to download the right software, struggling with connectivity as they tried to finish tutorials.'

During lockdown and its aftermath many of us found meetings on Zoom pretty wearing. How much more so if you are trying to meet a coursework deadline and really need to sit down and thrash out the argument of your essay, or the development of a new chapter in your novel. For the lecturer, too, so much is missed in a video-call: what Josie describes as 'tiny hesitations, bursts of enthusiasm' which you see in class and can usefully respond to, simply don't come across – especially if the student keeps the video call on audio only.

'Video calls can feel very invasive,' says Josie. 'Lockdown caught us unawares. Perhaps the student is in a space they don't feel comfortable in – the family kitchen, a bedroom. And video-calling a friend is very different from calling a tutor. What are the conventions? What is the etiquette?

'As a tutor, some of the important interventions were actually quite simple things, like patience. And one student may prefer to talk on Microsoft Teams, another on Zoom and another on Google Hangout. Giving them a choice can help a lot.'

All this – her expertise and the desire to empower her students – lies behind Josie's new book, and its ambitions.

'*The Multimodal Writer* addresses what I see as a very difficult problem for everybody. This thing – digital – has hit us all, and is already embedded in all our lives, in ways that go beyond anything that we can understand yet, and so we are all on the back foot, as a society and as individuals.'

None the less, for Josie this is a nettle to grasp. She wants to 'revivify confidence' in her students and readers, and is energised and excited by the digital turn and its limitless possibilities. How did she herself get into the new technology?

'I'm definitely not one of those people who goes out and buys the new thing straight away. And after all, a pencil was new technology. Everything is new to someone at some point. In that respect, *The Multimodal Writer* is highly personal, because it's addressing my own tussles: how do you get to grips with these new expectations?'

There's a nice moment in the book where she describes Mark Twain getting to grips with a new contraption, the typewriter. She uses this anecdote to reassure the reader hesitant about the whole business, pointing the way towards help.

Josie is an engaging person, on the page and in person. We first met at a party about twenty years ago: I knew few people there, but when I came upon her the rapport was instant. Not for nothing has she written a book about friendship, and it's clear that she has a great number of friends, many going back decades.

If I had to point to a single characteristic of her persona, it's her laugh: loud, frequent, incredibly infectious. I can remember her laugh at that party, and thinking: You're fun. But she's a serious person. Not long afterwards, I invited her to give a guest lecture to MA students at Middlesex University on the writing of *Poker Face*, her first novel, and she delivered something so thoughtful, and thought-provoking, that it wasn't long before she began teaching there part-time, and then became a permanent member of staff.

She is someone for whom opportunity has knocked quite often, and throughout her career she has seized and run with new possibilities: by her own definition, she is a multimodal person. But the image she uses of her deeply creative life is 'a braided set of threads'. It is perhaps not an accident that this phrase evokes associations with sewing and with childhood.

'*The Multimodal Writer* goes right back,' she says, when I ask about its origins, and in a book which contains charts, interviews, writing exercises and a wealth of referenced reading, it is the account of her childhood, much of it spent in a remote house on the North Yorks Moors, which many readers will particularly remember.

> When I was a child growing up in the Yorkshire countryside...I conceived of a 'proper writer' as someone who was a solitary full-time novelist, and this was my aspiration. When I wrote down stories in notepads...I was alone. Sometimes I would write in bed under the covers by the light of a torch, or at the kitchen table (if everyone was out)...

Solitude, the metaphorical equivalent of a room of one's own, was very important. But there were other significant influences on her development as a writer.

Custom-built bookshelves occupied a whole wall in the living room. From the age of about seven, she spent hours in front of them. 'I read voraciously.' The bookshelves contained the English classics – the Brontes, Hardy, George Eliot. They contained poets – Shelley, Emily Dickinson; they took her through the world, via William Faulkner, of writers who became seminally important to her, to Flaubert, Cervantes, Marquez 'and beyond'.

'There was no sense that I *should* read, or *had* to read, or that this book or that was right or wrong,' she tells me. 'I just made my way through in the way that suggested itself as I went along.'

At secondary school, although from an early age she considered herself an agnostic, she found Religious Studies compelling. The focus was on the Old Testament, whose stories were 'in structure, tone and delivery' so different from the texts they were studying for O-level English. 'I was entranced by the uncompromising sweep of the tales,' she writes, 'by the lists, the excess.' She was also interested in their authorship: books by so many different people treated as a single entity. 'I became interested in how, while observing particular genre conventions, a writer could express individuality, and maintain an identifiable voice.'

Someone whose first job was writing blurbs at Jonathan Cape, was, even as a child, drawn to blurbs, introductions and authors' biographies: they gave her, she continues, 'a feeling of interaction, perhaps even collaboration'. And she notes that the 'visceral pleasure' of that time was drawn not only from reading but also from the place in which she read, her bare feet sinking into the carpet, her cheek against the headrest of the armchair.

Acutely, Josie remarks that in contrast, although digital technologies have 'magical qualities', they can feel hard to get hold of. Once we feel we have 'physically got hold of' of them, 'then we can feel that we are performing them, rather than being performed by them.'

Outside that moorland house, about a mile away, lay another significant place of her childhood. This was Troll Bridge, a bridge not over water but a rut in the ground. Jumping drystone walls, running through a couple of fields and up past a silver birch wood to reach it, she would sit beneath this stone arch not with pen and paper, but simply with her own imagination, inventing stories.

'I managed to split myself,' she writes. 'I left the more ordered, rational side of myself at home. If I had consciously considered trying to become a writer while standing in front of the wall of bookshelves, I would have been too daunted to try to dream up my own story. Away from the shelves, in a landscape I loved, I was freed to be inexpert and play with narratives.'

Talk of 'splitting' the personality more properly belongs to psychoanalytic discourse, in which the 'split' individual is generally perceived to be in trouble. But what is notable about Josie Barnard is that although there are many parts to her working life

– her 'working practice', as she expresses it – she is absolutely not compartmentalised. On the contrary, that 'braided set of threads' is the apt image for connection. Seeing connections is very much the mark of a creative thinker, and if synergy (a word Josie uses often) is a working together of things, then synergetic defines her cast of mind.

She once wrote a piece for the art magazine *FIVE* (2004) in which she cleverly drew together two very different entities. Like several other contributors, she was asked to respond in any way she chose to de Chirico's mysterious painting *Melancholy* (1913), in which the sleeping Ariadne, abandoned by her lover, is shown as a lone statue on a pedestal in an Italian piazza. Josie's imaginative response was to make a metaphorical link with the Heroes of Telemark, a group of Norwegian members of the resistance in World War II about whom she had both written and made a radio programme. For their courage, their countrymen had placed them, too, on a pedestal, something they resisted. I shall return to this, returning now to that creative childhood.

Like the gazing at and choosing from those bookshelves, like the time spent inventing stories beneath a bridge on an empty moor, two other activities contributed to Josie's development as a writer.

> From the age of about ten, with a tenacity that was akin to the tenacity with which I read and made up stories, I pursued baking and sewing. I considered myself a tomboy (I made forts with haybales; I played target practice with an air rifle, shooting tin cans off fence posts). So this was suprising. Yet visceral pleasure kept me moving between sewing, baking and storytelling, weaving between them, enjoying the transitions....
>
> I drafted stories in an intense, focussed state; I felt blinkered, down a tunnel. By contrast, when I was baking or sewing, both when faced with errors (e.g. rolling pastry out on newsprint; sewing straight over an armhole) and in my attempts to find solutions, I could be

clear-sighted and pragmatic. I wanted to be able to apply
that clear-sighted pragmatism to my story-writing.

Metacognitive processes were at work. From the
cookbooks and sewing patterns I was learning techniques
and applying them as instructed. I was also experimenting
with transferring techniques... Making a piece of clothing
involves cutting up pieces of fabric and arranging them to
make a whole that fits a planned design. When working to
edit a story, I experimented with, literally, cutting up a
draft with scissors, rearranging passages until they formed
a more effective narrative.

'Effective narrative' is a modest way of describing the strength of
Josie Barnard's fiction.

Like *The Multimodal Writer*, her first novel, *Poker Face* (1996),
goes back a very long way. As a child, she once observed a
distraught neighbour arrive at the house, unable to cope with her
young, unruly children. Much later, while working at Jonathan
Cape, Josie wrote a short story about this incident, 'Mrs
Pickering goes up the road', in which a mother is on the point of
abandoning her children. The mother in the story does not do
so, any more than that frantic mother did, all those years ago.
But the notion of a mother who really does take the momentous
decision to leave remained as something which needed exploring at much greater length than a short story.

There is also more than an element of autobiography in this
novel. 'I haven't spoken about my parents' divorce very much,'
Josie says in our long conversation, and went on immediately to
describe the positives of that situation: going with her siblings to
jazz gigs where her mother was playing, going on tour to Italy,
spending time not just on the Yorkshire Moors but in London, as
well as on a much-loved beach in Devon.

But, like the children in *Poker Face*, she and her brother and
sister were brought up in a remote moorland house by her

father. Their mother left when Josie was nine. 'We were latchkey kids,' she says in an article about William Faulkner, in which she analyses the powerful effect of his novels on her adolescent mind. And in *Poker Face*, the mother has very much walked out.

> *'Bugger this for a lark,' our mum said. 'I've had enough.'*
> Yes. This is satisfactory. It is printed in my best hand,
> in my orange Junior School exercise book. I am pleased.
> It is my turn next to read out to the class.

This is how the novel opens, when Allie, the narrator, is nine years old. Consternation and embarrassment from the teacher follow as she reads to the class an account of her summer holidays. The class – which constitutes the entire rural primary school – contains Allie's little brother Max, and her younger sister Phyll, 'her two fingers and thumb rammed further into her mouth' as she reads on.

> *'I've had enough.'*
> She hadn't quite said simple sentences like that, but I
> had to cut it up because I can't remember everything ...
> *She kicked the blue tin train...*
> *'You're millstones round my neck...'*
> Dad didn't move at all.
> *'I'm leaving.'*

As a narrator, Allie has a voice as powerful as the voice of Holden Caulfield in *The Catcher in the Rye*. She is much younger, but her view of events is as restricted, while allowing us to see very clearly all that she herself cannot see, or express. She is a child who takes it upon herself to run the family in her mother's absence, growing up horribly fast, and her painful, passionate, unspoken love for her father – often irascible, emotionally closed off, as well as shut away in his study when he is not at work – is the most haunting strand of the novel, as she tries pitifully hard to accommodate his needs while she herself shuts down her face to the world.

> Today I am ill. Every so often it becomes necessary...I felt a coward and a cheat when he brought a slice of bread and cheese upstairs. He could have spent that time on a paragraph, maybe even a whole page... He examined me so caringly, I had to turn away.

Her loyalty to him is absolute: when a teacher tries to deal with her ragged fringe for a school photograph:

> Get off! I reel my head back. I'm not one of those dolls with hair you can grow and style. It's meant to be like this. It's my Dad's haircut. He couldn't get it straight the third, or fourth time. But it doesn't get in my eyes.

Through what are effectively three acts in the drama, the novel delineates Allie's difficult passage to young adulthood, through years in which she wears outgrown clothes, struggles with the love and (often) anger she feels for the younger children, and starts 'big school'.

'Since starting at big school I have a permanent poker-face. It is essential.'

She has a mask, hiding behind that fringe and her enormous specs: impassive, unreachable, concealing boiling emotion. But inside she develops 'the stretchy thing', like the tic which disturbed children sometimes suffer from, their body behaving in a way which reflects their sense of being out of control.

Within this bleak world – three motherless children living high up on the Moors, set apart from the life of the village below – are what Rose Tremain, in talking of her own work, once called saviour figures. Mrs Taylor, tut-tutting but solid and dependable, comes once a week to clean. Paul Cragg, a boy at both primary and 'big school', quietly watches over Allie: she notices and ignores him, but he comes to her rescue when needed. And then Scarlett Barr arrives.

This is her father's girlfriend. There have been a few before – 'colleagues', as he describes them, 'armed with compliments to win us over', sneaking into the cold spare room first thing in the morning, hoping this will persuade the children that it's where they've been all night. Allie is not deceived. They come, they go. Scarlett Barr is different. When she first comes home with him:

> He tries to pretend that everything's like normal, but he can't look anywhere but at this colleague. Neither can we, because we can't believe she hasn't weakened yet, and tried to ingratiate herself.
>
> Quite the contrary. It's with an objectionably relaxed flourish that she takes off her charcoal beret and shakes out a mane of glossy jet-black hair. With wool, multi-coloured striped fingers, she swiftly unbuttons her huge man's overcoat, and tosses it lightly into the wicker chair beneath the telephone – where Dad usually chucks his coat – and then she tosses her gloves on top, which is really pushing it. But Dad's only showing awed fascination.

And Scarlett Barr has brought no presents, makes no attempt to win over three hostile children. She asks their father to turn up the central heating. 'How dare she? This is one of Dad's ways of economising.' And then she suggests a game of poker. After the first shock – 'We practically choke. That's *gambling*.' – they settle down, and in moments she has won the younger ones over. Allie inwardly resists, but even she, very cautiously, begins to relax. 'I fear I am, against my better judgement, beginning to enjoy myself.'

Scarlett is very much her own woman: she comes and goes. But, after a fashion, she is here to stay, and towards the end of the novel she is the one to bring this disunited, troubled family together.

★

Josie spent years considering her way into a novel which in many ways resembled her own experience. She talks of her own initial resistance to autobiographical fiction: her assumption that it meant 'a splurge of raw emotion for which I had a rather English distaste'. This was over twenty years ago, when Josie was also aware of how such work might be received: as domestic, meaning 'small' or 'limited' and 'female' (or second-class). Now, although the autobiographical novel has long embraced classics – *David Copperfield, A Portrait of the Artist as a Young Man* – it seems to be considered something new: the word 'autofiction' is everywhere.

To consider how to approach writing *Poker Face*, Josie read very widely, inspired by Philip Roth's view that an author's fictional view of himself is essentially impersonation, and by John McGahern, who said simply, 'Fiction needs to be reimagined.' Both writers took the view that lived experience must be transformed. How to effect such a transformation is perhaps any autobiographical novelist's greatest challenge: Josie rose to it by embarking on what she describes as a literature review, a term more usually associated with a thesis.

'I had to supplement my memories with research into the issues and the historical period that I was planning to address,' she says. 'I needed facts, opinions, overviews, anecdotes and statistics, for example, to help me re-imagine the familiar. I applied research methods I associated with, and had applied to, non-fiction.' She is referring her to her two travel books on London and New York, commissioned and published by Virago.

What came to the fore in her reading was a feminist perspective on something that is often judged the ultimate taboo: a mother abandoning her children. 'Men leave their children, why not women?' Josie, 'a feminist now, and a feminist then', as she put it to me, began looking at what she realised was the very little literature dealing with women who leave children.

There is Ibsen's *A Doll's House*; Charlotte Perkins Gilman's *The Yellow Wallpaper*; Penelope Fitzgerald's remarkable novel *The Beginning of Spring*, set in the years leading up to the Russian Revolution. As well as these three important works, she was reading and thinking about classics of feminist literature such as books by Betty Friedman and Gloria Steinem which explored and recorded the frustrations of domestic life.

'A lot of very complicated things were going on in terms of how to plan and structure the novel,' was how she put it to me. 'Feminist literature, society's view of women, history of feminism around the 1960s and 1970s, and mapping on to that, questions of how to tell a story.'

She was up against a central aesthetic question. 'I realised that because women leaving children is generally considered so appalling, if you focus on that in the story, it becomes everything.' In other words, the mother herself becomes the central character – as Nora is in *A Doll's House* – leaving little room for exploration of the effect of her actions. The door slams at the end of Ibsen's play, and we know no more. What Josie wanted to do was enter the story in the aftermath. This is how Penelope Fitzgerald handles it in *The Beginning of Spring*, which opens with Frank Reid in Moscow reading a letter from his wife Nellie. She has already gone.

The mother has already gone at the opening of *Poker Face*, and it was Josie's work in radio, as well as her reading, which helped her effect this.

She had got into radio as a student. Reading Russian and Soviet Literature at Liverpool University, she and a fellow-student answered an advertisement to make an experimental series of programmes for BBC Radio Merseyside. She had a lot of fun and learnt a great deal about technique, later developed in her work for BBC Radio 4.

'In a radio feature, it's often the way pieces of speech or sounds are juxtaposed that creates meaning. If the radio presenter just explains everything, as a narrator might in a novel, it tends to seem clunky. Information has to be *revealed* on air, conversationally, by interviewees, with sound effects. So when Allie reads out her own essay, about what actually happened in her summer holiday, it's hearing another pupil's much jollier essay that helps her see why this might not have been a good plan. The teacher doesn't know what to say, so the increasingly agitated small sounds that she makes are worrying for Allie and reveal information about the class-room setting to the reader.

'If you've decided that the mother has to have left already, then the story is told by one of the children. And of course children have limited knowledge. So that was another thing I was negotiating. Decisions about whether to make it present or past tense, first or third person, were really important. I was drafting, drafting, drafting, and it wasn't until I had made those decisions that I was really able to get going.'

If reading about all this is enough to put the faint-hearted off the very idea of writing a novel, it must be said that not a breath of any of it shows in *Poker Face*. A lesser writer might have weighed down the narrative with undigested cultural history or polemic. What Josie Barnard achieved was the naked telling of distress by a growing child, and her own intense thinking about a feminist perspective is given in just a few lines, spoken by Scarlett Barr towards the end, as she and Allie build a bonfire. The house where the children grew up is being sold: all the accumulated rubbish and unwanted stuff must go. 'In many ways I admire your mother,' says Scarlett, addressing the rising flames.

> This absent-minded choice of subject matter is a surprise like a block of ice has been smashed into my face...
>
> 'Ten or fifteen years ago, it was inconceivable that a mother should leave her children... Your mother's

action could be interpreted as pioneering, feminist, even... It might be said that she acted with unusual courage... Of course, she clearly went quite bonkers.'

Allie is frozen by her words. But the violence with which throughout the novel she has often described both incidents and her feelings is reignited.

'My guts have been turned out on to the ground. They are palpitating, livid vermillion in the dirt... while I compose myself.'

Lines like this distinguish the novel, whose tough, compressed, hard-boiled prose is led by powerful imagery and powerful verbs: 'yank', 'snatch', 'grind', 'smash', 'grab', 'shove', 'screech', 'hammer'.

'Behind me Dad's plank door is snatched by vagrant wind. The screeching rusted metal of its hinges echoes loud around the empty house.'

'The window reflects at me that the collar saws my neck. The way I pinned my waistband tighter strangulates my breathing.'

Parts of speech are used idiosyncratically: 'reach up spindly', 'It savages my tongue', 'hoping a quaking plank will nightmare him into childish panic'.

'Barnard's short sharp sentences are like shards of glass,' said the *Guardian*. At least one influence on her style was the prose of William Faulkner. In an article about two of his novels written for *Slightly Foxed* in 2008, she points to *The Sound and the Fury*, and the way in which Benjy, the 'idiot' boy, sees the world. 'Leaves "rattle" around him; flowers "rasp" against him. [He] can "smell the bright cold".' Amidst the shards of glass in her own novel are rare but exhilarating moments of beauty.

'I look out over spreading fields of emerald glittering grass. Black-faced lambs kick their heels. A curlew calls from far away in the cornflower sky.'

In our conversation Josie was eloquent about the influence of the Yorkshire landscape – 'magically beautiful and frankly frightening' – on her development as a writer. Allie's own observation is acute, and Josie described the real seeking after truth which lay behind her research. 'I didn't feel I had managed to evoke a field closely enough, so I stood in a field.' But she had been standing in fields all through her childhood, had she not?

'Absolutely. But I didn't remember exactly how grass laces in on itself when it's a tussock. I wanted it to represent Allie's emotions, to show, but not tell her emotions. In order to get to what is quite a short paragraph of description, I took reams of notes in order to extract what would relate to Allie's state of mind.'

Writing this, her debut novel, 'took years, too many to admit to'. But this, very often, is what writing is. *Poker Face* won her a Betty Trask award; it was made into a short film for Channel 4; and it led to a new commission from Virago: to write a second novel.

Josie had begun thinking about *The Pleasure Dome* while researching *The Virago Women's Guide to New York*, commissioned in 1991 and published in 1993. She was already writing *Poker Face*, one more thread in the braid which so far had been made up of radio and print journalism, blurb and short story writing. Now she was weaving in travel.

In New York, in the post-feminist nineties, visiting strip clubs was considered to be a cool thing to do. For the women on stage, held post-feminist theory, it was a way of reclaiming their sexuality.

Josie wasn't convinced. 'That theory suits quite a lot of people who aren't the women stripping.' But she did go, she did absorb the atmosphere, and among her notes on many different aspects of the city made more and more on these clubs. By this time she had also been commissioned to write the *Virago Guide to London* (published in 1994). She began drafting scenes, feeling her way towards something more substantial, which turned out to be a novel. Characters began to emerge.

'I knew I had started *The Pleasure Dome* specifically when I was sitting at a London bus-stop one day, notepad in my pocket, staring at a billboard with a Wonderbra ad on it,' she tells me. 'I'd been reading Coleridge's poem *Kubla Khan* and Angela Carter's extended essay *The Sadeian Woman*. The Wonderbra billboard ran the width of a building. I was struck by how such a highly sexualised image of femininity had been normalised. The sight of the Wonderbra ad in such a workaday environment in combination with *Kubla Kahn* and *The Sadeian Woman* gave me title, setting, atmosphere. [My] main character was stripping off literally in her attempt to strip down emotionally to some kind of peace of mind. But she's misguided. The strip club she chooses to do this in is, in the words of Coleridge's poem, a "miracle of rare device, /A sunny pleasure-dome with caves of ice!"'

Belle George, twenty-three, tall, gangly, a complete and utter mess, is a tremendous central character. The daughter of a celebrated television presenter, Lilian White, who has just about managed the life of a single parent, she is woefully ill-equipped for life. Drinking hard, living in squalor in an outer-city run-down block of flats, Belle crashes through the world, stumbling from one dead-end job to another, falling over her own feet. At school, the one thing she did well was the Sports Day backwards egg-and-spoon race. Her skin is scarred from childhood accidents, she bites her nails to the quick, and struggles through most of her days with a permanent hangover. She is also, it is skilfully made clear, an attractive young woman who can, when necessary, look the business. Furthermore, she is immensely lovable: the reader is rooting for her at every turn. Where did she come from? How is her story told?

'Well, I think in all of us there's a sense that you're crashing through the world,' Josie says. She gives one of her great laughs, but then says seriously: 'I was heavily drawing on some internal stuff. This may sound clichéd, but I did want poetic truth. If you are going to do something that resonates, you are going to have to mine quite deep inside yourself. And I think that's why so many people find writing fiction so exhausting: you do have to go very deep, and allow yourself to be very raw.'

She does not talk directly about what she is drawing on, but both her novels are about maternal deprivation. In *Poker Face* the mother is absent, and the driving force is Allie's unexpressed love for her father. In *The Pleasure Dome*, Belle's painful adoration of her neglectful mother is what powers her every ill-judged action. And Xanadu's, the strip club where she is thrilled to be given a job, clearly fulfils her desperate need for a family.

In thinking once again about the whole question of writing autobiographical fiction, Josie continues in our conversation to unpack what needs to be done.

'The exhaustion has to be paced, and to really try and unpick all the emotions is really hard, and then to work to express that in prose...that was very much at the heart of both novels. Your own experience has to be transformed, so that by the time it's on the page it's not autobiographical any more. To get to that stage you have to go very deep into emotions, feelings, quite visceral responses.'

In talking like this, Josie is obliquely revealing a great deal about herself and her past. But she is a writer, and here a novelist, whose task is to make it 'not autobiographical any more'.

'How did I do that? Writing fiction involves working and re-working, transforming, re-shaping, until, very much in the same way that an initial pencil sketch on canvas is layered over with paint, any initial pencilled "facts" are impossible to extract from the finished work. It's a necessary part of the creative process. If a "fact" is left intact, it is almost certainly not doing its job. Each separate element has to support the narrative arc, develop character, evoke atmosphere.'

Josie talks about the very careful consideration she gave to voice, that which above all carries a novel. She writes in her PhD thesis:

I chose to make *Poker Face* first-person, present tense with the intention that this would keep the reader not merely close to the protagonist, but feeling as if they were *inside* the protagonist, peeping out. In a strip club, such peeping would be voyeuristic.

The Pleasure Dome is set in a completely different world. It's a world which is all about looking, but she wanted to avoid making the reader complicit in voyeurism.

Voyeurism is often facilitated by distance, [she continues]. Third person, past tense, for example, allows the reader to watch from a comfortable distance, so I knew that would be the wrong combination. Present tense denies the reader distance, but I rejected *first person*, present tense because this too can be voyeuristic. Voyeurism is often facilitated by confidence on the part of the watcher that they are hidden. I didn't want the reader to feel that. So, I used third person, present tense. While the *characters* might be able to remove themselves to a fantasy world in the alluring, claustrophobic setting of a strip club, my aim was that the use of present tense would make it harder for the *reader* to watch from a comfortable distance, voyeuristically.

And so it is that we observe the girls performing their acts in Xanadu's not through our own eyes, but through the eyes of the strippers themselves, who watch one another as they go through a routine, often with quite other things on their minds. Or we watch them through Belle's limited third-person perspective: here she is, just taken on, seeing a show for the first time.

The rising curtain sparkles with a golden constellation. The music drifts between traditional striptease – lots of jolly piano and plinky-plonk drum rolls – and up-to-the-minute electro beat, the wild mix telling her that she's in a different world.

An extremely proper, mildly amused male voice fills
the auditorium, confirming unreality.

'THEY'RE GLAMOROUS, THEY'RE SEXY,
EXTRA-ORDINARY. ARE YOU READY, LADIES
AND GENTLEMEN? FOR YOUR EYES ONLY...'

A dozen girls file on to the apron of the stage, twirl
silver-topped canes, take their top hats off, twirl them, and
put them back on. They do a bit of clumsy criss- crossing
between each other. They're mauvely indistinguishable.
They wiggle their notional coat-tails and file off.

Leaning forward, Belle frowns as if she must have
missed something. Just when she'd slowed down, the
show is speeding up.

A prop is there from nowhere: a furnace with tonguing
paper flames. A girl leaps out in a cap-and-braces saucy
stoker outfit, strobing red and orange. The music sharp-
cuts, and she is stripping...

The music is the stuff migraines are made of. Belle
presses fingers to her temples.

What more we learn about sex in this novel is not through gazing
lasciviously at the performing girls, but backstage, in the
crowded dressing room. Mae is a lesbian, Sue a single parent
who brings her little boy to work. There are many other strippers
at Xanadu's, and for all of them it's a way to pay the rent or, if
they're lucky, get an Equity card. This is why Sylvie is there: a
sweet, pretty, stagestruck little thing who misses her mum and
who comes to share Belle's appalling flat. Within moments she
has disinfected, cleaned, wiped, found a tablecloth and put tea
and a Battenburg cake upon it.

Belle's squalor, and the tenderness she feels for Sylvie,
becomes a sanctuary. For a couple of weeks Xanadu's has
offered everything she needs: friends, family, approval,
something she can do. Except that she can't: after a flying start
she ruins a number and is sent by her mates to Coventry.

In creating so engagingly and convincingly the atmosphere of that backstage dressing room, Josie was doing two things. She was mining feelings of self-doubt and anxiety that she could identify in herself, knowing that, as she put it to me, 'Those raw feelings are highly personal, but lots of people feel them. So it was also about working out the commonality. These young women have the usual fights and rivalries but of course are supporting each other.'

She was drawing not only on her observations of strip-club life but on her research into quite different communities. She was doing both a radio programme and a feature about the Bee-Keepers' Convention, and it is not hard to see the parallels: the hive as a world of its own, the keepers with their own special clothes, and special language. She was also researching police work in Manchester. 'The police are a very tight-knit group that society has very ambivalent feelings about. How they relate to each other, and deal with what is essentially a very claustrophobic and removed atmosphere – that also informed *The Pleasure Dome*,' she tells me.

And during the period of writing she also went to Norway, to meet another close-knit group, this time the extraordinary survivors of World War II who, in a daring raid, on skiis, and without firing a single shot, dismantled a German heavy water plant. They became known as the Heroes of Telemark, referred to already in this essay, immortalised in a film starring Kirk Douglas. But, as Josie found out for the feature she was writing, they felt uneasy about their status: 'We were just doing our job.' They didn't feel like heroes.

All these very different things lay behind the writing of this novel: multimodal work indeed. It is one of its achievements to show not only how much neglected Belle is out of step with life, but how vulnerable her mother is, too. Through an internal flashback, we are taken to the 'unwed mothers' home' where Lilian gave birth, realising 'with a post-birth rush of adrenalin', '*I want to keep my baby.*' 'I KEPT YOU,' she shouts at Belle, shaking her hard. She did at least do that, though it led to enduring stress for both of them.

The Pleasure Dome is a terrific novel, written, like *Poker Face*, in taut, compressed, energetic language. 'Squashed-up prose,' is how Josie's academic father has described her style, and there is a brilliance in the way the novel cuts from scene to scene, everything happening in the unwritten gap between. 'My writing takes a long time, refining and paring back,' Josie told me, 'and is something I work very hard on, and enjoy.'

Six years lie between the publication of her two novels, a testament both to the care with which they were written and to how much else was going on. With their success, the recognition that she was, as they say, someone to watch, Josie Barnard could have gone on to establish herself as one of the finest – and most intelligently self-reflective – novelists of her generation. She is very clear on why this hasn't happened yet. She's never stopped writing. 'It's in my bones.' She does have another novel quietly in progress, begun after *The Pleasure Dome* was published in 2000. But by then she had two small children.

'There's a reality check with children. You don't get those big blocks of time – the room of one's own. I'm full of admiration for people who write novels with young children, but I was not one of them. I had a good hard think about what I could achieve: how I *could* be fully there for them, but lay down lines that I could pick up.'

She was reviewing for the *TLS* and the *Independent*, so 'still essentially researching literature and narratives', as well as doing a lot of work for the BBC. 'I went ballooning, I did a whole range of things which took me into very different experiences, meeting very different people. It was a very expansive research period.' What she decided she needed now was a really big research project. 'Research is really important to me – it's not something separate from being creative.' What she began was a book about something she had always felt to be important: friendship.

★

The sheer quantity of research needed to write *The Book of Friendship* was daunting at first. Early on in the research period, Josie once fell asleep in the British Library, two stacks of books towering on either side. She was gently woken by a passing acquaintance. Conversational in tone, scholarly in scope, the book has a bibliography running to almost twenty pages and is itself almost twice the length of *Poker Face*. It was an enormous endeavour, broken up by making several BBC Radio 4 programmes, something which, as in the writing of *The Pleasure Dome*, both refreshed the author's mind, and served as helpful reminders when time felt short that she could indeed complete things. Perhaps this is an important part of multimodal writing practice.

The nature of resilience, and how you develop it, is another thread running through her work. The idea for this book came from her own struggle to make sense of friendship when she was a child, and, as an adult with many good friends, through the realisation that in our times, with small or fractured families, and people moving about, friendship has begun to assume a great, even esssential place in our lives. Yet there was little written about it: existing literature consisted either of academic works of moral philosophy or books adorned with flowers and kittens. She had identified a gap in the general market and what she wanted to write was a book which would fill it: wide-ranging, accessible and intelligent, with a strong narrative voice. She wrote a forty-page proposal, and was commissioned, once again, by Virago.

'This book is an exploration,' she writes in the introduction. 'I go down side alleys, I discover coves and glades.' It is divided into three parts: Beginnings, In the Thick of It and Onwards and Upwards. Within them, over twenty-six chapters, Josie engagingly introduces the reader to everyone from Aristotle and Kant to the Lone Ranger, via Tennyson and his love for Arthur Hallam; teen film; *What Katy Did*; the much-loved American television series *Friends*; Amy Tan's hit novel, *The Joy Luck Club* and Barrack Obama's election campaign, dominated by speeches about friends pulling together. It's immensely picku-pable, informative and absorbing, and was a publishers' call-in for the Samuel Johnson Prize.

But although it was published not so long ago, in 2011, even within the last few years the exponential growth of social media has transformed our ideas of friendship. 'In one way,' says Josie, 'the power of friendship has been diminished – everyone is in their own little world, removed physically and communicating remotely.'

Social media has also made us vulnerable. By the time she approached the end, Josie tells me, 'I was starting to see that friendship conducted via social media is a thing that can be mined for data. It has incredible status: peer recommendation can sell much more effectively than an advert. Companies can tap into it and make huge sales. So I was starting to think explic-itly then about new technology and how it's affecting, in that context, friendship, but also how it affects being a writer.

'One of the ways in which writing has been changed by the new technology – and this is quite well charted – is that, because people are primarily accessing a lot of material through their smart phones, the size of the screen is dictating quite a lot of writing: paragraphing, sentence lengths.'

Not long before Josie and I met for our first interview, the *Guardian* Review published a spot-on article by Richard Godwin about this new wave of writing. In 'How to speak internet', Godwin looks at a number of new young writers, and 'a distinc-tively minimalist style' which emerged at the end of the last decade by users of the micro-blogging site Tumblr.

'Capital letters were largely dispensed with, save for EMPHA-SIS; punctuation was largely notable by its absence; hashtags were used mostly for irony (#wild).'

He quotes a post from 2012:

> when did tumblr collectively decide not to use
> punctuation like when did this happen why is
> this a thing
> it just looks so smooth I mean look at this sentence
> flowing like a river

'It seems to me,' Godwin remarks, 'that any concerns about what the internet is doing to our collective mental health must be set against the poetry that it has simultaneously unleashed.'

It might be asked how that little blog-poem, beguiling though it is, differs from what ee cummings was doing over half a century ago. But cummings was a distinctive individual: what is happening now is sweeping through a generation.

Josie, who is now on the government's Digital Skills and Inclusion Working Group, is largely with Godwin in seeing the creativity and imagination found on writing disseminated via social media now.

'It's also the case that the book hasn't suddenly died. There are new markets, and podcasts have taken off. But one of the things about social media is that young people want to mark themselves out, in the same way a Punk might with safety pins and a mohican – it's something rebellious.

'And one of the ways of being rebellious is to decide that you're going to have a new take on grammar. So the lack of caps has its own set of rules. You're talking in a normal tone if you don't use them; the minute you insert a word that's all caps, you're shouting. Caps are still there, but they're deployed in a different way.'

Her only reservation is that among the things being challenged is close reading. 'I think that's much more disastrous than grammar. I think people are hopping about so much now between texts that their ability to sit down with a novel and read it closely – well, that's a precious human resource that's in danger of being lost.'

Her overall take on the digital turn, however, is positive. It's happened, it's affecting all of us, and imparting digital literacy is for her something of a mission.

'Online brings particular challenges to writers,' she says. 'One is non-linear narratives.'

On the page, writers have long embraced this challenge: from Laurence Sterne to William Burroughs, via James Joyce, Virginia Woolf and all their modernist and postmodern heirs – I think of Lucy Ellman – they have abandoned linearity, redefined the whole notion of story. But we're not on the page any more.

Working with her at De Montfort, Josie's students are writing web novels that weave between text, images and URLs. They are writing in smartphone-sized chunks of text, condensing a chapter to a couple of paragraphs. They are asked to think about visual story-telling, to tell a long novel – *Oliver Twist*, perhaps – in five Instagram posts. Or they might, says Josie, set a fairytale in a contemporary setting – nothing new there, but 'each of the goats in *Three Billy Goats Gruff* is assigned an appropriate platform (say Snapchat, Tumblr and Facebook) and the separate strands will work together to tell the full story.'

Hearing this, I'm reminded of 'the braided set of threads' which Josie uses in *The Multmodal Writer* as the image for her creative life. The child who told herself stories beneath a bridge on the North Yorkshire Moors; who cut up the written drafts to see if that worked better; who cut pieces of fabric against a sewing pattern, and who rolled pastry on to newsprint, learning from the mistake, became the novelist, the broadcaster, scriptwriter, critic and inspiring teacher, embracing the digital age and all it has to offer.

Further Reading

MICHAEL WALL

Hiroshima: The Movie, in *The Giles Cooper Awards*, 1985 (Methuen, 1986)
Amongst Barbarians (Samuel French, 1989)
Women Laughing (Oberon Books, 2000)

PENELOPE LIVELY
These are the books by Penelope Lively discussed in this essay, all published by Penguin Books.

A House Unlocked (2001)
Ammonites and Leaping Fish (2013)
Family Album (2009)
How It All Began (2001)
Life in the Garden (2017)
Making It Up (2005)
Moon Tiger (1987)
Oleander, Jacaranda (1994)
The Ghost of Thomas Kempe (1973)
The Purple Swamp Hen and other stories (2016)
The Road to Lichfield (1997)

HILARY DAVIES

The Shanghai Owner of the Bonsai Shop, Enitharmon, 1991
In a Valley of This Restless Mind, Enitharmon, 1997
Imperium, Enitharmon, 2005
Exile and the Kingdom, Enitharmon, 2016
'Shamans and Psychopomps', originally commissioned and published in 2015 by the Royal Literary Fund for its on-line magazine, *Collected.*
Writers Aloud (Royal Literary Fund audio) 2017
'Exile and the Kingdom: poetry and Pilgrimage', Agenda (2018)

Sebastian Barker: *Guarding the Border: Selected Poems*, Enitharmon, 1992
The Hand in the Well, Enitharmon 1996
Damnatio Memoriae, Enitharmon, 2004
The Erotics of God, Smokestack Books, 2005
The Land of Gold, Enitharmon, 2014

Denise Inge: *Happiness and Holiness: Selected Writings of Thomas Traherne*, Canterbury Press, 2008

Richard Wilmott: *The Voluble Soul: Thomas Traherne's Poetic Style and Thought* (Cambridge: The Lutterworth Press, 2021)

ANNA BURNS

No Bones, Flamingo, 2001, Fourth Estate, 2018
Little Constructions, Fourth Estate, 2007
Milkman, Faber & Faber, 2018
Mostly Hero [novella], Faber, 2019

Maureen E. Ruprecht Fadem: *The Literature of Northern Ireland: Spectral Borderlands*, Palgrave Macmillan, 2015

RUTH PAVEY

A Wood of One's Own (Duckworth, 2017)
Deeper into the Wood (Duckworth, 2021)

AFRA

Diana Nammi and Karen Attwood, *Girl with a Gun: Love, Loss and the Fight for Freedom in Iran* (Unbound, 2020)
Edward Said, *Reflections on Exile and Other Essays* (Granta 2001)
Write to Life poetry and prose is published by Freedom from Torture, originally in annual anthologies but now online. See freedomfromtorture.org

MAREK MAYER

The ENDS Report (Haymarket Press) endsreport.com
To find out more about the work of the Andrew Lees Trust:
http://www.andrewleestrust.org

ROY STRONG

The Roy Strong Diaries
Volume I *Splendours and Miseries 1967-1987* (Weidenfeld &
Nicolson, 1997, revised and updated 2017)
Volume II *Scenes and Apparitions 1988-2003* (Weidenfeld &
Nicolson, 2016)
Volume III *Types and Shadows (2005-2015)* (Weidenfeld &
Nicolson, 2020)
Selected Work
A Little History of the English Country Church (Penguin, 2007)
Self-Portrait as a Young Man (The Bodleian Library, 2013)
*The Elizabethan Image: An Introduction to English Portraiture
1558-1603* (Yale, 2019)

John Swannell: *Sir Portrait* (Frances Lincoln, 2015)

CHARLES PALLISER

The Quincunx, Penguin Books, 1989
The Sensationist, Jonathan Cape, 1991
Betrayals, Jonathan Cape, 1993
The Unburied, Phoenix House, 1999
Rustication, Norton, London and New York, 2013

ANTONY WOOD

Robert Chandler, ed. *The Penguin Book of Russian Verse* (2015)
Stanley Mitchell, *Eugene Onegin*, (Penguin Classics, 2008)
Antony Wood: *Alexander Pushkin: Selected Poetry*, Translated by
Antony Wood (Penguin Classics, 2020)
'The Carthorse, the Posthorse and Pegasus: My Relationship
with Pushkin', in A.D. Briggs *Alexander Pushkin: A celebration of
Russia's best-loved writer* (Hazar Publishing, 1999)

DARRAGH MARTIN

The Keeper (Little Island, 2013)
Future Popes of Ireland (Fourth Estate, 2018)
Penelope Mortimer *About Time Too* (Orion, 1979)
This is Not a Drill: An Extinction Rebellion Handbook (Penguin, 2019)
Saturday Lunch with the Brownings (Daunt Books, 2019)

JOSIE BARNARD

The Virago Women's Guide to New York (Virago, 1993)
The Virago Women's Guide to London. (London: Virago, 1994)
Poker Face (Virago, 1996)
The Pleasure Dome (Virago, 2000)
The Book of Friendship (Virago, 2011)
The Multimodal Writer: Creative Writing Across Genres and Media (Macmillan International Higher Education / Red Globe, 2019)
Richard Godwin, 'How to speak internet', *Guardian* Review, 12.10.19
Olivia Sudjic, 'Page Refresh: How the internet transformed the novel', *Guardian* Review, 23.1.2021

Acknowledgements

For permission to quote from works by the writers discussed in this book the author and publisher are grateful to the following publishers and individuals.

MICHAEL WALL

Japanese Style © Michael Wall (1982); *Headcrash* © Michael Wall (1986); *The Wide-Brimmed Hat* © Michael Wall (1987): by permission of Micheline Steinberg. *Hiroshima, The Movie* © Michael Wall (1985) from *The Best Radio Plays of 1985*, published by Methuen/BBC Publications, London, 1986; *Amongst Barbarians* © Michael Wall (1989) by permission of Nick Hern Books, London; *Women Laughing* © Michael Wall 1987, © The Estate of Michael Wall 1992, Oberon Books, 2000, used by permission of Bloomsbury Publishing Plc, London.
For all enquiries about the work of Michael Wall contact Micheline Steinberg at Micheline Steinberg Associates: info@steinplays.com

PENELOPE LIVELY

Oleander, Jacaranda, © Penelope Lively (1984); *A House Unlocked,* © Penelope Lively (2001); *Making It Up,* © Penelope Lively, (2005); *Ammonites and Leaping Fish,* © Penelope Lively, (2013), *The Purple Swamp Hen and Other Stories,* © Penelope Lively (2017); *Life in the Garden,* © Penelope Lively (2018) by permission of Penguin Random House, London.

HILARY DAVIES

In A Valley of This Restless Mind, © Hilary Davies, 1977; *Imperium,* © Hilary Davies, 2005; *Exile and the Kingdom,* © Hilary Davies, 2016, by permission of Enitharmon Press, London. 'Shamans and Psychopomps' © Hilary Davies 2015, in the Royal Literary Fund online magazine *Collected*, and statement in Writers Aloud (2017) by permission of the Royal Literary Fund, London. 'Exile and the Kingdom: Poetry and

Pilgrimage', © Hilary Davies 2018, by permission of Agenda quarterly (info@agendaquarterly.co.uk)

ANNA BURNS

Extracts from *No Bones* © Anna Burns 2001 and *Little Constructions* © Anna Burns 2007 reprinted by permission of HarperCollins Publishers Ltd, London; extracts from *Milkman* © Anna Burns 2018 reproduced by permission of Faber & Faber Ltd, London. Extracts from the American edition of *Milkman* © Anna Burns 2018, used with the permission of Graywolf Press, Minneapolis, Minnesota, www.graywolfpress.org.

RUTH PAVEY

A Wood of One's Own, © Ruth Pavey 2017 by permission of Duckworth Books.

MAREK MAYER

Extract from ENDS, February 2005 © Environmental Data Services Ltd, London.

AFRA

'Lampedusa' © the author, published in the *Guardian* Online, 2013, and on the Freedom from Torture website, 2013. Extract from Edward Said, 'Reflections on Exile' © Edward Said 2000, from *Reflections on Exile and Other Essays*, by permission of *Granta* Books, London.

ROY STRONG

The Roy Strong Diaries: Volume I *Splendours & Miseries 1967-1987* © Roy Strong 1997; Volume II *Scenes & Apparitions 1998-2003* © Roy Strong 2016; Volume III *Types & Shadows 2005-2015*, © Roy Strong 2020, by permission of the Orion Group, London. *Self-Portrait as a Young Man* © Roy Strong 2013 by permission of Roy Strong. Portrait of Roy Strong after Magritte © John Swannell 2015, from *Sir Portrait: Thirty portraits of Roy Strong*, Frances Lincoln Publishers, London, 2015, by permission of John Swannell.

CHARLES PALLISER

The Quincunx © Charles Palliser 1989 by permission of Penguin Random House, London. *The Sensationist* © Charles Palliser 1991 by permission of Jonathan Cape/Penguin Random House, London; *Rustication* © Charles Palliser 2014, by permission of W. W. Norton & Company, London and New York.

ANTONY WOOD

'The Carthorse, the Posthorse and Pegasus: My Relationship with Pushkin' from A. D. Briggs, ed., *Alexander Pushkin: A Celebration of Russia's Best-Loved Writer*, 1999, © Hazar Publishing, London, 1999. Extracts from *Alexander Pushkin: Selected Poetry* © Antony Wood 2020, Penguin Classics, Penguin Random House London. Lines from Stanley Mitchell's translation of 'The Bronze Horseman' in Robert Chandler, ed. *The Penguin Book of Russian Verse* © Stanley Mitchell 2015, reproduced by kind permission of Carla and Daniel Mitchell.

DARRAGH MARTIN

Extracts from *Future Popes of Ireland* © Darragh Martin 2018 reprinted by permission of HarperCollins Publishers Ltd. Extract from *About Time Too* by Penelope Mortimer published by Orion in 1979. © *About Time Too* 1979. Reproduced by permission of Sheil Land Associates Ltd.

JOSIE BARNARD

Poker Face © Josie Barnard 1996 and *The Pleasure Dome* © Josie Barnard 2000, by permission of Little, Brown Publishers; *The Multimodal Writer* © Josie Barnard 2019 published by Macmillan International Higher Education/Red Globe and reproduced with the permission of the Licensor through PLS Clear.

Every effort has been made to trace copyright holders and publishers of all works quoted in the text. Any omission will be corrected in future editions.